JUDICIAL POWER AND AMERICAN CHARACTER

JUDICIAL POWER AND AMERICAN CHARACTER

*Censoring Ourselves
in an Anxious Age*

Robert F. Nagel

New York   Oxford
OXFORD UNIVERSITY PRESS
1994

Oxford University Press

Oxford   New York   Toronto
Delhi   Bombay   Calcutta   Madras   Karachi
Kuala Lumpur   Singapore   Hong Kong   Tokyo
Nairobi   Dar es Salaam   Cape Town
Melbourne   Auckland   Madrid

and associated companies in
Berlin   Ibadan

Published by Oxford University Press, Inc.
200 Madison Avenue, New York, NY 10016

Library of Congress Cataloging-in-Publication Data
Nagel, Robert F.
Judicial power and American character : censoring ourselves in an
anxious age / Robert F. Nagel.
p.   cm.
Includes bibliographical references and index.
ISBN 0-19-508901-4
1. Judicial power—United States.   2. United States—
Constitutional law—Moral and ethical aspects.   I. Title.
KF5130.N34   1994
347.73'12—dc20
[347.30712]   93-41891

2 4 6 8 9 7 5 3 1

Printed in the United States of America
on acid-free paper

To William G. and Ethel M. Nagel

ACKNOWLEDGMENTS

The idea for this book began to take form when my first book, *Constitutional Cultures*, was still a draft manuscript. At that time several readers pointed out that the "mentality" of judicial review that I was attempting to describe might be the mentality not only of the legal profession but also, at least in some ways, of ordinary citizens. I could not satisfactorily assimilate this possibility into the writing that was already underway, but the thought was planted.

Eventually some other commentators energetically attacked that book. Although I appreciated the interest and insights of these critics, I was surprised at the extent to which a few seemed to view themselves as engaged in a kind of warfare. Reflecting on this vehemence also helped me to know what I wanted to say next.

A number of individuals have generously and thoughtfully commented on sections of *Judicial Power and American Character*. These include Paul Campos, Mark Loewenstein, Alfred McDonnell, Christopher Mueller, Gene Nichol, James Scarboro, and Pierre Schlag. Special thanks are due to those who read the entire manuscript: Akhil Amar, Lee Bollinger, Jack Nagel, Pru Nagel, Dale Oesterle, Michael Perry, David Smith, and Steven Smith. Different segments of this book were presented at the University of Colorado Law School and New York University Law School, and twice at Northwestern University Law School. I am grateful to the participants in those events, especially to Lea Brilmayer who commented insightfully and skeptically at two of them. My thinking also benefited from conversations with Terry Eastland and William F. Nagel. Katherine Gerland contributed useful research assistance in the final stages.

The University of Colorado provided me with a research leave that was essential to this work. Just as important, the secretarial staff at the law school has been highly professional and patient.

Early versions of chapters and parts of chapters were published as follows: 63 *University of Colorado Law Review* 945 (1992) (Chapter 2); 57 *University of Chicago Law Review* 633 (1990) (Chapters 3, 9); 6 *Constitutional Commentary* 289 (1989) (Chapters 3, 9); 84 *Northwestern Law Review* 858 (1990) (Chapter 3); 61 *University of Colorado Law Review* 685 (1990) (Chapters 4, 9); 61 *Tulane Law Review* 1027 (1987) (Chapter 4); 56 *Law and Contemporary Problems* 11 (1993) (Chapters 4, 5); *Public Values in Constitutional Law* (Gottlieb, ed., University of Michigan Press, 1993) (Chapter 6); 88 *Northwestern Law Review* 193 (1993) (Chapter 8); and 25 *Trial* 72 (1989) (Chapter 9). Material in Chapter 9 is reprinted with permission of *Trial* (December 1989), copyright the Association of Trial Lawyers of America. Much of Chapter 6 is copyright the University of Michigan Press and is reprinted with its permission. Chapter 3 and part of Chapter 9 are © 1990 the University of Chicago and are used here with permission. Finally, part of Chapter 3 is copyright Northwestern University and appears here with its permission. I should add that I tried out some specific phrasing in the *New Republic* (October 7, 1991) and *The Public Interest Law Review* (1993).

Boulder, Colorado   R. F. N.
February 1994

CONTENTS

JUDICIAL POWER AND AMERICAN CHARACTER

1

Introduction: The Court as Cultural Barometer

Part of the romance of constitutional adjudication is the illusion of the "landmark case." Under the reassuring influence of this innocent notion, the Supreme Court seems to float above the political landscape and from its lofty position occasionally pull our policies toward heaven. The moral ambiguities, the backsliding, the unintended consequences—these all pale in comparison to the vivid heroism of the Court's decision to intervene. Because political decisionmaking, which depends on our own virtue and luck, is sometimes frightening, often disappointing, and usually uncertain, the idea of the landmark case is a profound comfort. Whatever our own weaknesses, crucial policies are still possible; they can be imposed by an "independent" judiciary—and permanently at that!

As alluring as such a conception of the Court's role has proven to be, especially to legal academics, the facts paint a different picture. At least since 1957, when the political scientist Robert Dahl published a classic study, we have known that the Court usually follows, rather than leads, public opinion and the political branches.[1] Not only in the results that it decrees but also in the style of its thought, the Court's constitutional interpretations are often reflections of political currents and class interests that are no more elevated than the official positions of the American Medical Association or the editorials of the *New York Times*. For instance, *Miranda v. Arizona*, the famous case establishing the rule that criminal suspects must be warned of their right to remain silent, required that state and local police use a procedure already followed by the Federal Bureau of Investigation. *Griswold v. Connecticut,* which created a constitutional right to use contraceptives, invalidated a statute that no one had seen fit to enforce for decades. Even in one of its boldest decisions of this century, *Roe v. Wade,* the Court preempted a growing and highly respectable abortion reform movement that had already been effective in several state legislatures. In short, although the Court's major pronouncements may seem to come from on high, they often reflect and accentuate tendencies already underway in ordinary political life.[2] Even when the judicial decisions are, in one way or another, out in front of political decisionmaking, the Court's imprimatur is a good sign that important cultural trends are at work.

The Court, then, can be viewed as a kind of barometer of our political culture. This perspective reverses one of the predominant traditions of constitutional studies. That tradition (in which many of my writings have participated) asks how the courts have instructed or changed the rest of society; the judiciary is seen as an instrument acting on other institutions. However, those institutions also act on the judiciary. The courts are not only an instrument but also a reflection. Their work, therefore, can tell us something about ourselves. This book is a speculation about what that might be.

More specifically, it is a commentary on the relationship between the modern practice of judicial review and anxiety about moral decline. My theme is that judicial power is now a reflection of cultural self-doubt—that enforcement of the Constitution is a mechanism that expresses, even embodies, the people's misgivings about the state of their culture. Indeed, it is a mechanism through which we seek to escape our fears by participating in our own censorship.

Although many people—from Dan Quayle to Hillary Rodham Clinton, from Francis Schaeffer to Alasdair MacIntyre—have been saying that we are in a period of actual decline, my starting point is only that for some very good reasons we are anxious about our moral condition. It does not necessarily follow, of course, that doubts could not have been even more prevalent (and justified) in other periods of American history. Moreover, it does not follow from the observations made in this book that judicial review should have flourished during any such periods, for I do not argue that judicial review is a necessary response to a sense of moral inadequacy or that judicial review can function only as a reaction to cultural anxiety. I merely claim that this is one of the main uses to which we put the courts in the modern era.

Constitutional interpretations, as expressed in judicial decisions, are one reflection of our moral insecurity, but the modern practice of judicial review includes other important components. The Court's decisions are shaped in a variety of contexts, some plainly political. Perhaps the most prominent example is the process by which justices are nominated and confirmed. Chapter 2 examines the confirmation hearings on Clarence Thomas. I describe Thomas's dramatic confrontation with Anita Hill as a cultural event in which the often suppressed doubts about the strength of American character were bluntly uncovered. Quite independently of judgments about who was telling the truth, the hearings evoked questions about our inability to face issues honestly, our pleasure seeking, our lack of civic responsibility, and our moral opportunism. I relate each of these deficiencies to the recent record of the Supreme Court in an effort to show that the weaknesses we fear have been authoritatively present in the culture for decades. Perversely, both the hearings and the Court's record suggest that our highest rituals of legality reflect an absence of the moral preconditions for the rule of law.

I then describe Robert Bork's confirmation hearings as an imperfect but legitimate effort by the larger political culture to influence the direction of constitutional interpretation. My claim is that both Bork and his academic enemies are part of an elite that seeks to impose discipline on the distrusted political culture by reliance on abstract intellect. I try to show that this cerebral approach by itself is unattractive and that the hearings were useful to the extent that they exposed the intellectual habits of elite lawyers to broader influences and richer vocabularies. The Bork hearings, however, were only partially successful. I suggest that they fell short because of the continuing and disproportionate influence of legal theorists. This influence is ultimately a reflection not only of the elite's lack of confidence in the moral strength of the broader society but also of the society's lack of confidence in itself.

One consequence of our self-doubt, then, is intense ambivalence about political influence over judicial decisionmaking. I explore other manifestations of this ambivalence, including our conflicted attitudes toward local resistance to the Court's decisions. More specifically, in examining the justices' recent refusal to overrule the decision that established a right to abortion, I focus on their characterization of the political "fire" directed at that decision as illegitimate. I attempt to show both that this characterization is wrong and that it reflects our own deep fears about the capacity of the culture to sustain the rule of law.

I then discuss judicial efforts to deal with the pornography and flag-burning issues. My aim is to show that these decisions also are expressions of cultural self-doubt—that they are an unrealistic effort to convince ourselves that we can decide difficult moral questions without asserting any interest in the quality of the mental state of our fellow citizens. Despite efforts to disguise it, however, the Court's own decisions are inevitably based on visions of a desirable moral climate for our communities. In watching the Court's attempts to hide these animating visions, we can see our own need to escape the necessity for moral choice, a necessity that presents risks in any event but seems intolerably dangerous to people who fear their own weakness.

Next I introduce more explicitly the idea of Court as censor. I claim that in many decisions (involving sexist speech, school prayers, abortion, and racial integration) the Court embodies the same societal urges that have led to the "political correctness" movement. In these decisions the Court attempts to improve the minds of the people it considers morally inadequate by controlling the vocabulary used in public discourse. Another suppressive device in common use today is name-calling or political vilification. This tactic, too, can be seen in many constitutional decisions. In fact, the justices' frequent resort to it can be traced, oddly enough, to certain elevated and civilized aspirations that collide with the fact of deep cultural division. In the inability of moderate justices to define a restrained judicial role, we can see some reasons why even well-intentioned Americans do not seem able to resist invective or to tolerate disagreement.

In the final chapter, I propose that the essential technique of modern judicial review is itself a mechanism of censorship. The "principled" interpretation of our traditions is a device used to escape our full heritage and, therefore, ourselves. I develop this point by using a case that graphically depicts the "breakdown" of the modern family, and so I can relate the justices' use of "principle" to their attitudes toward cultural progress and decay. In the end, constitutional interpretation as practiced today turns out to embody the same defects of character that the Thomas-Hill confrontation put in front of us.

In all this there is much that will irritate the reader. To take a small example, you will have already noticed my use of the first person plural. In some contexts I refer to Americans in general as "we," and in others I refer to legal scholars that way. I recognize that this inclusive usage can seem presumptuous. I also recognize the enormous differences it glosses over. Yet saying what I intend would be difficult without the word *we*. One reason is that I mean to include myself in what I criticize. More important, if we never refer to ourselves as a political community, people will certainly be less likely to appreciate the limited ways in which we are such a community or might hope to become one.

To take a larger example, readers will be annoyed to discover that I make critical observations about many different judicial decisions and jurists. I criticize a decision that does not protect sexist speech, and I criticize an opinion that would protect sexual speech. I am negative about the case establishing the right to abortion and also about the decision that substantially cut back on that right. I lump together the liberal Laurence Tribe and the conservative Robert Bork. I see profound delusion and arrogance in the jurisprudence of the great progressive doctrinalist, Justice William Brennan, but I see the same in the work of the great common law incrementalist, Justice John Marshall Harlan. Making matters much worse, I do not in any specific way propose a better or more suitable role for the justices.

It would not make any practical difference, of course, if I were to make a prescription for judicial behavior. The modern forms of judicial review are solidly entrenched; constitutional interpretation is carried out as it is because of powerful historical and political forces. Accordingly, my objective is not to change the practice but to try to see it and the forces it reflects more clearly. What we cannot expect to change, we can still try to understand.

This is not to deny that some implications flow from the observations offered here. My view is that the Court is not a bastion of intellectual strength or civility or moderation. Instead, on balance it is a house of evasion, exaggeration, and intolerance. The Court is this way because we anxiously suspect that we have similar deficiencies in ourselves. It follows that to have a better Court, we need more confidence as a people. To have the capacity for the rule of law, we need better character. To have lawfulness, we need more politics. There is no shortcut through the judiciary that can substitute for self-respecting personal morality and vigorous political life.

2

Watching Ourselves: The Thomas Hearings and National Character

For three days in October 1991, millions of Americans watched in appalled fascination as the Senate Judiciary Committee considered Anita Hill's charges against Clarence Thomas. Given the mystifying nature of the confrontation between two apparently honest, capable individuals and given the public's normal interest in all things sexual, widespread attention to the televised hearings was to be expected. But our absorption had qualities of intensity and seriousness that suggest a deeper explanation. Certainly many viewers thought that they saw in the hearings a drama conveying something significant about our moral circumstances and political institutions. Thus, citizens across the country discussed the disturbing symbolism of fourteen white male senators sitting in judgment on a black man and a black woman. Many women found common ground in the angry thought that "they just don't get it." For their part, incredulous men for the first time began to take seriously the claim that coping with vulgar sexual advances is a pervasive problem for working women. Pundits wrote gravely about the decline of the confirmation process and, possibly, of the Supreme Court. In short, the public perceived the hearings as a moment of important cultural self-recognition.

But what should we have recognized about ourselves? Could we have seen anything of sustained significance in those fleeting, disturbing images? I believe the Thomas hearings do contain important cultural mean-

9

ing, but that meaning is not what most Americans were especially conscious of at the time or what many would prefer to acknowledge now. Indeed, a blunt description of the underlying import of the hearings runs the risk of sounding so portentous as to be (at once) an unlikely exaggeration and a clichéd truth. What I think we saw on our screens was symbolic confirmation of a very widespread intuition: that the American culture itself is in trouble.[1] Our country is threatened by something less tangible than social "problems" like unemployment and crime. Audacious experiments in equality and personal freedom do not seem to be working, and the signs of possible failure are discouragingly diffuse. Collectively, those signs amount to an emerging American identity comprised of self-deception, indecency, privatization, and moralistic impatience. Most of us, of course, do not think that this description applies to us individually or to the groups with which we identify, but we are condemning of other segments of the population and suspicious of the society as a whole.

The emerging overall conceptualization not only is dismaying in itself but also saps confidence in our capacity to cope with virtually all problems. Hence it is only natural that, in the course of ordinary life, we often attempt to avoid or downplay generalized claims about cultural deficiencies. In the focused, theatrical setting of those televised hearings, the forms of our anxiety could be seen but just as easily sloughed off.

Of course, to say that the Thomas confirmation proceedings should have evoked certain fearful beliefs is not to demonstrate the accuracy of those beliefs. One reason that cultural diagnoses are properly resisted is that, even when based on systematic descriptions, they involve perceptions and judgments that are complex and treacherous. To the extent that the public were to hold or adopt the kind of pessimistic interpretation offered here, the Thomas-Hill confrontation could represent a misleading moment of self-doubt rather than an insight. Ironically, however, the Supreme Court itself provides some evidence of the substantiality of the bleak cultural image that (at some level of dim recognition) drew me—and I suspect others as well—fitfully to the television. Decades of constitutional decisions tell us that what was suggested about us in those proceedings must be taken seriously. In fact, the Court has long been characterizing the disquieting values displayed there as tenets of our fundamental compact.

Inequality as Equality

Visually, the most striking aspect of the hearings was that a row of white male senators sat above—and in judgment on—a black man and a black woman. For some viewers, of course, this sight understandably triggered old and disturbing associations of racial inequality, but the picture was considerably more complicated and contemporary than this. After all, neither Thomas nor Hill appeared to be either inferior or subordinate. Both were experienced attorneys who had been trained at one of the nation's most prestigious law schools. Both were plainly proud, able, and articulate. Thomas was being nominated for a powerful and intellectually demanding job in the national government; Hill had held several significant official positions and was currently a law professor. Both were backed by coteries of advisors, as well as by significant political constituencies. In the way they were treated by the senators, it was obvious that these two witnesses posed as much of a threat to the members of the Judiciary Committee as those politicians did to them.

The physical confrontation between white politicians and black witnesses, then, connoted not only historical inequalities but also modern changes. In the presence and performance of Thomas and Hill, the public could sense the reality of progress in race relations—black people associating with whites at all levels, rising professionally, making political demands, talking back, exercising power. This complex scene, like our actual circumstances, was at once distressing and exhilarating.

In at least one respect, the televised images seemed, as if from a carnival mirror, to present a weird distortion of our actual circumstances. Even before Hill appeared, some liberal senators and commentators were opposing Thomas's nomination on the stated ground that he was being put forward only because of his race and that he was in fact unqualified for the high court. This reversed not only our usual expectation that liberals push hard, the niceties of race neutrality notwithstanding, for the advancement of blacks but also the widespread sense that conservatives are less committed to racial progress. Why were some Democrats talking about strict merit and some Republicans apparently unconcerned about it?

The most obvious answer, of course, was that in the Thomas hearings race was subordinate to broader ideological objectives and to shrewd political strategies. This basic reason for the somewhat comical switch was sufficiently plain to provoke a disturbing set of suspicions. These suspicions have had their elevated analogues in basic policy debates over the last several decades and their more personal analogues in private mutterings and veiled complaints.[2] The hearings put it right there in front of us: It is possible that much of the beneficent assistance provided to racial minorities in modern times may have chiefly promoted the interests of the benefactors; moreover, much of the apparent progress in racial matters may be superficial or even illusory. These two broad suspicions were manifest in doubts about Thomas himself. Was he being cynically used by Republicans and Democrats alike? And was he in fact up to the job?

These questions collapse into one gnawing doubt about the wave of racial preference that has swept across the country. Although it is certainly possible that favoritism on behalf of minority groups is leading toward racial equality, it is also possible that such favoritism is pushing members of all races to accept the terrible doctrine of racial inferiority. This doctrine can ultimately be resisted and rejected, but as a doubt it is inherent in the structure of affirmative action. It is inherent in the use of different and lesser evaluative criteria for minority group members, and it is inherent in the experiences created when relatively "unqualified" individuals struggle to work and learn under difficult circumstances.[3] This, one of the central doubts of our times, could not have been given a more painful representation than in the enigmatic face of Clarence Thomas, who of all the legions of lawyers was the one chosen for nomination to the Supreme Court and who over the course of interminable days had to fight to set aside serious accusations about his ability and his morality.

The possibility that affirmative action, which seems so essential and so decent, could be racist (in the sense I have just indicated) is exceedingly difficult to talk about. If accurate, it robs us of hope and forces our conversations precariously close to discredited ideas about inherent racial differences. It is a possibility that in our public consciousness we cannot entirely avoid and yet cannot entirely face either. Our solution is to march vigorously ahead with eyes averted. This has long been a central aspect of our political discourse at the highest and most authoritative levels. For example, in *Regents of the University of California v. Bakke,* decided in 1978, the Supreme Court approved certain forms of affirmative action in university admissions programs.[4] Justice Powell's opinion, while of debatable legal authority, has turned out to be highly influential through the years; indeed, his vocabulary is now a part of everyday policy making. Powell explicitly acknowledged that affirmative action programs might "only reinforce common stereotypes holding that certain groups are unable to achieve success without special protection. . . ." He met this and other objections, however, by emphasizing the goal of achieving diversity in an educational setting. For Powell, "diversity" had two significant characteristics. It turned race into a merit consideration, because minority status can itself be thought valuable if variety is the objective; and it obscured the extent to which race would be a determinative factor, because diversity can be achieved by taking race "into account" along with many other factors thought to be relevant to admissions decisions. Powell's position, with its strong differentiation between quotas and goals and its insistence that racial preference can coexist with individualized comparison, may be profoundly wise. If so, its wisdom arises in significant part from an underlying perception that our society needs to deceive itself on racial issues.

The other justices who in *Bakke* voted to approve affirmative action joined an opinion by Justice William Brennan. Like Powell's opinion, Brennan's acknowledged that the apparently "benign" use of race can "stereotype and stigmatize. . . . " Such programs can "reinforce the views of those who believe that members of racial minorities are inherently incapable of succeeding on their own." Brennan's reason for believing that affirmative action (at least in certain forms) does not stigmatize minority group members was, however, different from Powell's. Brennan wrote that the specific program at issue did "not simply advance less qualified applicants; rather it compensate[d] applicants . . . for educational disadvantage. . . ." This answer, or something like it, has no doubt been repeated in the minds of many of the beneficiaries of racial preference.[5] Brennan states this (as well as the rest of his argument) confidently, but his position is as much hope as fact. Even if minority students believe their admission is appropriate compensation for past wrongs, their pride can be badly damaged by special treatment.

As if recognizing that his main argument had oversimplified a complex matter, Brennan added a series of specific considerations. After noting various ways in which specially admitted students had to meet the same educational standards as others, Brennan concluded, "Since minority graduates cannot justifiably be regarded as less well qualified . . . there is no reasonable basis to conclude that minority graduates . . . would be stigmatized as inferior. . . ." Here Brennan's words stretch beyond the limit of what a judicial opinion can do. That one or more members of the Supreme Court believe a certain reaction would be unjustifiable or unreasonable has no bearing on whether people will in fact have that reaction. Reasonableness is a criterion in legal argument, but it is not what determines how we human beings regard ourselves or others. Individual self-respect and racial pride, especially, are not subject to cool assessment.

Brennan, in short, was kidding himself. Even the best analysis of a Supreme Court justice cannot bring order to the wilderness of racial perception and prejudice. Brennan could not know what he claimed to know; even less could he decree it to be so. Today we still do not know whether our pervasive reliance on racial entitlement is leading more to equality than to separation, more to achievement than to prejudice. The members of the Court who joined Brennan's opinion, like much the rest of our society, preferred the certainty that goes with self-deception to the anxiety that goes with a momentous gamble.

Offensiveness as Virtue

Aside from the racial connotations of the scene itself, the most obvious reason for our obsessive interest in the hearings was that the substance of Anita Hill's charges riveted us.[6] The words she attributed to Thomas were startlingly graphic and crude. She claimed (if anyone needs to be reminded) that he referred to pubic hair on a Coke can, the size of his penis, and sex with animals. These topics would be offensive to many people in many settings. However, a central principle of the Supreme Court's free speech decisions is that offensive communications are valuable.[7] The Court has said that "one man's vulgarity is another's lyric." It has praised tumult, discord, and offensiveness ("verbal cacophony") as a "sign of strength." It has given protection to words it described as a "scurrilous epithet" and an "execration." In contrast, the Court has repeatedly referred to impulses toward reflection and self-discipline with forbidding terms like "timidity," "chilling effect," and "self-censorship."

As a consequence, a drawing that depicted a minister as having had sexual intercourse with his mother in an outhouse is constitutionally protected. As a consequence, burning or (presumably) walking on an American flag is constitutionally protected. So is the word *fuck* on bumper stickers. So are concerts featuring songs that glamorize sexual brutality. So are pornographic magazines that contain pictures and words offensive enough to make the words attributed to Thomas sound, by comparison, tamely clinical. This cacophony, we try to convince ourselves, is desirable; indeed, if the Court is right, it is one of our defining virtues.

How, then, did the American public manage to be shocked by the sexually explicit conversation described by Professor Hill? The answer is, of course, that while vulgarity is legally protected on public streets, in commercial theaters, on the radio, in public parks, and elsewhere, it is not acceptable in the workplace. What is "robust expression" in most settings is "sexual harassment" at the job site. Accordingly, both Hill's testimony and the resulting publicity emphasized the possibility that Thomas had misused his position in an employment relationship.

The compartmentalization underlying this emphasis was central to our collective experience of the Thomas hearings. Although there were titillating rumors about the nominee's tastes in rented movie tapes, some felt sense of restraint kept this issue from being examined and publicized.

A few questions from senators touched on Thomas's sexual interests outside the employment context, but Thomas, appealing curtly to his right to privacy, easily cut these off. Similar, implicit constraints prevented any move to question his ex-wife. The Judiciary Committee, as well as the nation as a whole, walked the fine line between, on the one hand, a puritanical belief that sexual interests and communications are profoundly relevant to an individual's qualification for high office and, on the other, a hedonistic commitment to free expression and privacy. Only the sharp focus on the employment setting permitted us to have it both ways. What we knew (or should have known) about ourselves as we watched in apprehensive fixation was that in this and other ways our society is putting too much weight on the workplace.

After all, if it is relevant to interrogate judicial nominees about their relationships with employees, surely it would also be relevant to learn how they have treated spouses or lovers. True, Thomas happened to have had special statutory obligations relating to employment relationships, but it remains a fact that any judicial nominee's character (like any presidential candidate's character) could be illuminated in significant ways by information about intimate dealings. It is simply too late in the day to claim that personal traits, such as honesty or kindness or fidelity, are irrelevant to the task of judging.

Even if the workplace and the home cannot be distinguished on the basis of relevance to high office, we like to believe that differential treatment can be explained on the basis of varying privacy interests. By this view, people deeply *need* insulation in their homes but not in their offices. There is, of course, truth in this distinction, but it will not support the degree of compartmentalization that characterized the Thomas hearings. For one thing, our tolerance for sexual expressiveness is by no means restricted to truly private settings; as I have said, our law protects vulgar speech and behavior in a variety of public and commercial contexts. For another, it is easy to think of behaviors within a home or even bedroom that everyone would agree are fit subjects for official proceedings. Certainly incest and wife-beating are examples, and, presumably, marital rape is too.

No, we cannot easily reconcile our normal solicitude for self-expression and personal liberty with the special treatment that we reserve for sexually offensive speech in the workplace. It is possible, of course, that as a society we have taken this solicitude too far. This thought must have occurred to many Americans as they contemplated the nature of Thomas's alleged comments to Hill. Our commitment to individual freedom, however, is so pervasive and so elaborately rationalized that this perspective was to be resisted if possible. A more congenial possibility was that employment implicates uniquely important values. Premised (as they were) on the legal category "sexual harassment," the hearings pushed us to believe this. Simultaneously they offered troubling indications that in our culture both too much and too little is expected of work.

Careerism and Sexual Equality

Sexual harassment on the job is treated specially in our society for the plain reason that we have decided that it is crucially important to remove impediments to job opportunities for women. As a society, our choice is that it is more important to protect women from sexual pressure and vulgarity on the job than at the newsstand or along the street or in the home. As much as we prattle on about the importance of traditional motherhood or about the right of each woman to choose her own course in life, a massive social commitment is based on the assumption that the central path to self-fulfillment is through a paying job.

The Supreme Court has been an important part of this vast experiment. It was the judiciary—the very institution that has so assiduously protected the right to engage in offensive speech—that invented the unprotected category of speech called "sexual harassment" as an implied part of federal legislation against gender discrimination in employment.[8] Moreover, the Court's enforcement of the equal protection clause of the fourteenth amendment has consistently and explicitly been premised on the idea that "traditional" gender differentiation is usually "outmoded" and "invidious." In one typical decision, for example, the Court struck down a statutory distinction that permitted young women to purchase beer at an earlier age than young men.[9] How could the justices have concluded that this preference discriminated *against* females? Not only did the scheme grant a benefit to young women but also it intimated that young females are more mature, more responsible, and less dangerous than are young men. These traditional beliefs—or "stereotypes"—are not in themselves insulting or harmful to women; the Court could treat them as invidious only on the assumption that such expectations and perceptions are evil in that they encourage caution in women and thus subtly incline them toward the home and an unambitious domestic life.

Our national commitment to the economic and professional liberation of women is reflected in other cases, both peripheral and momentous. In *Roe v. Wade,* the 1973 decision creating a constitutional right to abortion, the justices depicted motherhood as a sad and limiting state:

Maternity, or additional offspring, may force upon the woman a distress-ful life and future. Psychological harm may be imminent. Mental and physical health may be taxed by child care. There is also the distress, for all concerned, associated with the unwanted child, and there is the prob-lem of bringing a child into a family already unable, psychologically and otherwise, to care for it.[10]

In its fifty pages of wandering philosophical and psychological discourse, the opinion contains no offsetting perspective; there is no talk of the unexpected pleasures of raising an "unwanted" child, no allusion to the dignity that can come from effort and sacrifice, and no account of the pain and regret that can arise from abortion. As Kristin Luker has shown in her perceptive book, *Abortion and the Politics of Motherhood,* the decision was deeply rooted in a worldview strongly associated with the values of modern careerism: rationalism, independence, freedom, self-fulfillment, and achievement.[11] She notes that even in its concession that a state may seek to protect the life of a viable fetus, the Court assumed that worth is a function of performance. Thus, *Roe*'s paradoxical posi-tion is that a state may preserve life in the womb only from the moment that the fetus has developed sufficiently to be able to survive outside the womb. In fact, the opinion goes further than this, for it explicitly defines *viability* according to the capacity of artificial medical devices to keep the fetus alive. A fetus, therefore, that has not "achieved" much physical devel-opment might still be worthy of state protection if the achievements of medical science are great enough. In its definition of *viability,* then, the opinion assumes that the products of human inventiveness can some-how invest human life with moral significance. The Court that wrote *Roe* in this way and the society that countenances one and a half million abortions a year both have boldly thrown their fate with modern moral psychology: Women are essentially the same as men, and accomplish-ment in a career is the way to self-realization for both.

Today these beliefs often pass as uncontroversial. Ruth Bader Ginsburg, who as a legal advocate and as a scholar pushed them far, was presented as a moderate when she was nominated to sit on the Court, and her confirmation provoked almost no interest or criticism. As unas-sailable as gender egalitarianism often seems to be, at least in polite com-pany, and as audacious as our society's commitment to it has been, these ideas are the source of much anxiety and doubt. This is evident not only in gross political terms (the prolonged failure to enact a federal Equal Rights Amendment and the rise of the pro-life movement, for instance) but also in the ambivalent arrangements that many Americans make as they live their own lives. Even feminist intellectuals have begun to rediscover and refashion the older understandings that females may experience life differently from males and may have distinctive kinds of contributions to make.

The Thomas hearings must have aroused nervous discomfort concerning these issues and may have threatened to make them unmanageable. As a witness, Anita Hill evoked sympathy in part because she appeared attractive, modest, and decent. She claimed to have been verbally assaulted by a salacious, aggressive man, and she, in effect, demanded vindication for herself and protection for others like her. In short, her appearance powerfully evoked a kind of neo-chivalry. The predominantly male Congress rode quickly to the rescue, gallantly expanding federal statutory protections. All this obviously trades on old, "outdated" stereotypes of female vulnerability and male strength, although today we rely on legislative schemes rather than personal codes and we guard careers rather than honor.

Neo-chivalry is a danger to the mind-set that has accompanied our massive commitment to gender equality. Usually, we are able to deny this incompatibility by insisting on the veneer of sex neutrality in the design of protective remedies. When this fails, we sometimes go to absurd lengths to rework the old instincts into acceptable, modern form. The Supreme Court, for example, once determined (sensibly enough) that it is constitutional for a state to discriminate between young men and young women in its statutory rape laws.[12] California, the Court said, could punish males (and not females) for engaging in sex with underage partners. Now, this distinction is undeniably bound up in a web of old beliefs—that males tend to be aggressive, that females tend to be physically weak and emotionally dependent, that intimate sexual contact has (or should have) different meaning for females than for males, and so on. The Court, however, awkwardly passed over such considerations with a reference to the "outdated" idea of chastity. The statute was justified, said our highest court, not by any such protective purposes but because its object was to prevent unwanted pregnancies. Females, the Court intoned, are sufficiently deterred by the threat of conception; that is, because men do not face the risk of pregnancy, only they need the prospect of jail time to control their procreative urges. If the Court is an accurate barometer of our times, we would rather convert the criminal law into a draconian population-control mechanism than acknowledge the disquietingly persistent moral instincts that continue to find their way into public decisions.

Hill's appearance came close to shaking these suppressed instincts into the open. Her testimony elicited from women a virtual chorus: "They just don't get it." Although no doubt this refrain was often taken to mean no more than that men do not understand how widespread sexual harassment is and how angry women are about it, the sentence had force because of its deliberate vagueness. The intimation was that male ignorance is profoundly open-ended. Indeed, it must have occurred to many men to wonder how they could for decades have worked alongside women in professional settings and missed what for women is a crucial fact of the work experience. This oblivion appeared to be so complete as to suggest that men must experience life on the job fundamentally differently from working women. What men thought of as jokes were cutting insults or acts of domination. What men thought of as flirtations were intimidating and oppressive. Behavior that men thought of as a natural part of the world of pressure, challenge, and conquest was out of place in a world that women expected to be ordered, decorous, and safe. In the brief moment of uninhibited anger that followed Hill's testimony, it became acceptable to think that, while working alongside one another, perhaps men and women are occupying different worlds of perception and feeling and expectation.

To believe that such varying subjective experience is possible is to put at issue most of the intellectual underpinnings of gender egalitarianism. If everyday events have such different significance for men and women, there is no reason to believe that achievement is understood or experienced in equivalent ways. Although no specific conclusions about appropriate sex roles necessarily follow from such doubts, a central article of contemporary faith is reduced to the level of question. Are conventionally defined careers a practical route to fulfillment for women?

Even to see this question written here will, I expect, provoke exasperation in some readers. Nevertheless, the question is a serious one, as is evidenced by the fact that it is often asked in its more acceptable form: How radically will (and should) professions like law and business be changed in reaction to the presence of large numbers of women who provide new skills, sensibilities, and needs? It is no wonder that we prefer the more optimistic version of the question. Our society has placed such weight on the morality of equality that we have been willing to alter our vocabulary, restructure our perceptions, redesign our families, and reshape our laws. Both collectively and personally we have risked much on unproven assumptions about women and work.

Perhaps it was because Anita Hill was a self-assured, successful professional depicting mistreatment on the job that she could evoke some of the subterranean doubts that have stubbornly accompanied the rise of sex-neutral careerism. How much, I wondered during those strange proceedings, do we not understand about the lives of working women? Indeed, watching Hill talk of her own career raised to the surface misgivings about whether careers, as they are now defined, can have enough moral significance for anyone, male or female.

Careerism and Responsibility

Hill testified that, despite Thomas's offensive behavior, she followed him from the Department of Education to the Equal Employment Opportunity Commission. Her explanation was partly that Thomas's behavior had improved and partly that she thought her position at Education was insecure. This issue was of obvious interest because, to the extent that her explanations seemed weak, it became more difficult to believe that Hill could have been mistreated by Thomas. The issue was also important in a less obvious way. Even if the explanations seemed believable (as they did to many people), her behavior was disturbing. In casting her professional lot with Thomas, Hill had decided that her job was more important than her obligations to the public.

Those obligations were considerable. If Thomas was guilty of sexual harassment, Hill certainly knew that he should not have been appointed to head the agency charged by law with preventing sex discrimination in employment or become a judge on the U.S. Court of Appeals. As a lawyer and a public official, Hill had a responsibility to citizens at large; as a feeling person she had an obligation to those women who might work for Thomas and might suffer in the ways that Hill said she had suffered. As it was, Hill waited some nine years to make her allegations publicly. Her own explanation for this delay was that "telling at any point . . . could adversely affect my career."[13] In fact, during those years her career benefited more than once from Thomas's position and connections.

If Hill had appeared to be an inept or venal person, this course of conduct might have seemed somewhat blameworthy but only narrowly significant. However, Hill's decision to testify at the confirmation hearings cast her in a heroic role. Moreover, she impressed her audience as an intelligent, decent, strong individual. She was well educated and successful. Therefore, Hill's prolonged silence could not easily be seen as a sign of any personal deficiency. If such an admirable person had placed her career ahead of her sense of civic responsibility, what can be expected of the rest of us? Bravely occupying center stage in a national drama, Hill paradoxically drove home a depressing message about how little selflessness we can expect of one another.

Four other respectable people—Susan Hoerchner, Ellen Wells, Joel Paul, and John Carr—testified that in years past Hill had privately confided information about Thomas's alleged misbehavior. All of these witnesses were lawyers, but not one had pushed her to make her accusations to the appropriate authorities. Their conversations with Hill had focused on her feelings and her career. To be sure, these attorneys had only limited responsibility. The decision to remain silent was Hill's to make and the advantages were hers to enjoy, but the privatization of concern among four separate, sophisticated lawyers was striking. Even when the issue was Hill's responsibility to come forward in 1991 when Thomas was first nominated to the Supreme Court, Judge Hoerchner did not urge disclosure. She testified, "I had no thought of should or shouldn't."[14]

It seemed, then, during the hearing as if an entire profession—indeed, the profession that dominates much of government service and has almost monopoly control over our system of justice—had lost its sense of public obligation. Or, more precisely, the unembarrassed testimony of these four suggested that the legal profession no longer even aspires to a role that transcends privately interested maneuvering. This dismal impression, of course, could be resisted in various ways. Those who identified or sympathized with Anita Hill could note that she was young and inexperienced during at least the early period of her decisionmaking. Perhaps more important, insecurity about a career is understandable for someone whose race and gender have long been obstacles to professional opportunity. But anyone inclined to this explanation was, nevertheless, exposed to the same dismal conclusion about the legal profession. To sympathize with Hill's delay in reporting her allegations about Thomas was to believe that large parts of Thomas's testimony were untruthful and damaging both to her and to our public institutions. For Hill's supporters, then, unbridled ambition and disregard for civic responsibility were personified in a powerful attorney's relentless pursuit of one of the nation's highest positions.

The hearings presented us, then, with differing possible pictures of the degradation of the legal profession. No matter what factual assumptions were indulged, some version of this impression was virtually unavoidable. The impression is worse because it has deep roots. Our culture exalts self-interest. Our psychology theorizes about self-actualization, our political science studies preference aggregation, our economics is built around utility maximization, and our jurisprudence is fixated on rights. Naturally, therefore, the reduction in the civic aspirations of the legal profession has not been a matter of shame or regret. It has, instead, been woven right into our constitutional law. As long ago as 1977, the Supreme Court declared that the advertising of lawyers' fees is protected by the free speech clause of the first amendment.[15] After analogizing legal services to commercial goods, the Court said that the listener's interest in commercial advertising "may be far keener than his concern for urgent political dialogue." With commercial purchasing thus elevated to (or perhaps above) the level of political decisionmaking, the Court addressed the possibility that a constitutional right to advertise might adversely affect lawyers' sense of professionalism. The justices acknowledged the historic view that law is a form of public service rather than a commercial trade but dismissed it as an "anachronism."

In short, the sense of diminished professional expectations that the hearings highlighted has been authoritatively present in our culture for many years. The reduction of law to a trade is important in itself, but it is more significant as a symptom of a widespread loss of idealism. This deeper loss is especially evident in our disdain for the politicians that we elect to office. Consider the scorn directed at the fourteen senators who comprised the Judiciary Committee. We knew that Hill's charges were serious and relevant, and we knew that these senators were obliged to hear evidence and to come to some determination. Yet we were angry with them for doing their jobs. Our resentment did not arise only in reaction to the fecklessness and hypocrisy that eventually characterized some of the performances of some of the senators. It began the instant we saw these politicians sit down to judge the credibility and morality of Thomas and Hill. It began visually, not substantively, for what angered many of us was the spectacle—the idea—of politicians presuming to apply ethical standards.

Distrust of politicians can, of course, indicate independence and vigor among the citizenry, but in recent decades skepticism has grown into a massive drag on representative government. In 1976, for example, the Supreme Court came to the rather astonishing conclusion that local patronage systems violate the free speech rights of government employees.[16] The Court emphasized that patronage penalizes political affiliation, which is true, but the Court's approach, focusing on how much public employment and political affiliation matter to individuals, privatized free speech. Speech is not merely a matter of the gratifications associated with self-expression or economic security. Speech has public functions that include helping to make government responsive to the people.

Rather than being antithetical to these public purposes of freedom of speech, patronage in many respects furthers them. It encourages party affiliation and activity, thus promoting political participation. It vastly increases the operational control newly elected officials can have, thus enabling electoral results to be translated into altered policies. Patronage, in short, is an affront to thoroughgoing cynicism because as a system it links politics in its most materialistic form to high public purposes. The Court, however, found this vision of politics to be another anachronism, outdated by the justices' opinion that merit systems can satisfactorily coexist with accountable government. By constitutionalizing civil service, the Court opted for a clean but despairing definition of the work of the politician.

The modern idea that ordinary, crass electoral politics are unconnected to high public functions has led to far-reaching changes in our institutions. The famous and acclaimed Watergate tapes case provides a sobering illustration.[17] This decision, as everyone knows, helped to drive an elected president from office. Until that dramatic event, it had been the common assumption that the constitutional remedies for misconduct in the Oval Office were all political: presidential oversight or (failing this) impeachment and removal by Congress or (failing this) repudiation by popular ballot. At the time of the Court's decision, the first of these had not worked but the second was underway; an apparently responsible committee of the House was investigating the conduct of President Nixon and his aides. The decision in *United States v. Nixon* proved to a relieved nation that this uncertain and prolonged process could be short-circuited. Corruption at the presidential level, we discovered, can be exposed and rectified by using independent grand juries and unelected federal judges.

The discovery of a nonpolitical solution to executive branch wrongdoing was so delightful that Congress soon set up a kind of prosecutorial civil service largely under the control of the judicial branch. This solution was fully institutionalized by 1988, when the Court validated the Ethics in Government Act, despite a range of strong constitutional challenges.[18] With this, we Americans had successfully neutered some of the most subtle and significant political judgments imaginable—judgments about when, how far, and at what cost high executive officials should be investigated and prosecuted. In determining that these decisions are not fit for elected leaders, we said how little we expect of our politicians. We also said how little we expect of each other.

The devaluation of politicians' work is graphically displayed during every judicial confirmation proceeding. The Senate's "advice and consent" function could ideally provide an opportunity for Americans to connect their ordinary experiences, values, and perceptions to fundamental issues of principle and wisdom. Through our elected representatives, our felt interests and aspirations could be communicated to the judicial nominees who will eventually determine the direction of our fundamental law. What have the federal courts done to public schooling? Have they reduced discipline and sapped local involvement? How much racial integration has been achieved, and should numerical balance be given more or less priority in the years ahead? Have the Court's separation of powers decisions on matters such as the legislative veto turned out to be, as many at first feared, harmful to maintaining accountability over administrative agencies? Have the privacy decisions strengthened or undermined family life? How serious an impediment has the exclusionary rule been to effective law enforcement? Has extension of free speech protections in areas like campaign finance regulation and defamation been healthy or destructive for our system of free debate? Are religious minorities being treated fairly in our schools and other public places? Is affirmative action essential to racial equality or a threat to the self-respect of minority group members? Such are the questions raised by the nomination of people like Robert Bork, Clarence Thomas, and Ruth Bader Ginsburg.

Instead of debating pivotal questions of value and fact, questions that involve politicians in their high roles, members of the Judiciary Committee pretend they are not senators. Like justices or law professors, they talk about penumbras and natural rights, the intent of the framers, the place of *stare decisis*. Or, like trial court judges, they try (with ostentatious and ineffective efforts at avoiding hearsay and other irregularities) to conduct trials about individual guilt or innocence. Or, like a civil service board, they weigh professional qualifications. Any role can be imagined and played except a role that would invest politics itself with real stature and significance.

Moralism and Opportunism

Although they conveyed to us clear indications of how far we have devalued the public responsibilities of lawyers, politicians, and citizens, the Thomas hearings nevertheless had an aura of sticky moralism. Senators claimed to be appalled by the sexual explicitness in Hill's allegations. (Senator Simpson referred to "this foul, foul stack of stench."[19]) The nominee was stern in denouncing invasions of his privacy, and at one point he condemned the whole process as a "high-tech lynching." The chairman was boyishly eager in his efforts to keep the proceedings "fair."

The combination of political cynicism with personal self-righteousness was vividly captured by an exchange that occurred late on Sunday night during the testimony of John Doggett. A sense of anticipation had been building for this witness. Earlier press accounts made his story sound both excitingly strange and potentially important. Had Hill fantasized about romantic relationships with men? Had she displayed inappropriate anger at imagined rejections? As tantalizing as such questions were, Doggett's testimony turned out to be a dud. After spending an inordinate amount of time talking about himself, Doggett told a story that did more to confirm his own egoism than to discredit Anita Hill. Most observers knew at once that Doggett was not a crucial witness, but not Senator Howard Metzenbaum.

Metzenbaum thought Doggett worth discrediting. When his moment to ask questions arrived, the senator turned immediately toward his aide to get a damning piece of evidence. He then demanded to know whether nine years earlier Doggett himself had not sexually harassed a young woman. This question and the "evidence" that it was based on quite appropriately sent Doggett into a fury. The question was a smear. It was based on an aide's telephone conversation with someone who had not testified, had not been sworn, and would not appear for cross-examination. Worse, as Doggett himself angrily pointed out, the smear was an unwitting reenactment of one interpretation of the basic structure of the hearings themselves: If a black male appears as a political threat to white liberals, locate someone who will make charges of sexual misconduct. Metzenbaum's reflexive, casual use of this tactic appeared to confirm the worst suspicions of Thomas and his allies.

No amount of scurrying by Chairman Biden to shut off Metzenbaum's line of inquiry could suppress the wider implications of this play within a play. Senator Metzenbaum's self-assured ideology had been vividly communicated in this and earlier confirmation hearings. It was clear that, for him, there could be only one acceptable direction for the Supreme Court; for him, the judicial role was simply and only to advance the agenda of the Democratic left. The morality of this position being certain, Senator Metzenbaum felt free—indeed, he felt obligated—to pursue his ends by all available means. Thus, in the image of this earnest man we all could see the depressing truth that the genesis of much of our political immorality is in our simplistic moralism.

Americans are a legalistic people, and we especially revere our fundamental law. However, our own impatience for results is causing us to doubt that there is security in rules or integrity in processes. Institutions and procedures matter little to the impatient moralist. If we want, for example, a right to privacy, that is enough ground for finding it where the constitutional text is silent. We hardly even think of the amendment process; that procedure, which is workable and authoritative and available, would require something of ourselves.

For decades now we have demanded that the courts expand, delete, and distort the Constitution, and the judiciary (honored by the significance of the invitation) has complied. As a result, whole libraries of modern constitutional interpretations can be reduced to this sentence: Anything can be forbidden or permitted if there is sufficiently good justification. If impeachment seems impractical or uncertain, it is permissible to substitute the criminal process. If the president seems unwilling to see that the criminal law is faithfully executed, we can entrust this executive function to a new hybrid branch of government. If there is a good reason for the government to regulate the speech of participants in the electoral process, principles of free speech are not offended. If there is not a sufficiently good reason for the government to regulate flag desecration or pornography, principles of free speech are offended. If it seems necessary, federal judges can raise taxes, operate public schools, or administer state prison systems. If it seems unnecessary, newly elected mayors cannot install employees of their own political persuasion. All means must be justified, but the end is always the justification.

As a society, we have demanded so much of law that the idea of law is in disarray around us, replaced by expediency and desire. In the end, law requires us to believe in ourselves, in our strength as individuals and as a culture. It requires that we be able to face what we are doing. It requires that we practice decency and moderation. It requires a capacity for civic responsibility. It requires a moral sense that is mature and restrained. We are fast losing the belief that as a people we have these traits. This loss is what I began to understand as I watched Clarence Thomas's confirmation hearings, and I suspect it was a real, if unacknowledged, part of the meaning of the hearings for many Americans. It is why the opportunity for public deliberation about who should sit on our Supreme Court, the institution that most symbolizes the rule of law, has become such an eerie spectacle.

3

Shaping Law: Elitism and Democracy in the Bork Hearings

Whatever else it may involve, law is a matter of restraint and, therefore, of character. Basic legal practices, such as the consistent application of rules and the impartial evaluation of evidence, require that desire be held in check. During the Thomas hearings, procedural fairness seemed, like a rider on a bucking horse, to be a light, almost ridiculous presence patently subordinate to large political forces and objectives. No one who watched Senator Metzenbaum question John Doggett could fail to see that much of the Judiciary Committee's proceedings were, in this sense, lawless. I suggested in the last chapter that this recognition should have triggered larger self-doubts, for as a society we have demanded too much of even our highest judges and our most fundamental law; we have wanted so much that we have jeopardized the complex and reciprocal expectations of forbearance that make law possible or even imaginable. Our own character is at issue, and our legal system stands in danger of being revealed as a charade.

Because law requires the disciplining of desire by self-control and intellect, it is sometimes thought (especially within the educated classes) to follow that law is the opposite of desire and that intellectualism is the crucial trait for a culture that aspires to legal norms. The most prominent advocate of this position is former judge Robert Bork, who in 1987 suffered through a prolonged inquiry at the hands of the Judiciary Com-

mittee only to have his confirmation to the Supreme Court rejected by
the Senate. In *The Tempting of America,* Bork argues forcefully that these
events amounted to the "political seduction of the law," a victory for the
modern "heresy" that judges should implement their sense of morality
rather than apply law.[1] The lawless qualities in the Thomas hearings, then,
can be viewed as subsequent corroboration of Bork's interpretation of
his own confirmation proceedings. This equivalence, however, is too
simple. Robert Bork's intense and frustrating ordeal did have much in
common with Thomas's experience, but the cultural meaning of the Bork
hearings was also different and, in some ways, more optimistic.

Bork against the Mainstream

At the time of his nomination to the Supreme Court, Bork personified
the law as a discipline and a profession. He had been the Alexander Bickel
Professor at Yale Law School, the Solicitor General of the United States,
and a judge on the Court of Appeals of the District of Columbia. He had
written important books and articles on legal subjects and had argued
significant cases in the courts. Moreover, during the hearings, Bork presented himself as resolutely cerebral. At least in a loose metaphoric sense,
his defeat did represent rejection of "the Law."

Early questioning by Senator Biden on the right to privacy put Bork
on the defensive throughout the hearings. It is worth examining one of
these exchanges to remind ourselves why "Law" had so little appeal.[2]
Biden began by asking whether Bork believed "that the government has
as much right to control a married couple's decision about . . . a child
. . . as . . . to control the public utility's right to pollute the air." Bork
replied that "where the Constitution does not speak—there is no provision
. . . that applies to the case—then a judge may not say, I place a higher value
upon a marital relationship than I do upon an economic freedom." Biden
suggested that under Bork's view, economic freedom "has no more or less
constitutional protection than the right . . . to use . . . birth control. . . ."

Bork then retreated to criticizing how the Court in *Griswold v. Connecticut* had derived the right to use contraceptives. Biden tried to elicit
Bork's opinion on whether a right to privacy exists in the Constitution
and Bork continued his attempt to confine the discussion to his criticism
of the reasoning in *Griswold.* Biden, seemingly weary, then asked:

> Well, let me say it another way then. . . . Does a state legislative body, or
> any legislative body, have a right to pass a law telling a married couple,
> or anyone else, that behind . . . their bedroom door . . . they can or can-

not use birth control? Does the majority have the right to tell a couple that they cannot use birth control?

To this admirably blunt question, Bork replied, "[T]here is always a rationality standard. . . . All I have done was point out that the right to privacy, as defined or undefined by Justice Douglas, was a free-floating right that was not derived in a principled fashion from constitutional materials." Against this vague and intellectualized answer, Biden counterposed Douglas's eloquent language: "The right of privacy [is] older than the Bill of Rights. Marriage is a coming together for better or worse, hopefully enduring, and intimate to the degree of being sacred. . . ." Bork replied that the quoted language was not "the rationale of the case [but only] rhetoric. . . ."

The senator's questions, obviously, were not compelling because of anything in the Constitution; indeed, Biden did not allude to specific language in the document. Nor was his position strong substantively. He did not, for instance, show what was wrong with Bork's claims about the parity—as a matter of legal authority—between privacy and economic freedom. Nevertheless, it is easy to see how and in what way Biden "won" this argument. He made Bork seem downright stodgy. Bork's emphasis on the defects in *Griswold*'s reasoning seemed cold and irrelevant to everyone whose predominant concern is that police not invade bedrooms. The passage from Justice Douglas is sufficiently moving that Bork's focus on its narrow legal significance seemed obtuse. In short, Biden's questions were powerful because they highlighted Bork's willingness to ignore and frustrate the public's heartfelt desire for a constitution that protects sexual privacy. Biden, who sometimes seemed genuinely amazed at Bork's criticisms and doubts, was the appealing child. Bork was always the somber adult, querulous and unmoved by the evident pleasures of moral affirmation through creative interpretation.

The perspective of the child was sufficiently ascendant that senators unembarrassedly jettisoned one traditional source of legal constraint after another. For instance, Senator Arlen Specter, who was one of the most intellectually self-assured members of the committee, repeatedly cast doubt on whether the Constitution should mean what its authors intended it to mean.[3] Adopting arguments that are fashionable in academic circles but not usually in the political arena (where it is more typical to revere the Founding Fathers), he suggested that the intent of the framers may be impossible to identify and that "law does not depend on an understanding of original intent." He even asserted that the school desegregation decision of 1954, *Brown v. Board of Education*, was "at sharp variance with what the Framers had intended." He also argued that our "consistent tradition" is for judges to protect values not found in specific constitutional language. As replacements for history and legal text, Specter alluded to the conscience of the people and to the justices' "feelings" about the needs of the nation. At one point, he went so far as to claim a popular "consensus by the tradition of our Court" that judges should rule even though they have no law upon which to base their decisions.[4]

Much in the hearings, then, supported Bork's view of the symbolism of his rejection. Senators were impatient with process, authority, and constraint. There was in the air a giddy sense that judges should just do good. As Bork urged in his book, all else seemed to fade in the bright and insistent light of moral certainty. From this perspective, Bork seemed, indeed, to represent law as discipline and his opponents seemed to represent politics as desire.

Oddly, however, this perspective can be reversed. Some of Bork's most vociferous and articulate critics accepted this dichotomy between law and politics but switched Bork's characterization. Professor Laurence Tribe, for example, testified that Bork's ideas set him apart "from the entire 200-year-old tradition of thought about rights that underlies the American Constitution."[5] He questioned whether Bork was promoting "a consistent philosophy of judicial restraint rather than personal values." Another prominent legal scholar, Ronald Dworkin, reacted to Bork's defeat by asserting, "Bork is a constitutional radical who rejects a requirement of the rule of law that all sides . . . had previously accepted."[6] He accused Bork of "the jurisprudence of fiat" and of seeking to apply, not law, but "the prejudices of the right."[7] In this mirror image of Bork's interpretation of the hearings, his critics claimed that the Judiciary Committee stood for law as discipline in rejecting a nominee who represented politics as desire.

A crucial area of agreement can be detected beneath these competing accusations. Both Bork and his academic antagonists understand constitutional interpretation as an essentially intellectual activity to be superimposed over majoritarian politics. Bork sees himself, the lonely proponent of principled legality, as standing boldly against a modern consensus that favors merging law and politics. His critics define the mainstream in terms of principle and accuse Bork of standing outside it as a covert practitioner of conservative politics through judicial power. Both sides are united in disapproving of fiat or the politicization of law. This area of abstract agreement casts doubt on whether either Bork or his opponents are right in thinking that Bork is outside the contemporary jurisprudential mainstream. If, as I am about to argue in more detail, the mainstream is characterized by shared assumptions about the primacy of intellect in law, Bork and his rivals *are* the mainstream.

In the remainder of this chapter, I argue that a mainstream does exist and that it consists of Bork and the academic elite that urged his rejection. My point is that, at their best, the Bork hearings represented the commonsense recognition that, although law requires discipline and intellect, it grows out of desire and experience; that is, the hearings repudiated not only Bork but also the mainstream of which he is part. To see this is to understand not only what was useful about the hearings but also where they fell short.

Bork as the Mainstream

Roughly 40 percent of American law teachers proclaimed their opposition to the appointment of Robert Bork to the Supreme Court.[8] In *The Tempting of America,* Bork claims that this opposition revealed the legal academy's subordination—even rejection—of legal norms, and he argues that this devaluation of law is part of a broader anti-intellectual movement based within the universities. Moreover, he insists that this movement poses a grave threat to our constitutional system and, more generally, to the health of our political culture. Bork argues that those who are most responsible for intellectual values lie in order to achieve their immediate political objectives and that they systematically engage in cynical fabrications in order to displace the right of the people to govern.[9]

Bork refers to judicial "civil disobedience" and "limited coups d'état." He describes the doctrine of substantive due process as "utterly illegitimate"; he labels the process of deriving rights from such sources as "the essential nature of all free governments" as "preposterous" and "judicial despotism." He criticizes the application of the desegregation principle to the federal government ("social engineering") and the reapportionment decisions ("disregard for the Constitution"). He condemns not only the work of Justice William Brennan but also that of Justices Samuel Miller (who adopted a position that would lead to "despotism"), Oliver Wendell Holmes (for the *deferential* standard of review proposed in his *Lochner* dissent), John Marshall Harlan (for his "entirely legislative" arguments based on tradition), William Rehnquist (for "judicial revisionism"), and Antonin Scalia (for assuming an "illegitimate power" when he derives rights from the most specific tradition available). Bork, it seems, is just about the only nonheretic.

No doubt, it is offensive for Bork to claim the mantle of reasonableness for himself while condemning the work and ideas of so many responsible and intelligent jurists; nevertheless, if this posture were simply a matter of combativeness, it might be overlooked as the kind of excess common (as Bork himself knows well) in politics, for his is not primarily an academic book. Bork means what he says, however. He has insisted for many years—including in testimony before Congress—that the courts are engaged in a pattern of illegal conduct.[10] The fact is that Bork believes that his approach to constitutional law is right and that just about every other current jurist and scholar is wrong. Thus the problem with Bork's book is not the extreme phrasing it contains but the towering intellectual self-assurance it displays.

We have, however, seen that kind of self-assurance before. It is evident, for example, in Laurence Tribe's generalization about "the entire 200-year-old tradition of thought about rights that underlies the American Constitution." Since Tribe presumed to speak on behalf of an entire 200-year tradition, it is not especially surprising that in the same statement he testified for all of those who wrote and ratified the Constitution (saying that "no understanding of the Constitution could be further [than the theory of original intent] from the clear purpose of those who wrote and ratified the Constitution"). Or that he spoke for all of "105 past and present Justices of the Supreme Court" (none of whose views were as "radical" as Bork's). Or that on occasion he has purported to know the thinking of all respectable legal scholars on controversial issues, or that, like Bork, he is very often certain about the true meaning of complicated constitutional provisions.[11]

Bork, the former Alexander Bickel Professor from Yale is, then, excessively definite, harshly critical, and heroically confident, and in these characteristics he resembles the Tyler Professor of Constitutional Law from Harvard, who resembles the distinguished professor of jurisprudence from Oxford. Recall that after Bork's nomination, Dworkin, like Tribe, presumed to speak for everyone and invoked the idea of heresy: "Bork is a constitutional radical who rejects a requirement of the rule of law that all sides . . . had previously accepted." Harsh criticism? Dworkin wrote that Bork's philosophy is "not just impoverished and unattractive, but no philosophy at all."[12] Certainly not all of the professors who opposed Bork's nomination recognized in his arrogant intellectualism something familiar, but it is safe to say that a very large number of law professors (including me) try to stake out positions that are different from everyone else's, criticize uninhibitedly, and generally write with a degree of authority to which we are not entitled.

Bork may seem unique, nonetheless, in that his condemnation of judges and the authority of their decisions is so complete; it is one thing to be intellectually confident but another to call recklessly into doubt so much of what courts have done for many years. We academics may all be self-assured, that is, but only Bork is outside "the mainstream." This response underestimates the force and ambition of scholarly commentary. Bork is at odds with much legal authority when he criticizes the doctrine of substantive due process, and his specific criticism of judicial reliance on tradition does seem extreme, separating him from positions taken by even Justices Harlan and Scalia. Still, these criticisms are not more far-reaching than John Hart Ely's devastating work on the same subjects.[13] Michael Perry's early writing depicted virtually all of modern constitutional law as illegitimate except insofar as it was justified by some functional theory that had never been imagined, let alone adopted, in any decision that I have read.[14] Bork rejects much authority, both scholarly and legal, but he could not reject more than Mark Tushnet does in his respected book.[15] In criticizing the privacy cases, does Bork repudiate more precedent than the academic critics who took on the hundred-year long refusal of the Court to enforce the free speech clause? More than the progressive realists when they condemned pre-1937 activism on economic issues? Or the process theorists, who described the main work of the Warren Court as usurpation?

Everyone knows that in constitutional law not only scholars but also judges defy whole lines of authority. In the face of specific constitutional text and many decisions directly to the contrary, Justices Brennan and Marshall insisted over and over again that the death penalty is inherently unconstitutional. Well they might, for many solidly established doctrines have been discarded, including separate but equal, the nonapplication of the Bill of Rights to the states, economic due process, the "bad tendency" rule in free speech cases, the political question doctrine in reapportionment and prison cases, and so on. Moreover, many of the Court's most important decisions—think of *New York Times v. Sullivan, Miranda v. Arizona, Griswold v. Connecticut,* and *Roe v. Wade*—were new departures, reversing long-held understandings on the basis of sometimes casual and occasionally incomprehensible references to prior cases. In a country that in the first half of its history saw very little judicial review and during the second half saw it often exercised in lurching defiance of precedent, Bork's willingness to rethink case law puts him in the company of many eminent jurists.

It is possible to try to differentiate Bork from this critical tradition on the ground that the destruction of theory and doctrine is usually accompanied by some positive suggestion so that the resulting innovations in case law have a creative kind of integrity; they are usually linked, or they are supposed to be, to a "better" view of the Constitution. But Bork does offer a positive theory—original intent—and his theory even has established lineage. Moreover, Bork's argument is precisely that this approach would align the cases better with the Constitution as it is properly understood. Like most theorists and judges, he justifies apparently radical recommendations by claiming that they represent an underlying continuity, a realization of the true Constitution.

Probably the least attractive aspect of Bork's iconoclasm is that, although intended to be intensely serious, it sometimes verges on being frivolous or even nutty. He asserts, for example, that for the past fifty years the Court has never had a departure from the framers' intent in order to establish "an item on the conservative agenda." (Never? Is it so clear that the framers of the equal protection clause intended to restrict the authority of local governments to assist disadvantaged racial minorities? Did the authors of the free speech clause think they were protecting commercial advertising and campaign expenditures of corporations?) He writes as if irresponsible political tactics are practiced only by the left and as if there are no exceptions or qualifications to the rule that "activists of the 1960s" have "only contempt" for responsible politics. He depicts the *Griswold* litigation as a cabal of Yale professors battling for the cultural validation of their sexually libertine values.

This problem runs deeper than conspiratorial themes, for those themes betray a general willingness to believe too quickly in the novel or unconventional idea. Indeed, some of the book's fundamental claims are doubtful because they rest so heavily on the challenging abstraction and ignore the ordinary and concrete. As correct as Bork's criticism of *Griswold* may be in principle, it just seems fanciful to conceive of the right to privacy as a threat to our form of government. Such an allegation places too little value on what Bork purports to respect: a sense of history and the public's common sense. The public, after all, has had experience with the right to contraceptives for considerable time now and senses in that experience no real danger. More generally, what most undermines the sense of outraged urgency in Bork's argument that the rule of law is in jeopardy is his own survey of political judging in American history. According to that history, the rule of law has been in jeopardy since *Calder v. Bull* in 1789.

The vice of being overattracted to generalizations and principles is what Bork ascribes to his former colleagues. He is right. Law professors tolerate and reward abstract writing that is every bit as quirky, conspiratorial, and doomsdayish as Bork's.[16] Space limitations preclude anything like a full set of illustrations. Certainly much of the free speech literature is characterized by exaggerated fears and extreme claims. Scholarly evaluations of the Burger Court were often notable for their conspiratorial cast. The commentary on abortion, exemplified by Tribe's reference to abortion laws as "the power to sentence women to childbearing,"[17] is often strained and sometimes hyperbolic. The brilliant, the imaginative, and the unlikely abound in our images of judges—as moral prophets, as intellectual Hercules, as protectors of democracy, as Christlike parable tellers, as saviors of "the very regime itself at some awful moment of supreme peril."[18]

My own favorite academic argument is Richard Wasserstrom's extended analysis of the question whether a good society "would be one in which the individual's sex was of no more significance . . . than is eye color today."[19] Noting that such a society would be incompatible with almost all sexual differentiation—"Bisexuality . . . would be the typical intimate, sexual relationship . . ."—Wasserstrom hesitates in his endorsement. He has to admit, after all, that "substantial sexual differentiation is a virtually universal phenomenon in human culture." This fact, he says, might be a basis for an "argument" if "where there is a widespread, virtually universal social practice . . . there is probably some good purpose served. . . ."; Wasserstrom, however, concludes, "This is an argument, but it is hard to see what is attractive about it."

The virtue of Wasserstrom's analysis, like Bork's, is its bold, imaginative quality. The disadvantage is that it elevates the conceptual over the experiential and historical, and thereby achieves goofiness. Bork's constitutional jurisprudence may be thought demonstrably wrongheaded by more scholars than share my opinion of Wasserstrom's thinking on sexual differentiation. However, widespread rejection of his theory does not set Bork apart—not from Herbert Wechsler or John Ely or Laurence Tribe or Ronald Dworkin or Roberto Unger. Bork is different, if at all, only in that *his* demonstrably weak theory also strains against much of our shared experience with the Court's current practices. To insist on an interpretive approach that would require the dismantling of so much of what has come to seem normal and acceptable has, like Wasserstrom's musings, the quality of being unmoored and unserious. The facts are that political judging is pervasive, has accomplished some good, and is counted on by many people. Although they are less deeply established than the fact of heterosexual attraction, these facts, too, ought to count for something. Bork's book does not make much provision for such considerations; when it does, he becomes (perversely) even less distinguishable from other legal scholars.

Constitutional scholarship is fanciful and adventuresome, but in the end it usually comes home to the Court. So does Bork.[20] It turns out that Bork believes *Brown v. Board of Education* is quite consistent with the framers' intent. Unreasonable sexual distinctions can be objectively determined and are unconstitutional. The reapportionment decisions, although not required by equal protection, fortunately are dictated by "what the Founders meant by a republican form of government." Many distortions of real constitutional meaning, like the post-1937 commerce clause cases, have to be lived with because of respect for precedent.

Indeed, what at first appears to be a forbidding jurisprudence of original intent, can—if you blink—transform itself into a conventional methodology not much different from Tribe's or Dworkin's. The giveaway comes early in the book when Bork praises *Marbury v. Madison* and *McCulloch v. Maryland* and describes Chief Justice John Marshall as a faithful expositor of constitutional meaning. To those who understand the enormous liberties that Marshall took in his highly political decisions, this is a jolt but less so after Bork fully explains his theory of interpretation:[21] Judges ought not make policy "not fairly found in the Constitution. . . ." But judges must engage in policy making when they apply constitutional values to specific cases, and moral philosophy assists judges in deciding "whether a new case is inside or outside an old principle." Although principles must be applied rather than invented, they must be applied so as to keep them relevant in a changing world. Judges should use "the principles in the text." These principles are to be understood as the Framers intended, but if intention is unclear or unknowable, they should be inferred from "the general language of the clause" and defined at the level of generality that "the words, structure, and history of the Constitution fairly supports." Two conscientious judges engaged in this difficult task can arrive at opposite results in the same case; nevertheless, they are sufficiently constrained if they seek "the best understanding of the principle enacted."

Bork, then, should not be misunderstood when he repeatedly and confidently refers to what is actually "in" the Constitution.[22] He does not conceive of our fundamental charter as a box that can be opened and examined; the definiteness of his legal conclusions must be understood as expressing the conscientious character of the complex and difficult mental process that is legal interpretation.

Bork's methodology, understood this way, is not frivolous or radical. In its essentials it is the conventional approach, aspired to by most justices and endorsed by mainstream theorists like Tribe and Dworkin.[23] The weakness of this method is the weakness that Bork identifies but does not apply to his own version of the theory: It provides no significant constraint and thus raises the suspicion that interpretations reflect class and partisan biases. Moreover, Bork's interpretive method invites the same serious charges that Bork makes against many others when he asserts that their interpretations are hypocritical and that their "law" represents deceit. For Bork, as for other elite theorists, interpretation is difficult and serious work, and its results are properly framed in terms of true meaning. Given the inevitability of suspicions about political agendas, such conclusive phrasing inevitably sounds manipulative to a nonbeliever.

Hence, Bork is like most law professors not only in his vulnerability to the severe accusation of deceit but also in his willingness to make the charge. He repeatedly asserts that jurists and scholars use constitutional doctrines as fabrications to cover their left-wing political objectives. Ronald Dworkin calls these charges "shrill and mendacious," meanwhile suggesting that Bork's jurisprudential agenda is to advance "right-wing dogma."[24] For reasons that require considerable explanation, Dworkin does not think he is conceding anything about his own commodious interpretive approach when he describes Bork's as sufficiently loose to permit a political agenda to masquerade as constitutional imperatives. Conversely, exactly the same can be said of Bork and his assertions about the political objectives of people like Dworkin.

Bork, Dworkin, and Tribe all point to the same kind of evidence in denying any covert political agenda.[25] Bork tries to establish his good faith by repeatedly acknowledging that judicial usurpations have in the past had right-wing objectives and by criticizing conservative theorists like Richard Epstein and Bernard Siegan. Similarly, Tribe's testimony on Bork emphasized that he had supported the conservative nominees Sandra Day O'Connor and Antonin Scalia. Dworkin proclaims himself satisfied that Anthony Kennedy, although conservative, does have the makings of a judicial philosophy and is fit for the Court.

Bork and the leading mainstream theorists, then, are alike in the fundamental riddle they present (and in knowing that they present it). To what extent do they believe their own interpretive claims? To what extent are those claims coldly cynical? My opinion is that, at some level, they all believe their own claims and are not hypocrites or liars. I suspect that this opinion would be greeted by knowing guffaws in faculty lounges around the country; if I am right in this suspicion, then unfortunately there is more truth in Bork's general assessment of the academy than we probably will care to dwell on.

The reason for my benign view is not especially benign. It seems likely to me that the inspirational but terrible hold that ideas can have over people is even stronger for those who especially value abstractions and pride themselves on intellect. Justice William Brennan, I think, does believe that in the constitutional text there is a "sparkling vision" that is inconsistent with the death penalty, just as Ronald Dworkin believes that constitutional principles prohibit restrictions on homosexuality. For them, as for Robert Bork and many other powerful minds, there is a real

Constitution, and it would be a dereliction of duty not to enforce it no matter who disagrees or how many object. This fierce ambition, this submission to abstraction, can be viewed as a weakness, even as a dangerous weakness, but it does not differentiate Bork from those who define the mainstream.

Given Bork's devotion to the abstractions of legal interpretation, one of the reasons frequently given for opposing him was startling. Judith Resnik, for instance, testified that Bork "is hostile to the very act of adjudication . . . [and] disdains and distrusts judging itself."[26] Resnik was referring to Bork's judicial opinions, in which she saw a tendency to decide more than necessary and to limit the extent to which courts hear claims of wrongdoing. Since many great jurists have displayed one or another of these tendencies, Resnik's accusation was perplexing. (Did Justice Brennan hate judging? Justice Holmes?) It seems even more perplexing after the appearance of *The Tempting of America* because the book is such an urgent effort to save judging—and law itself—from an oblivion that Bork plainly and intensely fears.

In at least one way, however, the book does suggest that Bork may be "hostile to the very act of adjudication." Bork savages not only exotic judicial inquiries proposed by academics but also ordinary doctrinal analyses of the sort judges actually employ every day. Consider, for instance, the requirements that legislation serve a legitimate governmental interest and be substantially related to its objectives. Bork says of the first: "No theory of the legitimate and important objectives of government . . . is even conceivable." Of the second, he says that usually the social sciences cannot provide an answer and that in important cases, "[d]epending on which way the government states the objective, the law will be impossible to strike down or impossible to uphold." Bork writes as if he is making a rebuttal to a limited theoretical proposal, but in fact his rebuttal calls into question a great mass of constitutional doctrine. Accordingly, it might be fair to say that he hates (or at least rejects) judging as it is now widely practiced.

Like so much of what can be criticized in Bork's writings, the nature of this somewhat oblivious hostility to judging confirms how indistinguishable he is from the mainstream. Bork himself often chides scholars for not facing up to the implications of their arguments on judicial review. For example, he quotes Paul Brest's assertion that "all adjudication requires making choices among levels of generality on which to articulate principles and all such choices are inherently non-neutral."[27] Bork replies that, if this were correct, "we must either resign ourselves to a Court that is a 'naked power organ' or require the Court to stop making 'constitutional' decisions." Similarly, in responding to Justice Brennan's skepticism about the possibility of accurately determining the intent of the framers, Bork writes: "The result of the search [for intent] is never perfection; it is simply the best we can do; and the best we can do must be regarded as good enough—or we must abandon the enterprise of law and, most especially, that of judicial review."[28] In short, both Bork and mainstream theorists can be accused of coming very close to the conclusion that judicial review is illegitimate and should be abandoned.

Although *The Tempting of America* contains much that is useful and admirable, its deficiencies provide a number of sound reasons for doubting that Bork should have been elevated to the Supreme Court—or indeed that the mainstream scholars he so resembles should be in the future. The book displays, as I have said, an overconfident intellectualism, a stridently critical instinct, an attachment to theory that subordinates the wisdom of experience and the weight of practice, an affinity for the novel and audacious that verges on being fanciful and conspiratorial, and strong but unexplained devotion to independent judicial power. Although the Bork hearings were a complicated political event, in their most attractive light they can be seen as representing the rejection of this "mainstream."

Meeting the Enemy

To hear the academic mainstream tell it, the Bork hearings were a high-level academic conversation about jurisprudence and moral philosophy.[29] Thus, Bruce Ackerman describes the hearings "as a part of this ongoing project in self-government" under a Constitution that provides us "with institutions and a language by which we may discriminate between the passing show of normal politics and the deeper movements in popular opinions which . . . ultimately *earn* a democratic place in the constitutional law. . . ." Ronald Dworkin says the hearings were "an extended seminar on the Constitution" and humbly urges that they represent a rejection of "crude historicism" and an acceptance of his own "jurisprudence . . . of principle." And Laurence Tribe writes that the ideal is a "concerted, collective effort by the upper house of Congress to articulate a vision of the Constitution's future, and to scrutinize potential Justices in that vision's light."

At first it seems natural that, if the Senate is to understand its function as influencing something so august as constitutional law, it should gravitate to the most familiar and reassuring model for guiding its deliberations. That model, obviously, is judging. The effects of this gravitational pull of high legal culture were evident everywhere. Senators were praised in the press for their learned questions on textualism, judicial restraint, the place of *stare decisis* in constitutional law, and other matters of legal philosophy. There were elaborate debates about arcane legal doctrines, including the proper standard of review in gender discrimination cases—senators talking about "tiers of scrutiny"!—subtle variations in the clear and present danger test, and the relationship between fifth amendment due process and fourteenth amendment equal protection. Senators' brows were furrowed about penumbras and the ninth amendment, about the containability of the category "political speech," and about the objectivity of the reasonable relationship test as compared to that of the rationality test.

Someone has to advise the senators on how to participate in judgelike conversations and on how to evaluate the nominees' answers. Who better than the elites of the practicing bar and the academy? Is Bork outside the mainstream of legal thought? Better ask those who make up the mainstream. Hence, not only the general values but even specific pet theories of a few eminent professors—theories about the unenumerated rights of the ninth amendment or the breadth of the principle at stake in *Griswold*—momentarily masqueraded as deep political consensus. This professorial influence accounts for what seems in retrospect to be the dreamlike quality of much of Bork's interrogation. Did members of Congress actually welcome judicial readiness to negate legislative decisions and to invite such actions on the basis of the fact of an individual's existence? Did politicians repeatedly take positions that could be characterized as supporting judicial solicitude for such politically controversial causes as homosexuality, subversive speech, and obscenity? All these lines of questioning did occur,[30] and in the argumentative, intellectualized atmosphere of the hearings, they did not seem to create political embarrassment for senators. Nevertheless, they do not exactly have those qualities of stolid common sense and moderation that we like to think characterize the general public's instincts. The questions certainly reflect views that are fashionable in academic circles. It is a sad and (on second thought) puzzling irony that purposeful effort to expose the Court to democratic influence should result in enhanced power for elite groups that already have a disproportionate influence over the shape of the law.

Legalized discourse, however, did not entirely replace normal politics during the Bork hearings. Although some of the tactics were rough and unfair, we must look to some of these injudicious moments to see what was rejected during these extraordinary proceedings. One of the most useful parts of the hearings was the exchange on *Griswold v. Connecticut,* the contraceptive case, which I described at the beginning of this chapter. Another was the exchange on *Shelley v. Kraemer,* the decision that invalidated racially exclusionary covenants in housing. Bork's doubts about the reasoning in these decisions did not put him outside the mainstream; intellectually, those doubts and arguments put him near the heart of the law's commitment to clarity, consistency, and principle. In both instances, arguments that seemed strong in the nation's law school classrooms and in its legal journals seemed weak in the arena of politics. Why?

The reason, obviously, was that what counts in political life is different from what counts in the legal culture. In politics, ideas and justifications matter less and they matter differently; consequently, interest in nuance and abstraction seems suspicious rather than admirable. The position on *Griswold* that seemed powerful to the public had little to do with theories of interpretation or the ninth amendment. What was compelling was that people have come to expect some judicial protection of their sexual privacy and that they want such protection. The position on *Shelley* that seemed powerful had little to do with the legal mainstream's views on the doctrine of "state action." What was compelling was that racial exclusion in home purchasing is no longer usual or expected, and that the interest of minority groups in integrated housing has gained wide acceptance and legitimacy. It seemed quirky, if not sinister, for a nominee to dwell on explanations in an arena where widespread perceptions of normalcy, intense desires, and strongly felt interests are what matter.

By exposing legal thinking to broader political values and forms of discourse, the Bork hearings provided a useful testing ground. Unfortunately, the legalization of discourse during the Bork hearings crowded out much of the politics, giving nonlegal standards only occasional and implicit force. Little information was developed, in all those days of witnesses and questioning, on the actual effects of the Supreme Court's doctrines and decisions. A few representatives of law enforcement organizations spoke about crime and dangers to police officers, black politicians emphasized the importance of the changes that the Warren Court achieved in the South, and the economist Thomas Sowell offered an opinion about the effects of affirmative action. In contrast, an overwhelming proportion of the witnesses were law professors who spoke of philosophy and doctrine, and these subjects also dominated the senators' statements and questions.

If the senators had spent less time on bottomless jurisprudential and doctrinal issues, they could have spent more time exploring whether the performance of the Court during the last ten or twenty years has been good for the country and how that performance might be improved. The legal culture is properly concerned with ideas, but the political culture is properly concerned with the consequences of ideas—with the everyday effects of abstractions on perceptions, aspirations, and self-interest. The

Bork hearings were at their best when they created a political forum—a place where the answers that dominate in the legal culture were not fully satisfactory and where legal discourse seemed limited and sounded tinny. In short, at their best the hearings rejected the idea that law should be the exclusive preserve of abstract thinkers. At their best, they rejected the sharp distinction between experience and intellect, between desire and discipline, between politics and law.

Ironically, it may be that Robert Bork's jurisprudence of original intent was his own effort to reject these same dichotomies. Near the end of his book, Bork says:

> The attempt to define individual liberties by abstract moral philosophy, though it is said to broaden our liberties, is actually likely to make them more vulnerable. I am not referring here to the freedom to govern ourselves but to the freedoms from government guaranteed by the Bill of Rights and the post–Civil War amendments. Those constitutional liberties were not produced by abstract reasoning. They arose out of historical experience. . . . Attempts to frame theories that remove from democratic control areas of life our nation's Founders intended to place there can achieve power only if abstractions are regarded as legitimately able to displace the Constitution's text and structure and the history that gives our legal rights life, rootedness, and meaning. It is no small matter to discredit the foundations upon which our constitutional freedoms have always been sustained and substitute as a bulwark only the abstract propositions of moral philosophy. To do that is, in fact, to display a lightmindedness terrifying in its frivolity. Our freedoms do not ultimately depend upon the pronouncements of judges sitting in a row. They depend upon their acceptance by the American people, and a major factor in that acceptance is the belief that these liberties are inseparable from the founding of the nation.[31]

Bork's jurisprudence thus can be seen as a rhetorical argument, the purpose of which is to sustain a set of mythical beliefs and emotional ties necessary for the protection of individual liberty. Viewed this way, his position has both appeal and gravity; it is an argument, made for a high purpose, that is based on plausible assumptions about the deep underpinnings of successful democratic institutions.

During his confirmation battle, part of Bork's failure was that this side of his philosophy remained hidden. Indeed, it remains largely hidden even after the publication of *The Tempting of America.* To see Bork as someone who believes the people are the ultimate guardians of their rights requires overlooking his opposition to most available political checks on the judiciary; to see him as a political rhetorician requires overlooking his announced disdain for expressive writing; to see him as someone whose aim is to shape and reinforce the sentimental bases of political community requires overlooking his insistent reliance on logic and abstraction.[32] It requires, that is, differentiating him decisively from the academic elite that calls itself the mainstream. Because he did not successfully accomplish this differentiation, Bork was repudiated and so, implicitly, was that elite. It is odd but understandable that the scholarly "mainstream" should have participated in this repudiation, turning on Bork with the special fierceness that goes with self-hatred. Like other Americans, the professors had to convince themselves that one of their own was really very different before they could vent their dismay.

What is more perplexing was the eagerness of members of the Judiciary Committee to rely heavily on legal theorists whose instincts and vocabulary so resembled those of the nominee they were rejecting. Why did senators embrace the style of intellectualism that they were exposing as unattractive? This question is not only about the senators but also about their constituents. Why did we tolerate (even reward) the spectacle of political representatives talking the arid language of law professors while they were slighting matters of readily understandable importance?

Part of the answer must be that many Americans would have found it unnerving to have their representatives openly and directly confront issues of value and consequence. A sustained examination of such issues in a political arena would have laid bare the fact that the future shape of constitutional law depends on what we have experienced and what we want. It depends, that is, on what kind of a people we are. The thinking of the mainstream of the legal academy represents one kind of flight from this knowledge. As unattractive as that method of escape may be, we (professors and citizens both) often find it necessary. It is more reassuring than watching ourselves.

4

Marching on Constitution Avenue: Public Protest and the Court

Most legal theorists, of course, would deny that Robert Bork's intellectual instincts and style resemble theirs and that this similarity was an important, legitimate reason for keeping him from the Supreme Court. However, in at least one respect, Bork and his critics are undeniably alike. To the extent that they can influence the content of the dialogue that formed the public aspect of the confirmation process, Bork, Tribe, and most other academics encourage the jurisprudential and doctrinal focus that I criticized in the last chapter. Bork's complaint about the process is that it became too political, and Dworkin's defense is that the Judiciary Committee in fact conducted an "extended seminar." Here, at least, is common ground on what confirmation hearings should be.

This agreement is remarkable because, while our constitutional system contemplates considerable insulation for federal judges, the nomination and confirmation provisions explicitly provide the opportunity for political influence. The belief that even this opportunity should be utilized as a seminar suggests how deep the consensus is within the mainstream about the primacy of intellect in constitutional interpretation. It follows powerfully that the irrationality and emotionality of politics should be excluded from the decisionmaking of judges *after* they are appointed. Near the beginning of *The Tempting of America*, Bork appealed to this consensus by evoking a "disturbing" image:

> My [judicial] chambers . . . were on the third floor of the United
> States Courthouse and overlooked Constitution Avenue. Twice a year . . .
> I watched massive marches come down that wide street, one by anti-abor-
> tionists and one by pro-abortionists. . . . [T]he demonstrators march past
> the House of Congress with hardly a glance and go straight to the
> Supreme Court building to make their moral sentiments known where
> they perceive those sentiments to be relevant.[1]

To Bork these demonstrations are evidence that many Americans are
coming to accept what he calls the "major heresy" that judges are not
bound by law.

No matter what his academic opponents might say about the rest of
Bork's legal philosophy, they would agree that this picture of direct political pressure on the Court is disturbing. Indeed, it is disturbing for
anyone who values the rule of law. Like the Thomas hearings, the image
provokes underlying anxieties about our culture. As a people, do we want
too much? If we lose our inhibitions against making direct political demands on judges, can we maintain a legal system?

At the most elementary and important level, we know that, whatever
a lawsuit should be, it should not be a plebiscite or a lynching. At a more
rarified level, we suspect that political pressure is inconsistent with judicial review itself, for in one way or another most theories of judicial review turn on the belief that judges have something unique to contribute
to public decisionmaking and that the nature of this contribution is closely
tied to political insulation. These theories emphasize different virtues—
the capacity to remain faithful to constitutional text, to apply law neu-
trally, to protect minority participation in the democratic process, or to
develop coherent moral precepts—but they all have significant appeal and
they are all put at risk by explicit political pressure.[2]

Naturally, judges from all sides of the ideological and jurisprudential
spectrum are emphatic in their disapproval of political pressure on the
courts. Justice Harry Blackmun, the author and staunch defender of *Roe
v. Wade,* started that opinion by writing that the judicial task was "to resolve the issue by constitutional measurement, free of emotions and predilection."[3] He assured us, "We seek earnestly to do this. . . ." More recently,
in condemning legislative efforts to thwart or limit the right to abortion,
Blackmun alluded to the history of massive resistance to desegregation in
the South and affirmed that as "judges . . . we are sworn to uphold the law
even when its content gives rise to bitter dispute."[4] In *Webster v. Reproductive Services,* Justice Antonin Scalia, who is perhaps the sharpest judicial
critic of the right to abortion, lamented the Court's failure to overrule *Roe
v. Wade* and charged that postponement of an authoritative decision "dis-
torts the public perception of the role of this Court." Scalia continued:

We can now look forward to at least another Term with carts full of mail from the public, and streets full of demonstrators, urging us—their unelected and life-tenured judges who have been awarded those extraordinary, undemocratic characteristics precisely in order that we might follow the law despite the popular will—to follow the popular will.[5]

If he is right about nothing else, then, Bork is right that it is disturbing to imagine our law being made in response to clamor in the streets. But Bork is only partly right. No one—not the academic mainstream, not the general public, and not our jurists—behaves in ways that are consistent with this important, yet limited, intuition.

Judges as Politicians

The position that overt political pressure should not influence constitutional judgment becomes puzzling as soon as we recognize that, even as they decry demonstrations and resistance, the justices try to provoke and control political reaction to judicial decisions. Consider Justice Blackmun. He was surely sincere in saying that his effort would be to decide the abortion issue "free of emotion" and independent of "bitter" public disputes, but listen to these extraordinarily impassioned and revealing passages from his dissenting opinion in *Webster*:[6]

> Never in my memory has a plurality announced a judgment . . . that so foments disregard for the law. . . .
>
> Nor in my memory has a plurality gone about its business in such a deceptive fashion. At every level of its review . . . the plurality obscures the portent of its analysis. . . . The . . . opinion is filled with winks, and nods, and knowing glances to those who would do away with *Roe*. . . .
>
> I fear for the future. I fear for the liberty and equality of the millions of women who have lived and come of age in the 16 years since *Roe* was decided.
>
> . . . .
>
> It is impossible to read the plurality opinion . . . without recognizing its implicit invitation to every State to enact more and more restrictive abortion laws. . . .
>
> . . . .
>
> Thus, not with a bang but a whimper, the plurality discards a landmark case . . . and casts into darkness the hopes and visions of every woman in this country. The plurality would clear the way again for the State to conscript a woman's body. Of the aspirations and settled un-

derstandings of American women, of the inevitable and brutal consequences of what it is doing, the plurality . . . utters not a word. The silence
is callous. . . . The plurality invites charges of cowardice and illegitimacy
to our door. I cannot say that these would be undeserved. . . .

. . . .

> For today, at least, the law of abortion stands undisturbed. For today,
> the women of this Nation still retain the liberty to control their desti-
> nies. But the signs are evident and very ominous, and a chill wind blows.

Notice that Blackmun accuses the plurality of inviting the enactment of
restrictive abortion laws even though the plurality opinion bears only in
very limited and indirect ways on the wisdom or desirability of such legislation.[7] Notice that he writes as if the plurality had utterly abandoned *Roe*
and had decided to approve the harshest restrictions on abortion even
though the plurality itself expressly rejects both positions.[8] Notice, finally,
that Blackmun refers repeatedly to women as a unitary group—"American women" and "the women of this Nation"—and speaks in the most
incendiary terms of their liberties, their interests, and their bodies. It is
implausible in the extreme to read Blackmun's opinion in *Webster* as being
addressed primarily to his colleagues on the bench. He is addressing women
in the general public, and his evident purpose is to convince them that the
plurality opinion should be read in the most ominous possible way. Why
would he do this if not to arouse a political reaction to *Webster?*

It is an arresting fact that a highly conscientious judge can—with respect to a crucially important issue like abortion—bitterly criticize political pressure on the Court and also make transparent efforts to mobilize
that pressure. Yet this fact is not grounds for any special criticism of
Justice Blackmun. Consider Justice Rehnquist's dissenting opinion in
Texas v. Johnson.[9] This case, about which I will have much to say in Chapter 6, created a first amendment right to burn an American flag. In the
past, Rehnquist, like Blackmun, had strongly resisted the notion that constitutional interpretation should be based on public opinion and political influence,[10] but in *Johnson* Rehnquist protested the majority's holding by quoting Ralph Waldo Emerson's "Concord Hymn," Francis Scott
Key's "Star Spangled Banner," and John Greenleaf Whittier's "Barbara
Frietchie." He rehearsed bits of American military history with references
to the American Revolution, to hand-to-hand combat at Iwo Jima, and
to the landing at Inchon. Think what you will of Rehnquist's dissent; it
was not addressed primarily to lawyers.

As is also true of Blackmun's opinion in *Webster,* the natural and pre-
dictable effect of the kind of rhetoric used by Rehnquist was to foment

political opposition to a judicial decision. In the case of flag desecration, that opposition appeared in the form of outraged editorials, a new federal statute (which was later also struck down by the Court), and talk of a constitutional amendment. In the case of abortion rights, the opposition could be seen in exaggerated newspaper accounts of the meaning of *Webster,* in an outpouring of political support for organizations and candidates committed to abortion rights, and in a proposed federal statute codifying *Roe v. Wade.* It was against the background of all this political activity that the Court reconsidered its position on both flag desecration and abortion.

When the Court reconsidered its earlier decisions, the justices explicitly took notice of intervening political events. In defending the constitutionality of a new federal flag desecration statute, the government argued that Congress had recognized a "national consensus" in favor of prohibiting flag burning. In *United States v. Eichman,* decided within a year of the enactment of the Flag Protection Act of 1989, the Court noted and rejected this argument.[11] In *Planned Parenthood v. Casey,* decided three years after *Webster,* the Court explained in florid detail (which I will describe in the next chapter) why the political "fire" that had been directed at the Court's abortion decisions should not cause a reversal of *Roe.* In contrast, the interests of those whom Justice Blackmun had sought to arouse were treated solicitously by the Court, which noted the cost that reversal would impose on "anyone who approve[d] . . . a constitutional decision where it [was] unpopular or who refuse[d] to work to undermine the decision. . . ." To these groups the Court said it had undertaken to "remain steadfast."[12]

It cannot, of course, be said with absolute certainty that the Court in *Casey* was affected by the political pressure that Justice Blackmun's opinion in *Webster* may have encouraged. On the issue of flag burning, the Court resisted whatever pressure Rehnquist's opinion may have helped to arouse. It is clear in both cases, however, that the Court did not ignore those political messages. Moreover, the process of reconsideration is not yet complete. Indeed, Justice Blackmun's opinion in *Casey* is an anguished effort to influence subsequent political decisionmaking. As in *Webster,* his rhetoric is plainly aimed not at lawyers but at the general population. ("But now, just when so many expected the darkness to fall, the flame has grown bright.") Again, he attributes the worst motives to those who voted to overrule *Roe.* ("I fear for the darkness as four justices anxiously await the single vote necessary to extinguish the light.") If there is any doubt about what Justice Blackmun is trying to influence, he removes it at the end of his dramatic opinion:

[T]he distance between [overruling *Roe* and reaffirming it] is short—the distance is but a single vote.

I am 83 years old. I cannot remain on this Court forever, and when I do step down, the confirmation process for my successor well may focus on the issue before us today. That, I regret, may be exactly where the choice between the two worlds will be made.[13]

Justices Blackmun and Rehnquist were not oblivious to the incendiary qualities in their respective opinions. Nevertheless, they would probably deny any specific intention to provoke marches, to affect the kind of mail delivered to the justices, or to influence the confirmation process. Normally, however, people are assumed to intend the natural consequences of their actions.

Let us assume that the justices intended only to influence public opinion generally—that they were simply attempting to be persuasive before the broad audience of the American public. Unless the members of the Court are impervious to the views of American citizens, this attempt is, in effect, also an effort to influence subsequent judicial deliberations. I will return soon to the question of whether it makes sense to distinguish between specific form of pressure, like marches down Constitution Avenue, and diffuse forms of pressure, like general public opinion. But now this much is clear: Justices as different as Blackmun and Rehnquist write opinions in a way designed to affect the amount and type of political activity directed at the Court, even while believing that the Court should not be affected by external pressure.

Opinions that speak of "cast[ing] into darkness the hopes and visions of every woman in this country" or that quote "Barbara Frietchie" may be unusual, but fomenting political pressure on the judiciary is an unavoidable part of judging. Every idea, Holmes said, is an incitement. Every persuasive opinion necessarily helps to shape the political climate, which in turn shapes the Court's deliberations. The fact that *Brown v. Board of Education* was a unanimous opinion (or that the Little Rock desegregation decision, *Cooper v. Aaron,* was individually signed by each justice) reduced some political pressures and increased others. Even a tightly reasoned, legally powerful dissent—say, Justice Brennan's in *National League of Cities v. Usery,* the Court's short-lived effort to define and enforce a principle of state sovereignty—will encourage vehement academic commentary. Law review articles are not marches, but the dominant opinion in academia, like general public opinion, is a form of pressure that can help to induce the Court to change direction.[14]

The issue, then, is not whether the justices should write in ways that have the effect of altering the constellation of social and political pressures on the Court. They cannot avoid doing so. Nor is the question whether they should intend these pressures to influence judicial deliberations. They can avoid this intent only by convincing themselves—against considerable historical evidence, not to mention an elementary understanding of human nature—that judges are not influenced by such pressures. The issue is whether the kinds of pressures so often condemned (such as marches and bags of mail) are significantly different from the kinds of pressures usually tolerated or approved (say, widespread political consensus or the opinions of the Harvard law faculty).

Marching and Advocacy

As a way to begin considering this question, let us return for a moment to Justice Blackmun's opinion in *Roe v. Wade*. Remember that he began with the statement that the Court was earnestly trying to avoid emotion and predilection, to decide "by constitutional measurement." Those sentences are directly followed, not by any references to constitutional principles or text, but by this statement: "[B]ecause we do [earnestly seek to avoid nonconstitutional influences], we have inquired into, and . . . place some emphasis upon medical and medical-legal history and what that history reveals about man's attitudes toward the abortion procedures over the centuries."[15] Indeed, the pages immediately following deal with the beliefs of the Greeks and Romans about abortion, the meaning of the Hippocratic Oath, the history of both English and American positive law, and the positions of the American Medical Association (AMA), the American Public Health Association, and the American Bar Association (ABA). I count some twenty-three pages of such material before the Constitution is again mentioned (and then only to concede that its text does not mention a right to privacy).[16] Those twenty-three pages are an effort, according to Blackmun's words, to avoid extraneous influences, to find some constitutional measurement.

Now, Blackmun is not unique in his claims about what is relevant to constitutional "measurement." On the contrary, virtually every member of the Supreme Court in recent years has subscribed to the view that political and moral traditions are relevant to defining constitutional rights.[17] But this wide consensus presents a perplexing question: No matter how they are derived and defined, why are such traditions more appropriate vehicles for measuring the Constitution than are marches down Constitution Avenue? At first glance, the kinds of sources we are talking about—common law principles, philosophical and religious writings, policy recommendations of professional groups—are simply individual or collective opinions about right public policy. That is precisely what is carried on the mail cart to the justices, and precisely what is manifested by political demonstrations in the streets. In fact, opinions that we usually dismiss as "political influence" have the advantages of being current and strongly held. The opinions that we dignify with the word *tradition* are often outdated and faded. At the very least, one would think that if the opinions of the Romans or the early history of state abortion laws is relevant to constitutional measurement, current views should be too.

At such a point, jurists and academics usually start making distinctions, but I find it hard to locate any that are especially helpful. The most obvious distinction turns on the relevance of the type of opinion expressed.

Substantive Relevance

It might be thought that a consensus of respected scholars on a legal question should influence the Court's deliberations but not the chanted slogans of marching feminists or the bottles containing fetuses held out by anti-abortion demonstrators. This kind of distinction seems intuitively strong to many people, but these intuitions depend on implicit and controversial theories about appropriate sources of constitutional meaning. In the days before law faculties turned so much of their attention to Wittgenstein and Habermas, academic opinion might have been thought relevant under a theory, like Bork's, holding that the Constitution should be interpreted according to a rigorous application of legal precedents and historical evidence as to the intent of the framers. Because Justice Blackmun's constitutional interpretation in *Roe* relies on the positions of the AMA and the vicissitudes of state regulation, it is clear that he, at least, does not adopt any such restrictive theory of constitutional meaning. Nor do any of the other justices.

It is difficult to see why the technical knowledge held by the medical profession is relevant to establishing constitutional meaning but not the chants of women who have been patients and not the direct observation of a fetus in a bottle. There is reason to think, in fact, that Blackmun does think that information about raw events is relevant; he may well believe, for example, that seeing an individual in a permanent vegetative state is important to deciding whether there is a constitutional right to die.[18] If constitutional law is supposed to represent profound public morality, as many now claim, I cannot see any reason why Justice Blackmun is not right if he does believe that emotional reactions to direct observation of the subject matter are relevant. I doubt, for example, that a decision about the morality of the death penalty would be fully informed without seeing an execution carried out. Demonstrations on Constitution Avenue are proxies for direct observation. The angry, fervent marchers with their bullhorns and their placards are telling the justices how it felt to them to observe and experience abortion policy in action.

Perhaps it is wrong to think that constitutional law should represent judgments about the morality and wisdom of various public policies, but I know of no one, including Judge Bork, who will argue that such factors should be entirely excluded. It is mysterious that there can be such broad agreement on this point and yet we can still find widespread hostility to the idea that judges should note and be duly influenced by street demonstrations.

Pressure and Persuasion

Even if it is true that the kinds of experiences communicated by political demonstrations are often relevant to the moral decisionmaking that is now a part of constitutional interpretation, it might be that there is an identifiable type of influence—suggested by the very word *pressure*—that is irrelevant under widely shared assumptions about appropriate sources for constitutional law. There is a difference, one would think, between demonstrations or letters that seek to persuade (even if on the basis of emotion, raw experience, or some other unconventional argument) and influence that does not depend on any argument about appropriate legal meaning. Thus, a threat on a judge's life seems to make no claim of any kind about the proper content of the Constitution; its message is "Rule my way no matter what the law should require because, otherwise, I will harm you." As latitudinous as the standards for deriving constitutional meaning have become, there is still a consensus that physical threats are not relevant to interpretation. It might be that this consensus extends to a more general principle: Influence that does not depend on persuasive force is inappropriate. For example, a street demonstration might be labeled pressure to the extent that its message is "Rule our way because there are many of us" or "Rule our way because we are important people."

Because most efforts at influencing the Court incorporate at least some form of legal or moral argument—no matter if abbreviated or crude—this distinction between pressure and persuasion rules out very little. Moreover, even when there is no express argument about law or morality, there can be implicit argumentation. The size of the crowd that masses together on Constitution Avenue is itself an argument unless how many people share a certain ethical position is irrelevant to moral decisions. (It is hard to see why in due process cases it is thought to be important how widespread a tradition is and how long it has been entrenched, except on the assumption that the extent of agreement is an appropriate consideration.) The identity of the protestors can also be relevant unless moral advice from a group of liars or criminals should be as weighty as the opinions of right-living citizens. (Perhaps some judgment of this sort lay behind Blackmun's reliance in *Roe* on the opinions of professionally respectable groups such as the AMA and the ABA.) Indeed, even physical threats can amount to moral arguments unless a fervently held position is entitled to no more moral weight than a lukewarm belief. (Certainly the willingness of civil rights protestors to break the law during the 1960s attested to the seriousness of their ethical claims.) To say that political pressures contain implicit constitutional arguments is not to say that all such pressures ought to be acceded to; sometimes the impolite or garbled or threatening arguments made in the streets ought to be ignored. They should be ignored if they are poor arguments or destructive arguments—but the word *pressure* ought not blind us to the persuasive elements that do exist.

Formal Authority

A third distinction turns on the amount of formal authority represented by those who would pressure the courts. At the high end of this scale would be political influence expressed in constitutional amendments or in the nomination and confirmation of federal judges. In both of these instances a formal governmental mechanism allows for political influence over the courts. Lower on the scale would be the enactment of federal statutes and the exercise of presidential vetoes. Lower yet might be state statutes, the common law, and so on. Political influence expressed in these and other ways may or may not be relevant to establishing "correct" constitutional meaning, but such influence is at least authorized in some degree. Hence the Court sometimes defers to congressional judgments on how to enforce the equal protection clause and to state legislative judgments on the justification for various policies that infringe on rights; indeed, the Court goes so far as to look to established patterns in state law to define individual rights under the due process clause. By way of contrast, letters to judges and marches in the streets can be described as the actions of private individuals who have no authority to shape our positive law.

This distinction does not explain either observed behavior or felt intuitions any better than the distinctions based on substantive relevance. In *Roe* Justice Blackmun, for instance, relied on resolutions and positions of the ABA and the AMA, although those groups are not authorized to make law, whereas in *Thornburgh* he bitterly denounced the actions of various state legislatures in establishing restrictive abortion policies. Moreover, even if Blackmun and other judges consistently honored the formal authority of other governmental institutions, it would not follow that they should ignore nongovernmental sources of opinion. Although private individuals and informal groups are not authorized to establish legal meaning, this lack of authority does not necessarily disqualify them from influencing the formal mechanisms that do establish the positive law. Public opinion appropriately affects, for instance, the judgment of senators on whether Bork should sit on the Supreme Court; why should that same opinion, insofar as it relates to issues like judicial enforcement of unenumerated rights, not also be heard by the sitting justices?

Informal Authority

A fourth distinction emphasizes informal authority. I am referring to the quality of the decisionmaking process that underlies a particular form of influence. Some theorists have proposed, for instance, that the Court should defer to state legislative enactments when there is evidence of public-spirited deliberation, and it may be that public opinion expressed during the Bork hearings should be permitted to affect the Court because those opinions were qualified and transformed in a responsible, thorough public hearing.[19]

Informal and formal authority sometimes track one another, but not always. Perhaps in *Roe* Justice Blackmun listened to the positions taken by organizations like the AMA, which have no formal authority, because they are large and provide opportunities for full and informed debate. In contrast, street demonstrations often reflect relatively unorganized and sudden expressions of opinion; letters represent only the views of single individuals who may be writing without thought or consultation.

It is even sometimes suggested that informal authority can make up for irregularity and illegality. Thus Professor Ackerman has proposed that the legislative innovations of the New Deal have the force of a constitutional amendment (and thus should greatly influence judicial decisions) even though Roosevelt never proposed any amendments and did not even successfully pack the Court.[20] For Ackerman, the massive, mobilized political consensus that developed around the need for affirmative, regulatory government carries its own informal moral and political authority. Similarly, he argues that the fourteenth amendment should heavily influence judicial interpretations despite the fact that the lawful processes of amendment were significantly abused. He claims that the legal force of that amendment arises from the extraordinary nature of the public debate, from the transformative power of focused and inspired public opinion.

One problem with the distinction based on informal authority is that it is likely to be wildly inaccurate. Debate in the ABA may be full and thoughtful or it may be posed or even fraudulent; a single letter may reflect a foolish impulse or the most careful internal moral dialogue. Moreover, the same decisionmaking process can be complex enough to justify very different characterizations. Ackerman emphasizes how the Civil War amendments resulted from deep intellectual and moral deliberations, but they also resulted from (as he acknowledges) brute military and political force. To shift the example a great deal, law review articles might be given low weight because they are typically written by cloistered eccentrics and edited by inexperienced students, but they also can be characterized as the product of a focused, thoughtful collegial discourse. Given the room for error and choice in characterization, emphasis on informal authority is treacherous. To some degree, it inevitably reflects judgments about how correct, not how deliberative, a form of political pressure is. Justice Blackmun, being only human, is inclined to reject the informal authority of state legislatures that oppose his conclusions about abortion; he sees their decisions, like armed resistance to desegregation, as illegitimate expressions of emotion and hostility. Then again, it would be only natural for him to welcome supportive demonstrations by advocates of freedom of choice.

Legalism, Realism, and Edwin Meese's Heresy

The confused and ambivalent state of our attitudes toward political pressure on the courts was vividly captured by the vociferous reaction to Attorney General Edwin Meese's notorious speech, "The Law of the Constitution," which he delivered in the fall of 1986.[21] His argument proceeded along these lines: (1) The Constitution itself is not the same as the judicial opinions that interpret it; (2) the legal authority of the Constitution is superior to the legal authority of judicial interpretations; (3) Supreme Court opinions should be subject to criticism and revision because they may not always be faithful to the document that they interpret; (4) therefore, citizens and government officers should form their own independent and critical judgments about the meaning of the document. Meese tied these points to the well-known position that Supreme Court decisions are binding only on the parties to the case and on executive officers responsible for enforcing its decrees. He claimed that a more expansive view of the impact of judicial opinions would inhibit the formation of the sorts of critical opinions that might help correct judicial errors.

Although certainly not entirely uncontroversial, much of Meese's argument was either plainly true or of respectable heritage. Neither journalists nor legal academics, both of whom frequently criticize the Court for misinterpreting the Constitution, are in much of a position to deny any of the first four points. The notion that the legal effect of judicial decisions should be narrowly confined to the parties is a debatable but serious position.[22] Meese's effort to connect this position with the need to foster critical evaluations of judicial opinions is not altogether convincing but hardly sinister or revolutionary. Nevertheless, much of the public reaction was hysterical in tone.[23] Anthony Lewis, a prominent and sophisticated commentator, characterized Meese's argument as a "calculated assault on the idea of law in this country." Others claimed that Meese was "encouraging defiance" and was "contemptuous of the Court." The urge to condemn Meese's speech was so powerful that some observers, who admitted that he had raised legitimate issues, actually suggested that such weighty matters should be discussed only by intellectuals, preferably university professors.

It is tempting to explain this outpouring of criticism on partisan grounds. Indeed, the jurisprudential mythology holding that judicial interpretations should not be influenced by "nonlegal" considerations can be—and is—trotted out whenever a message from the political world is disagreeable. Prochoice people object to the possibility of the justices being influenced by those bottles holding fetuses, and Justice Blackmun rails against state legislative resistance to *Roe;* some prolife people claim that feminists should not be marching down Constitution Avenue, and Justice Scalia worries about the mail he will be receiving after *Webster.*

In the same way, scholars and journalists attack Meese for saying things that they recognize as important when raised by others. They calmly admit that eminent jurists from John Marshall to William Brennan have emphasized that constitutional meaning should have a political component and that interpretation should be an institutionally shared enterprise; they know that this tradition has been embraced by statesmen like Jefferson, Madison, and Lincoln and (in one version or another) has been expounded by such scholars as James Thayer, Alexander Bickel, and Jesse Choper. Indeed, most commentators are proud of monumental decisions, such as those desegregating the public schools or limiting defamation protection for public officials, that were decided by justices acutely aware of people marching in the streets. They approve of the political resistance to the Supreme Court's early opposition to New Deal initiatives, and they applaud the Court's eventual validation of expanded national authority over commerce. More specifically, they know the impressive lineage of the argument that Supreme Court decisions should be viewed as binding only on parties to the case. Nevertheless, they are outraged when Edwin Meese, the appointee of President Reagan, traffics in these aspects of our constitutional heritage.

More is involved here, however, than partisan distrust and posturing. Meese's critics are articulating a deep and real ambivalence that pervades our constitutional traditions. They are not simply using this ambivalence for their political purposes. They are, I think, in fact subject intellectually and emotionally to it. Like many other sophisticated participants in constitutional debate, they at once believe in political influence over legal interpretations and object to such influence. They, like the American jurisprudential tradition out of which they argue, are intensely legalistic at the same time that they are profoundly realistic.

When we react as pure legalists, even the most accepted forms of political influence seem objectionable. Theoretically, a proposed amendment could be inconsistent with basic constitutional provisions or with some deeper spirit in the overall document.[24] (It is difficult to imagine in our system a blunt holding that an amendment is "unconstitutional," but certainly a new provision could for similar reasons be emptied of any significant meaning.) Although the argument is not common anymore, some still urge that the Senate's advice and consent function should be limited to consideration of technocratic qualifications rather than philosophy, ideology, or probable voting patterns.[25] To the extent that traditional legal materials and methods are thought to be properly determinative of constitutional meaning, it is regrettable to have influence from any group or institution for which such legal values have low priority.

When we react as pure realists, however, even the most irregular forms of influence seem potentially useful to judicial decisionmaking. The reenactment of a statute already held unconstitutional can be justified as providing the courts with an opportunity for sober second thought. The prospect of violent resistance to a decree is a relevant consideration if the courts should seek to preserve their institutional prestige or to take care for the physical safety of members of the plaintiff class; violence itself, as I have said, can be seen as a sign of heartfelt conviction.[26] If practical or political considerations should be an important part of judicial interpretations, disagreement arising from virtually any "real-life" circumstance is relevant and potentially important information.

Because our interpretive practices are both legalistic and realistic, incongruous positions on political influence are always starkly evident. Many will agree (with a knowing wink) that, of course, courts must follow the election returns and react to other significant signs of the times; indeed, it is commonplace to assert, as Justice Brennan phrased it, that judges should have "a decent regard for public opinion."[27] But we fear for the rule of law when masses of people march in front of a judicial building. Observers believe it is only sensible for the Senate to guess how a judicial nominee is likely to vote by asking about their personal lives, their political philosophies, and their opinions on famous cases, but most disapprove when senators ask directly how a hypothetical case should be decided.[28] (In this instance, the ambivalence is so acute that during confirmation hearings intellectually rigorous nominees, such as Bork, slide back and forth from moment to moment, first loftily denouncing questions that call for judgments about how cases should be decided and then matter-of-factly volunteering such answers.[29]) Jurists who would be offended by a personal letter about a pending case take home law review articles that are, in effect, extended pieces of legal advocacy; judges who would never dream of utilizing out-of-court evidence do not hesitate to rely on pre-judicial experiences or on conversations with their clerks.

We compartmentalize our legalism and our realism—and then carry both with us at the same time—for the simple reason that they seem utterly incompatible and yet both seem utterly necessary. Once we assert that judicial review should be predicated on political insulation and traditional legal materials, we cannot justify constitutional decisions that seem morally right and politically necessary. Once we admit that some political reactions should be noticed and evaluated by judges, there does not seem to be any satisfactory way to define the kinds of pressures that are appropriate and those that are not. If they are legalistic, constitutional interpretations will for the most part be either trivial or pernicious. If they are realistic, there may be no distinctive judicial function—a possibility that, given our actual history, is distressingly likely. We want and need a constitutional "law" that is responsive, but what we want and need triggers the deepest fears of lawlessness and breakdown. Hence, Edwin Meese could be bitterly denounced as a dangerous radical by critics who conceded much of his argument as self-evident. Although Meese himself took refuge in a reassuringly formalistic conception of constitutional interpretation, his argument rudely reminded us that the fundamental law, our anchor in a moving sea of moral passions and conflicting interests, in fact grows less from the document than from us. For better or worse, it grows from our raw demands and disagreements, even from our resistance to judicial decisions.

5

Speaking before All Others: Interpretation as the Suppression of Disagreement

The outraged criticisms of Attorney General Meese's speech described in the preceding chapter have their judicial analogue in the Supreme Court's reaction to state laws challenging *Roe v. Wade*. In 1992, twenty years after *Roe* was decided, the Court emphatically reaffirmed the holding that abortion is a constitutionally protected right in *Planned Parenthood v. Casey*. Noting the sustained public resistance to its initial abortion decision, the Court said that to overrule *Roe* while "under fire" would threaten "the character of a Nation of people who aspire to live according to the rule of law."[1] Referring to the rest of us, the justices continued: "Their belief in themselves as such a people is not readily separable from their understanding of the Court invested with the authority to . . . speak before all others for their constitutional ideals."

Here, as in a late-night fit of drunken sentimentality, is revealed an important and disturbing truth about the self-image of some members of our high Court. They believe that judicial sovereignty over constitutional issues is essential, not just to the Court's power or to the practical workings of government, but to our sense of ourselves as a people. Our submission to the authority of the Court—which is to "speak before all others"—is crucial to our very character as a nation. In a mystical transposition, we are obligated to let *it* define *us*.

Like the criticisms of Meese's speech, this outpouring of self-important romance is a reflection of deep anxieties about the rule of law in a
country where the fundamental law is so plainly political in purpose and
derivation. These anxieties are entirely understandable, especially now.
In important areas (such as abortion rights, criminal procedure, religious
freedom, and school desegregation) the Supreme Court has been narrowing rights for some two decades. Much of this constriction has followed the expression of political opposition to earlier, more expansive
judicial decisions, like *Roe.* No matter what the justices assert or believe
about the legal justifications for these cutbacks, it is possible that this
opposition has been a significant consideration. Many Americans, not
just those in the legal elite, instinctively recoil at the thought of precious
constitutional principles being diluted in response to democratic pressure. Generalized fears about the rule of law are natural enough in our
present circumstances.

If political opposition has affected judicial interpretations, it seems
likely that the most influential form of resistance has been official acts
of state and local government officials. I am referring to the kind of resistance that occurs when state authority is exercised in ways that are
premised on disagreement with the Court's reasoning or conclusions but
are not directly defiant. I shall call this "local recalcitrance." A prime
example is the "fire" directed at the Court's abortion decisions—the enactment over the past two decades of legislation burdening the right to
abortion.[2] Some of these restrictions, although significantly different
from the criminal prohibitions invalidated in *Roe v. Wade,* are nevertheless hostile to the spirit of that decision. They implicate state interests
that were not explicitly considered in *Roe,* or they attach somewhat different weights to individual and state interests than did the Court. They
are arguably inconsistent with the "law" of *Roe*'s trimester system (but
only arguably so). These laws are aimed at limiting the right first announced in *Roe* and can be seen as efforts to obstruct and eventually
reverse that decision.

Local recalcitrance, obviously, has been a widespread and significant
form of resistance to the Court's decisions. It can be observed at the street
level when police officers give *Miranda* warnings in a hurried, mechanical tone. It can be seen in the grudging responses of many school boards
to desegregation decrees; these responses are not necessarily segregative but they do slow or complicate the achievement of a full "root and
branch" remedy. It can be seen in various subtle strategies for encouraging prayer and other religious activities in the public schools. In each
of its legal settings, local recalcitrance consists of acts that are aimed at
legitimate objectives—at protecting parental authority over minor chil-

dren, securing confessions to crimes, accommodating the exercise of religion, or providing neighborhood schools. Nevertheless, these acts reflect a different and arguably inconsistent set of priorities from those underlying the relevant judicial decisions.

We are ambivalent in our attitudes toward local recalcitrance in the same way that we are ambivalent about all forms of political influence on courts. For example, the Court sometimes uses local recalcitrance as an ordinary opportunity to define the limits of a prior holding,[3] and under certain assumptions this kind of interpretive "dialogue" certainly makes sense. It is at least possible, after all, that in some circumstances judges might have something to learn from nonlawyers even on traditional aspects of legal interpretation.[4] For example, the restrictive judicial constructions of the text "commerce among the states" prior to 1937 were not necessarily more sophisticated than the competing interpretations common in the political arena. Similarly, the historical claim that the establishment clause was intended to create a high and impregnable wall between church and state was received with justifiable skepticism by many outside the judicial system.

More important, it is certain that formal legal materials are not sufficient bases for interpretations involving matters like abortion, police practices, school prayer, and school desegregation. Decisions in these areas, as in much of modern constitutional law, are thought to be appropriately influenced by judgments about such matters as political and social history, moral philosophy, psychology, education, organization theory, medical science, sociology, economics, and so on.[5] State legislatures, police departments, and local school boards undeniably have access to information and experience relevant to such issues. The political response to *Roe v. Wade,* for instance, provided a troubling rebuttal to the Court's initial itemization and evaluation of possible state interests in the regulation of abortion. The original trimester scheme seemed to overlook the possibility of public objectives related to such values as parental authority, marital harmony, and informed consent. The Court's refusal to note and consider state legislative reactions posing these issues would amount, under the realist view, to willful blindness.

Sometimes, however, the Court treats local recalcitrance as irrelevant or illegitimate. This assessment is often announced as if its bases were self-evident. It is occasionally accompanied by loose analogies to violent defiance and embellished with expansive bromides about the meaning of *Marbury v. Madison.*[6] Given the highly political nature of the considerations that are unquestionably relevant to modern constitutional interpretation, unrefined arguments from legal formalism are plainly unsatisfactory. But more promising justifications can be pieced together. The nature—and limits—of these justifications must be examined before the propriety of local recalcitrance can be fairly evaluated.

The Rule of Law

A relatively sophisticated "rule of law" justification begins with some structural principles. It is commonly thought that resistance from state and local officials is different from disagreement that is manifested by the political branches at the national level.[7] Under the theory of separation of powers, consideration of (and even deference toward) the constitutional judgments of the Congress and president are natural inferences from their coordinate status. Such inferences are especially strong when authority over a specific area is textually committed to one of those branches, as is the case with enforcement of the right to equal protection or the regulation of commerce. In these areas the Court has shown a willingness to consider resistant judgments of the other branches. By way of contrast, the formal acts of state and local governments are (of course) subordinate to federal law. It is true that the substance of certain constitutional provisions may require consideration of state legislative activity, but in these instances state actions are believed to be relevant merely as an objective measure of some social fact. For example, the pattern of state capital punishment laws is relevant to whether this penalty is "unusual" under the eighth amendment, and customary expectations about a particular form of privacy are relevant to the meaning of "search" under the fourth amendment. But as judgments, as acts of disagreement with interpretations of the Supreme Court, it is argued that state laws are at best irrelevant and at worst illegitimate.

They are illegitimate, according to the structural argument, not only because of the supremacy principle but also because of the nature of constitutional limitations and judicial review. It is said that constitutional principles are necessarily checks on momentary majoritarian pressures and that the advantage of judicial enforcement is that federal judges are insulated from—rather than responsive to—politics. To give in to disagreement, then, would defeat the entire enterprise.

These structural claims are supplemented by a pragmatic argument about the role of courts in maintaining the legal system. This second part of the rule-of-law justification asserts that even at the national level resistance to authoritative judicial determinations is permissible only for practical issues surrounding the choice of means, not for ultimate judgments about legal meaning. In explaining its decisions allocating authority to enforce the Constitution, the Court has rather consistently adhered to this distinction,[8] and significant justifications can be asserted for this version of the "myth" of judicial finality. If the idea of "dialogue" were taken so far as to legitimate political efforts to curb or overrule judicial decisions about the meaning of the Constitution, every defiant official act would have the effect of something like a petition for rehearing. Acts prompted by disagreement would be rewarded by judicial attention. Every decided case would invite a cycle of resistance and revision.

The pragmatic argument emphasizes that the function of adjudication is to resolve disputes, not to engender endless controversy and uncertainty. Moreover, the purpose of judicial review in constitutional cases is partly to articulate clear and enduring principles. Ultimately the rule of law requires more than official compliance with judicial decrees; it requires widespread habits of mind that conceive of the announced law as being authoritatively settled even as it evolves.[9] For all these reasons, recalcitrance (it is claimed) should be excluded as a consideration in legal interpretation.

This second component of the rule-of-law argument does not depend on the assumption that courts should refer only to traditional legal sources or that they should monopolize the interpretive function. It acknowledges that legitimate political influence can occur, but insists that generally such influence should occur prior to adjudication. It is at this stage that legislative and executive officials must, as a part of their duties, say "what the law is," and these decisions should be respected by judges.[10] Comity at this stage does not reward disagreement or destabilize judicially announced law. Thus in separation-of-power cases it is considered appropriate for courts to take into account prolonged executive and legislative practices.[11] But once the Court has, for example, invalidated the legislative veto, continued resort to this practice by Congress should not count in subsequent adjudication.[12] Still less should courts consider local recalcitrance on abortion and desegregation.

The realist critique of judicial finality is largely based on the observable fact that written opinions and decrees are neither the only nor the last source of constitutional law. The rule-of-law argument that I have just sketched acknowledges that the law develops from many sources and that it continues to develop after each judicial decision. The argument, which is based on constitutional structure and text as well as on practical claims about the functions of adjudication, purports to be consistent with actual practices. It asserts both that judges do not normally treat local recalcitrance as a legitimate interpretive consideration and that they should not.

It may be that this rule-of-law argument seems compelling, perhaps even obvious. Here, it might be thought, is at least the beginning of a clear understanding of when intellect should confine desire, of why law must be kept separate from politics. The remainder of this chapter casts doubt on this assessment. I describe in more detail how the judiciary has used tradition to define due process rights, and I then outline how it has expanded its definitions of rights in reaction to popular resistance to prior rulings. These two interpretive practices are so widespread as to be responsible for a great part of our modern constitutional law. I will urge that they cannot be reconciled with the rule-of-law argument and that, to the extent that they can be justified, judicial consideration of local recalcitrance is justified too, even when rights are narrowed as a consequence.

Legal Traditions and Constitutional Rights

The use of tradition to define constitutional rights has been effectively criticized (as all of our interpretive techniques have been), but it remains a major tenet of modern jurisprudential orthodoxy. Judge Robert Bork's objections to it were one major reason that those hundreds of law professors opposed his nomination to the Supreme Court.[13] It was said, remember, that Bork's position set him apart "from the entire 200-year-old tradition of thought about rights that underlies the American Constitution."[14] Whether or not this sweeping claim is accurate, the range of justices who in modern times have relied on tradition to define rights is impressive; it includes Earl Warren, William Douglas, William Brennan, Arthur Goldberg, John Marshall Harlan, Warren Burger, Lewis Powell, Thurgood Marshall, Harry Blackmun, William Rehnquist, Antonin Scalia, Anthony Kennedy, Sandra Day O'Connor, and John Paul Stevens. The thinking of many authoritative jurists, eminent scholars, and important politicians converges on the ideas that the Constitution protects implied rights and that these rights should be defined in significant part by judicial examination of our traditions.

This consensus coexists with broad agreement that judges should not constrict rights in response to local political resistance of the type I am referring to as "recalcitrance." I cannot assert, of course, that exactly the same people hold both views, but there is little doubt of substantial overlap.[15] It is not too much to say that these are two of the dominant tenets of our legal culture.

At least superficially, these tenets involve opposite evaluations of the role of local lawmaking in constitutional interpretation. This is so despite wide variation in how judges go about defining our national traditions. They have, as I noted in the last chapter, examined everything from the beliefs of the Greeks and Romans to the positions of the American Public Health Association to recent changes in social morality and private behavior. But judicial descriptions of our traditions virtually always take into account local positive law.[16] Hence, one of the important tenets of constitutional adjudication (that judges should consider local lawmaking when identifying those traditions that define constitutional rights) appears to be in considerable tension with a second (which holds that in defining constitutional rights, judges should not consider local lawmaking if it expresses strong disagreement with prior judicial decisions).

This tension might not involve real contradiction. Certainly, the pragmatic argument for interpretive stability suggests some reasons for different treatment. When the positive law is used in defining our constitutional traditions, there is little risk of engendering a chaotic cycle of revision. Although there is a remote chance that statutory changes may be encouraged by the knowledge that courts pay attention to them when interpreting the due process clause, this possibility is attenuated. After all, changes in the law are motivated by many factors, and they would influence the courts only as a small part of a long history. By definition, however, recalcitrant acts (at both the federal and state levels) express dissatisfaction with specific case outcomes. Therefore, they are relatively likely to be encouraged by anticipated judicial receptivity. Moreover, public officials whose acts were motivated by disagreement with the courts may be inclined to overestimate the impact of their recalcitrant decisions. Thus any acknowledged consideration of these decisions in a judicial opinion may promote additional resistance.

Furthermore, to the extent that the objective is stability in announced meaning (or the appearance of stability), there is a relevant difference between federal and state recalcitrance. Although stability can be undermined by revisions initiated by congressional or presidential actions, the institutional sources for this instability are at least limited to two branches of government. In contrast, the innumerable jurisdictions at the state and local level provide a vast reservoir for recalcitrant action. These disparate authorities are not disciplined by the institutional and political checks that exist for the national government. It may be, therefore, that the practical need to foster compliant mental habits and to articulate clear, lasting principles is especially great when federal courts review the actions of state authorities.

The need for interpretive stability, however, is not the only consideration. The reasons why traditions are relevant to constitutional interpretation are, to some extent, also reasons why recalcitrant local lawmaking should be considered. Judges refer to tradition (including the positive law) in part because their task is to identify liberties that are especially important or "fundamental."[17] Tradition represents an accumulation of public and private judgments about the moral or political significance of a particular freedom and thus is relevant to the substance of the decision facing the judge. It is, of course, always open to question whether any particular aspect of received tradition represents wise moral choice, but it is not necessary for an interpretive source to be infallible for it to be worth consulting. Moreover, even morally doubtful traditions have the advantage of expressing continuing consent—of representing "the Constitution" as actually understood and lived by the people.[18] At any rate, judges aspire to make their differentiations between ordinary rights and fundamental rights on some basis other than their own personal predilections.[19] This is intended to give assurance that judicial determinations are bounded (by the external standard that has been consulted) and authoritative (or, at least, of greater weight than a personal opinion, impulse, or emotion). Traditions, at a minimum, are comprised of the behavior and thought of many besides the judge.

These justifications suggest that patterns of local lawmaking should be relevant even when they are recalcitrant. Of course, it is possible to say that official acts in response to (and in disagreement with) judicial decisions do not represent deeply embedded judgments about wisdom or morality. They can be described as sudden and untested reactions to current controversies. Recalcitrant lawmaking, that is, might be simply too new to be included as a component of tradition. This position is unconvincing for at least two reasons. First, there is no reason to exclude the possibility that recalcitrant acts can be efforts to reconstitute some version of older understandings and practices. Indeed, much of the popular dissatisfaction with the Court's modern decisions has been based on deeply traditional views on such matters as family values, sex roles, educational methods, religion, and neighborhood life.[20]

Second, it is an obvious oversimplification to conceive of tradition as unchanging and old. Experience accumulates by way of experimentation and adaptation. Contemporary political behavior, including official recalcitrance, is a part of our collective life and is relevant to understanding our underlying traditions. This, presumably, is why justices as different as Brennan, Blackmun, and Scalia all have examined patterns of modern statutory change when depicting legal traditions.[21]

To the extent that judges utilize tradition in constitutional interpretation to assure some degree of democratic consent, the exclusion of recalcitrant acts is counterproductive. Whether political traditions are static or changing, recalcitrance at least suggests that an earlier judicial decision contradicts the understanding of some segment of the public. There may be reasons in a particular case why a wave of resistance does not indicate any lack of deeper consent, but these reasons will be offered only in response to candid consideration of the extent and significance of local recalcitrance.

It is, needless to say, highly controversial whether resorting to tradition can provide authoritative standards that are bounded and external to the judge. Tradition, like other sources of legal meaning, can be transformed within the mind of the judge. Nevertheless, our current practices commit us to hope that tradition can provide at least some objectivity. One would think that to the extent any legal justification (including tradition) effectively constrains judges and commands general respect, reconsideration ought to be proportionately less risky both institutionally and intellectually. Possibly, embattled judges who ignore dissent could appear to be the faithful and impersonal expositors of the law, but they are at least as likely to appear arbitrary and willful. In the original abortion decision, Justice Blackmun's lengthy description of our legal and moral traditions was an earnest endeavor to "resolve the issue by constitutional measurement, free of emotion and predilection." Ironically, however, nothing undermined and unmasked this effort at objectivity more than his later venting of personal outrage at decades of local recalcitrance, which he could see only as illegitimate defiance.[22] Calm deliberation about disagreement, in contrast, can convey a sense of confidence that is consistent with the ideal of objectivity.

In short, the reasons usually offered for utilizing tradition in constitutional interpretation also weigh in favor of taking local recalcitrance into consideration. More important, those reasons seriously undermine the structural aspect of the rule-of-law argument. Recall that this part of the argument contrasts recalcitrant acts of the coordinate branches of the national government with local recalcitrance. The argument concedes that judicial deference to federal decisionmakers is often appropriate (because of their assigned duties under the Constitution) but denies that deference is appropriate to state authority (because it is subject to the supremacy clause). Even if state and local acts can sometimes be relevant as independent data, they are not considered relevant as expressions of judgment about constitutional law, which should be defined independently of majoritarian pressures.

Our practice of using tradition (including local law) to define constitutional rights is at odds both with this sharp distinction between federal and state authority and with strict countermajoritarianism. In this practice, state laws are consulted because they represent a cumulative view about what freedoms are fundamental. This means that the judgments of state authorities are relevant on the constitutional issue itself. Indeed, justices sometimes describe unenumerated or implied rights that are derived from tradition as predating and underlying the written Constitution. Justice Douglas, whose words were later thrown up against Robert Bork, found the constitutional right to use contraceptives in "a right to privacy older than the Bill of Rights."[23] Plainly, this approach assigns to state and local decisionmakers a direct role in giving meaning to the Constitution.

Contemporary judges and scholars who approve of this role must believe it is consistent with separation of powers and the supremacy clause. As a matter of logic it is certainly possible for the exercise of state authority to be inferior to federal law and yet still be a constituent element of that superior law. Indeed, if it is correct—as our use of tradition in due process cases assumes—that both official and private actions at the local level should make up some part of the fundamental law, then federal judges are obligated to give effect to those local actions as a part of their obligation to give effect to the Constitution itself. The supremacy clause, under this view, actually requires consideration of and even deference to the exercise of state and local authority. Moreover, constitutional limitations are not to be defined entirely independently of majoritarian preferences; part of the judicial function is to understand how those preferences bear on our deeper political traditions.

This logic is borne out by the distribution of authority in the text of the Constitution. The rule-of-law argument is wrong in its assumption that only the coordinate branches of the national government are assigned duties that necessarily involve constitutional judgment. Just as Congress is assigned the power to regulate commerce among the states and the president is given limited authority over foreign affairs, the text specifies some national duties for state governments and for the people. State legislatures, for example, have final authority to determine "the Places of chusing Senators."[24] The states appoint presidential electors "in such Manner as the Legislature thereof may direct."[25] States must decide, as an initial matter, what it means to give full faith and credit to the official acts of other states.[26] The exercise of state regulatory power can require legal judgments by the states and their people about what powers were "not delegated" to the United States;[27] in fact, one fundamental purpose of state governments in the constitutional scheme is to provide a "counterpoise" against federal officials when they ignore limitations in their assigned roles.[28] Finally, the people, who retain rights that are not enumerated,[29] must continue to decide what it is that they have retained. In sum, the use of state and local laws to help define our constitutional traditions is fully consistent with the constitutional structure. This use therefore severely undercuts a significant part of the argument against judicial consideration of local recalcitrant acts.

From this, of course, it does not follow that federal courts should treat local recalcitrance as an interpretive consideration. It does not even follow that they should consider recalcitrance at the local and national levels as legal equivalents. The pragmatic component of the rule-of-law argument may satisfactorily explain (at least for some) not only why judges should view recalcitrant laws differently from other political acts but also why they should discourage recalcitrance by state officials more than recalcitrance by federal officials. There is, however, another widespread modern judicial practice that throws the pragmatic argument for stability into doubt. This is the strong tendency of courts to expand rights in the face of actual or anticipated disagreement. This practice deserves separate consideration.

Political Resistance and the Expansion of Rights

The prevalent instinct to condemn the Rehnquist Court for narrowing rights in reaction to political resistance is not disturbed by extensive reflection about how those rights came to be widened in the first place. The truth, which I believe is well known but usually left unspoken, is that the same constitutional rights that are now being constricted were once enlarged as a judicial response to local recalcitrance. When it is raised to the surface, this fact presents some difficult questions. What justification might there be for judges treating official disagreement as a reason to expand the definition of rights? If such a justification exists, would its logic imply that sometimes disagreement can also be a reason to restrict the definition of rights? Before addressing these questions, I shall try to explain how we can know that one highly significant interpretive consideration behind the modern "rights explosion" has been recalcitrant local action.

The Practice of Expanding Rights

It sounds odd to say outright that judges have enlarged rights because public officials have disapproved of them. Widespread approval of a decision, of course, might be a reason for augmentation, just as it might be prudent to back away from a decision in the face of disagreement. The judgment of others is always relevant as a form of validation, but it would seem perverse to be fortified by dissension. Perversity, however, is sometimes rewarded. Many of the modern Court's most admired decisions have met resistance that was eventually discredited. Southern opposition to *Brown v. Board of Education,* now a part of our national folklore, was fervent and sometimes ugly, but was largely overcome.[30] Initial indications that President Richard Nixon would defy a grand jury subpoena for the Watergate tapes caused serious concern, but he finally did comply with the decision in *United States v. Nixon*.[31] It is hardly implausible to think that people, including judges, want to be admired for their courage and morality. Consequently, it is not unlikely that for many federal judges a dominant aspiration has become to confront some aspect of the general culture and to transform it by force of the superior virtue represented by the Constitution.[32]

In fact, engendering and surmounting disagreement have become significant aspects of the judiciary's role. The concept of the judge as heroic social reformer has not been left to the private imaginings of jurists. This ideal has been portrayed in admiring biographies and has been rationalized in elaborate academic commentary.[33] It is embodied in the achievements and the reputations of progressive judges like Frank Johnson, Frank Bazelon, William Wayne Justice, Earl Warren, William Brennan, Thurgood Marshall, and Harry Blackmun. As I will describe in Chapter 8, the ideal has also been a major influence on moderate and conservative justices, including the second John Marshall Harlan and Sandra Day O'Connor.

The allure of heroism may be obvious, but how is it possible to know that in specific cases judges have actually expanded rights in reaction to official disagreement? The answer in at least some classes of cases lies in the Court's own explanations. These types of cases are not minor or aberrational. Together they have been and continue to be a significant factor in our modern constitutional jurisprudence.

Impermissible Motivation

In some constitutional decisions, disagreement is cast as an illicit motive and thus is explicitly treated as an interpretive consideration. The Court, for instance, has long said that under the establishment clause state statutes "must have a secular legislative purpose." As a consequence, whether laws were motivated by a desire to foster religion has been an important (and sometimes determinative) consideration. One of the Court's duties, of course, is to determine what particular governmental actions impermissibly foster religion. When local authorities desire to induce a reversal of any such determination, their motive can be said to be (by definition) the fostering of religion. This means that a law *not otherwise in violation* of the establishment clause can be found to be invalid on the ground that it was motivated by disagreement with an earlier judicial determination.

This logic can be seen at work in *Wallace v. Jaffree,* where the Court invalidated an Alabama statute that had authorized public school teachers to announce periods of silence "for meditation or voluntary prayer."[34] The Court said that the actual purpose of the state had been "to characterize prayer as a favored practice" and "to return prayer to the public schools."[35] Now, the terms of the statute neither endorsed prayer nor returned official prayers to public schools. In fact, what the statute itself permitted—for students to meditate or pray during a moment of silence—was not unconstitutional. The Court in *Wallace* was quite clear about this, as it had to be, because to allow all thoughts except prayerful thoughts would itself be unconstitutional. So, if the effect of the statute was to permit something that is perfectly legal, why should the motives of the legislators have mattered?

One possible answer is that motivation changed the effective meaning of the statute. True, if communicated to students, legislative intentions could have converted permission into endorsement. Certainly the literal message "you may pray" can be understood to mean "you should pray." For example, if the speaker has just finished a sermon, the permissive words could convey something even stronger than encouragement. The words alone, if uttered with a certain intonation, could also be received as an endorsement. But consider the evidence the Court offered about legislative motivation. State senator Donald Holmes, a sponsor of the bill, inserted in the legislative record a statement that it was an "effort to return voluntary prayer" to the public schools. This same senator later confirmed in sworn testimony before the federal district court that this was his objective. Moreover, an earlier piece of legislation had already authorized (in fact, had required) a moment for "meditation." Because, according to the Court, "meditation" includes prayer, the later addition of "or voluntary prayer" could have been intended only to send the "message of State endorsement and promotion of prayer."

It may, I think, be safely assumed that neither school students nor their teachers normally study official legislative records or the transcripts of trials in federal court. Any student who had read the words of the 1984 statute and then critically compared them with the language in previously existing legislation was surely exceptional. Therefore, even if the Court was correct in its claims about the motivations of the state legislature, it was not correct in assuming that the basis for those claims had been communicated along with the statutory language itself. The Court did not, in short, explain why students or teachers would understand the 1984 provision as an endorsement of religion.

In what sense, then, were legislative intentions relevant? Perhaps they were constitutionally impermissible, but why? Putting aside the possibility that disagreement with the Court's school prayer decisions is per se improper, the most likely answer is that, because members of the Alabama legislature wanted to circumvent or reverse the 1962 decision that first invalidated official school prayers, the Court understood the moment of silence statute as a first step in a campaign that could eventually lead to an unconstitutional result. This, however, is to say that an action legal in itself can become illegal because it is motivated by disagreement.

Wallace v. Jaffree is not unusual. In the murky judicial business of characterizing official motivation, disagreement with the courts can often be discerned as one indicator of illicitness. For example, in *United States v. Eichman,* the case that reaffirmed and extended the year-old holding that flag protection laws violate freedom of speech, the Court treated the political groundswell that preceded Congress's action as evidence that the purpose of the law was to suppress unpopular messages.[36] Similarly, in *Thornburgh v. American College of Obstetricians,* the Court alluded to the history of recalcitrant state abortion regulations as evidence that the purpose behind one state's "informed consent" rules was to "intimidate women" and "to deter" abortions.[37] In cases like *Columbus Board of Education v. Penick,* local school boards around the country have been found guilty of "segregative intent" because they had "failed to heed their duty" to achieve racial balance after *Brown v. Board of Education.*[38] In each of these cases, rights were extended into new territory. Flag desecration laws became invalid even when they did not single out offensive conduct. The freedom to decide whether to abort grew (temporarily, it turned out) to include a right to have physicians decide when to withhold unpleasant but truthful information.[39] The right to attend schools on a nondiscriminatory basis expanded to overlap substantially with a right to attend racially balanced schools. Perhaps these extensions were wise; certainly, the dominant opinion in the practicing bar and the legal academy supported them. We should, then, face up to the implications of the fact that they were justified in part by reference to official disagreement with prior judicial decisions.

Risk Valuation

Lawyers tend to project the perspective of the time of adjudication backward onto the time of action. We are in the habit of saying that official acts were either "constitutional" or "unconstitutional" because a judge later found them to be so. From the perspective of the governmental decisionmaker, however, it would often be more accurate to speak in terms of risk of illegality. I am not referring to the vagaries of trying to predict a judge's eventual decision. I mean that often "unconstitutionality" is a compound condition, and no single official is in control of all the components of that condition.

Consider, for example, a school board in a district that at one time segregated its students. As I indicated in the preceding section, it would violate the equal protection clause for such a board to perpetuate racial imbalance by adopting a neighborhood school policy if the motivation for this decision were to resist the goal of integration.[40] Suppose that board members vote for a neighborhood placement plan and do so with the expectation that continued racial imbalance will result. Can they know that this conduct is unconstitutional as the vote is cast? Although they can know something about their own motivations, they cannot be sure whether the expectation of racial imbalance will be fulfilled. This will depend on the decisions of others, including zoning officials, real estate agents, and parents. The most that can be said is that the vote helps to create a risk of a constitutional violation.

Obviously, public officials who disagree with a judicial decision will be relatively likely to make decisions that create a high risk of violation. They may value certain countervailing considerations more highly than did the judge, or they may have greater tolerance for factual uncertainties; they may hope that any unconstitutionality that does result will lead to a reinterpretation, or they may simply care little about obedience to a legal principle that seems incorrect. In any event, judges faced with this form of recalcitrance have a strong incentive to broaden the range of prohibited behavior so as to reduce the risk of violation.

This dynamic has been a major and explicit factor in the modern judiciary's expansion of rights.[41] The most famous and clearest examples have arisen in the context of criminal law enforcement. For example, because police need to be deterred from illegal searches and interrogations, judges must exclude illegally seized evidence and un-Mirandized confessions from criminal trials.[42] These requirements rest heavily on the need to instill "respect" for the constitutional value and to assure full compliance.[43] The problem, as recounted in great detail in *Miranda,* is not merely that the police are likely to coerce confessions in the "traditional sense" but that they skate too close to the edge, engaging in tricks and strategies that can turn out (in particular circumstances or with particular suspects) to be coercive.[44] Police, in short, take unacceptable risks. That is a major reason why custodial interrogation is "inherently" coercive and why prophylactic warnings are necessary.

The criminal procedure cases provoked much attention because the decisions themselves specifically distinguish between the substance of the constitutional rights involved and the instrumental measures that the Court was proposing as useful in protecting those rights.[45] It is especially clear in these cases that the area of proscribed conduct has grown larger than what the Constitution itself requires. In many more ordinary cases, however, the dynamic of risk management can also be seen to be at work. In virtually every area of modern constitutional law, principles are ambitiously operationalized with easily remembered aphorisms, bright-line rules, hard categories, illustrative dicta, or elaborate doctrines.[46] These everyday judicial techniques are employed in order to educate, to inspire, to intimidate, and to control. This is thought to be necessary for many reasons. One is that the public and its officials do not sufficiently appreciate the constitutional values enunciated by the Supreme Court and are—if left to their own devices—likely to take unacceptable risks with those values.

Built into modern interpretive methods, then, is a strong hedge against disagreement. If judicial decisions are believed to represent the substance of "the Constitution," this hedge is by definition also part of that substance.[47] Viewed this way, it is not possible to say that otherwise legal behavior is being proscribed due to disagreement; unlike the illicit motivation cases or the prophylactic criminal procedure cases, there are no independent standards acknowledged in the Court's own opinions by which the behavior can be termed "constitutional." But usually opinions do distinguish ultimate principles, values, or objectives from implementing rules and doctrines. Indeed, the latter are justified by reference to the former. Thus, it is the objective of "robust" public debate that justifies the malice standard in certain classes of defamation cases; it is the importance of the value of personal autonomy that (once) explained why restrictions on abortion must serve "compelling governmental interests" and (now) explains the "undue burden" standard. Even within the terms of the judiciary's interpretations, there is slippage between constitutional and judicial standards. Some part of this gap is made up of proscribed behavior that is "unconstitutional" only because of anticipated disagreement.

Motivated Incompetence

One of the most striking and far-reaching aspects of the modern rights explosion is the extent to which the Constitution has been construed to require complex regimens of governmental initiatives. Courts have ordered that prisons be built, that new mental health programs be implemented, and that school systems be transformed. Federal judges have controlled a spectacular range of governmental decisions; they have done so often and in jurisdictions across the country.[48] The phenomenon has formed a central part of public experience of modern judicial power.

From the beginning of the debate over these "institutional injunctions," it has been noted that many of the specifics in the decrees are not required by the Constitution itself.[49] No one thinks that our fundamental compact establishes—either directly or by implication—the right of inmates to have their food prepared by cooks with bachelor's degrees in diatetics or the right of school students to have petting zoos and swimming pools.[50] Such requirements are remedial rather than substantive; they are justified as means toward constitutional ends.

The connection between institutional injunctions and local resistance is well known.[51] The courts, it is often said, are forced to take over an expanding set of functions and to make increasingly detailed decisions because the responsible government officials are responding slowly, inadequately, or not at all. This general account lumps together many forms of behavior that can result from disagreement and treats them all as failures that justify further judicial intervention.

Somewhere within this set of resistant behaviors is the category I have been referring to as "recalcitrant." A warden might, for example, hire new prison guards in compliance with the terms of a decree, but then not train them properly. A school board might reassign teachers without anticipating the need to counteract a drop in their morale. These lapses can be described as motivated incompetence. By "motivated" I do not mean defiant. To create change in complex institutions requires more than submission. It requires will, foresight, enthusiasm, and energy. An official who disagrees with a court's interpretation of the Constitution naturally tends not to be fully enlisted in the court's project. Although such a person's oversights can be (in a sense) motivated by disagreement and although such mistakes can undermine the objectives of the decree, they do not necessarily interfere directly and they are not necessarily intended to interfere. In any particular setting, the forms of resistance to judicial orders are varied and they are matters of degree. Judges cannot be expected to sort out precisely what is producing failure. Motivated incompetence, like other forms of local recalcitrance, is therefore treated as one more reason to control an ever-widening complex of otherwise legal conduct. As remedies expand, rights are redefined to be vague enough or broad enough to be commensurate with the orders. Therefore, like statutes that are unconstitutional because they are enacted with "illicit" motivation and like the prophylactic measures used to prevent dissenting officials from risking constitutional values, institutional injunctions demonstrate that federal judges have responded to officials' disagreement by expanding rights.

The Justifications for Expanding Rights

The various ways in which courts expand rights in reaction to disagreement are all questionable. It can be asked, for example, why (as a matter of substantive constitutional law) it should have mattered that Alabama legislators wanted to endorse prayers in the public schools if all they did was authorize private moments for meditation or prayer. Similarly, even if local officials are putting constitutional rights at risk, by what authority does a court try to prevent constitutional violations before they have occurred? And after violations have occurred, are there *any* limits on the authority of federal judges to take over local governmental functions in a potentially endless quest for full correction? These questions are difficult, but one basic answer is offered to each: The constitutional obligations of public officials may be expanded in order to vindicate rights as defined by the judiciary. State authority is displaced when its exercise threatens federal constitutional values, that is, when legislation has as its aim the subversion of an announced constitutional value, or when discretionary acts create a risk of constitutional violations, or when local decisionmaking is ineffective in correcting violations. In essence, this answer is the structural part of the rule-of-law argument; it asserts that state authority must be subordinated to the supreme law as enunciated by the federal courts. Whether or not the answer is fully satisfactory in this context, the practices that it justifies are solidly in place and widely accepted.

As a justification for expanding judicial protections, the answer is familiar. But why would it not also justify constricting the constitutional obligations of public officials? If the objective (for example) is to prevent the return of official prayers to public schools, it might be that religiously motivated legislation should be permitted as long as it stops short of accomplishing that return. Such legislation could make the exclusion of official prayers more acceptable and thus might reduce outright defiance. If the objective is to prevent the risk of involuntary confessions and illegal searches, it could be that the widest possible range of investigatory techniques should be allowed. Broad local discretion, if effective in securing convictions, might reduce the pressures and frustrations that lead to unconstitutional abuses. If the objective is full implementation of complex institutional reform, it might be that the will and initiative of local leaders could be best enlisted by insulating them from detailed oversight and the threat of displacement.

These possibilities, of course, are all doubtful under some assumptions and in some circumstances. The same can be said of the opposite strategy: Expanding obligations can vindicate underlying constitutional rights on certain assumptions and under some circumstances. The expansion technique apparently strikes many jurists and academics as being sounder.[52] This judgment is defensible but hardly justifies the harsh condemnations of judicial retrenchment that coexist with a generally uncritical acceptance of the established practice of judicial aggrandizement. What is at stake, it turns out, is not the principle that constitutional law is supreme but the relative efficacy of two different protective strategies.

What can account for the doomsdayish terms in which objections to retrenchment are often expressed? Why do scholars fear that rights are being "destroyed" and that the Constitution is "vanishing"?[53] Why do justices brood about undermining "the character of a Nation of people who aspire to live according to the rule of law"?[54] These terms are suggestive of deep anxieties about the durability of our constitutional system, which is portrayed as being in disarray and under ferocious attack. A second justification for the expansion strategy, then, is the openly pragmatic part of the rule-of-law argument. The point is not that expanding rights assures their actualization as required by the principle of federal supremacy. The point is that expanding rights in the face of disagreement prevents chaotic cycles of revision in the announced law. It creates respect for courts as the expositors of law, and it promotes clarity of principle, which generates public understanding and, eventually, agreement. Under this view, what is at stake is not merely the implementation of preferred judicial policies, but the fragile social and psychological supports for the rule of law itself.

How, exactly, might expanding constitutional obligations in reaction to local recalcitrance be expected to accomplish these deeply reassuring goals? The most obvious answer emerges from contrasting the consequences of the two strategies, retrenchment and expansion. Constricting rights (and correlative legal obligations) rewards disagreement and thus invites further recalcitrance. In contrast, expanding rights increases the costs of recalcitrant action by increasing the obligations of public officials. Disagreement is thereby discouraged. The announced law is protected from further political pressure, and the public is encouraged to develop respectful and compliant attitudes.

The difficulty is that this assumes there will be no cycle of revision caused by mounting displeasure. It is certainly possible that as unpopular constitutional meaning is expanded, political dissent will be provoked, triggering more expansion and more disagreement. As a matter of recent history (not to mention common sense), this possibility is quite real. The *Roe* trimester scheme can be understood as an effort to forestall recalcitrant state legislation by predetermining the outcome of many possible future cases, but this expansive strategy provoked especially intense opposition.[55] Subsequent efforts to expand on *Roe*—invalidating paren- tal consent requirements, informed consent laws, and so on—only made the effective meaning of the right to privacy even more unacceptable to segments of the public. The result cannot be described as stability or respect for the rule of law.

As a matter of political prediction, the strategies of expanding and restricting rights both have some potential for discouraging local recal- citrance but also for encouraging it. It may be that lawyers tend to over- estimate the extent to which the rule of law depends on respect for courts and on stability in announced constitutional meaning. The history of judicial review in the United States is remarkable for the amount of political opposition engendered by the courts' decisions and for frequent, significant variations in announced doctrine. As I have argued elsewhere, judge-made constitutional law seems to have more to do with change than with durability.[56] Stable understanding of constitutional values and popu- lar commitment to those values are probably a function far more of social and political life than of judicial interpretation. Even in the most elevated reaches of our legal system, there is no escaping the centrality of our character and our culture.

6

Pursuing Visions: Interpretation as Moral Evasion

The constitutional decisions of the Supreme Court are political not merely in the sense that they are based on considerations that go beyond the traditionally legalistic but also in the more specific sense that they take account of political reactions to judicial interpretations. This is, I have suggested, simultaneously widely known and widely denied. It is both a commonplace and a heresy. It is desirable and intolerable. As the abortion cases demonstrate, it happens most dramatically while being denied most emphatically.

It is not surprising, then, that the Court's constitutional opinions, both liberal and conservative, are often written in a way that masks significant considerations. These opinions tend to be long, detailed, and professional. Consequently, the cases indicate a direction and a sense of urgency without revealing any animating vision or underlying judgment. The stream of words is insistent but fundamentally ineffective, baffling. Sentences, paragraphs, pages are massed to distinguish, say, "core political speech" from "commercial speech" or "symbolic speech," yet the doctrinal consequences of these categories often appear to be (despite the sound and fury) inconsequential or nonexistent.[1] Moreover, even where some doctrinal difference can be identified, the outcomes of the cases often cannot be traced to those differences.

It is tempting to try to understand the Court's categories and their accompanying legal tests as inchoate indicators of more primitive assessments and inclinations that "actually" explain the decisions and provide, at least to the trained lawyer, a basis for prediction. But the opaque words of the opinions are largely ineffective in communicating whatever larger values might justify the predicted results. The demand in a particular subset of cases for a "substantial governmental interest," in contrast to a "legitimate" or "compelling" one, conveys almost nothing about what the basis for judicial predispositions might be. The Court dispatches teeming armies of words and distinctions and propositions, but the battles— if there are any—are out of sight.

Although criticism of this kind is widespread, the characterization just given is, in at least one sense, excessively bleak. It ignores the discernible impact that the Court's legalisms sometimes seem to have. Certainly, academic debate about doctrine is frequently vociferous in a way that would be unlikely if the Court's words were utterly remote and uncommunicative. It might be replied that law professors attach their ardor to surprising objects in the same way that ideologues are aroused by minor deviations. However, politicians, journalists, and even members of the general public sometimes find great significance not only in case outcomes but also in doctrinal justifications.[2] Presumably such people see, if only dimly, some expression of real fears and hopes under the surface of the words of the modern case law.

In this chapter, I closely examine two opinions written by the foremost modern practitioner of doctrinalism, Justice William Brennan. My purpose is to show that the important interests often at work in judicial decisions are indistinguishable from the kind of interests that the federal courts frequently find to be suspicious when asserted by the other branches and layers of government and, furthermore, that the reasons for this suspiciousness apply with special force in the circumstances of constitutional adjudication.

To refer to this sort of public objective (whether judicial or legislative), I borrow from Justice Brennan the term *unfocused interest.* Appropriately enough, this phrase is dry and unexpressive, but it directs attention to the powerful images that drive the justices and that deeply engage the rest of us. The phrase is a key that allows us to see how even highly doctrinal constitutional decisions are judgments about us as a people. They resolve, not legal disputes, but cultural struggles that are dangerously uncontainable in their implications. Legal thinking and doctrinal explanations hide—but do not eliminate—these dangers. Our society's continuing heavy reliance on judicial power suggests that it is not only the justices and the mainstream of legal advocates who find this obscurity comforting. We Americans in general seem to be afraid to keep the nature of our collective moral decisions in focus.

Sexual Speech and Moral Climate

The idea of "unfocused" governmental interests is one of the pervasive themes of modern constitutional analysis.[3] In one version or another it appears in decision after decision: when the Court declares a governmental objective to be vague, insubstantial, speculative, or dangerously "boundless." The specific word itself, however, has been used only rarely. Justice Brennan employed it in his dissent in *Paris Adult Theatre I v. Slaton*.[4] He was describing the governmental interest asserted to justify a prohibition against adults viewing obscene films in commercial theaters. Having just acknowledged that states have authority to regulate not only health and safety but also "the morality of the community," Brennan quickly distinguished the moral objectives behind suppressing obscenity as "ill defined" and "speculative." The state's interest in regulating morality is, he argued, lawful but inadequate to justify the suppression of obscenity. In contrast, "strong and legitimate" interests—perhaps the welfare of children and the privacy of adults—might justify controls over the methods of distribution of obscene material.

The distinction between "unfocused" interests and "strong" interests, then, was a tentative effort to establish a hierarchy of public purposes. The word *unfocused* was part of a justification for the relatively low legal weight that Justice Brennan would assign to the state interests behind at least certain "moral" regulations. It is possible to see in this argument traces of a general distinction between definitive governmental interests that can be rationally justified and weak interests that are unprovable or "only" moral. In one form or another, this distinction is deeply rooted and widespread in both the case law and legal theory, so much so that in some circles the word *moral* has weak, sentimental, or irrational connotations.[5]

To the extent that Brennan's analysis deprecates moral regulation, perhaps it trades on these associations. But the distinction between "moral" and "rational" public objectives, which Brennan seems in places to be making, does not withstand reflection, including his own. He acknowledges, for example, that profoundly important laws, such as those that abolish the death penalty, are grounded in part "on a concern about the morality of the community." Surely, the two potentially "strong" state interests that Brennan mentions in connection with regulating obscenity (protecting children and privacy) reflect important moral values and could serve to define a society's character. It is necessary, then, to understand Brennan's proposed hierarchy in a slightly different way; his position must be that some state interests are "strong and legitimate," not because unprovable moral interests are absent, but because they are present in an identifiable way, that is, in a "focused" way. Under this reading, the category "unfocused interests" is an effort to distinguish unimportant *moral* regulation from important *moral* regulation.

If "unfocused interests" are not defined by the presence of either individual or collective moral considerations, what does define them? Brennan's discussion emphasizes the intangible and uncertain kinds of consequences that can be traced to exposure to obscenity. There is "little empirical basis" for a causal connection between obscenity and sexual deviance or crimes. It is only "speculative" that repressing obscenity would build a moral community, and, in any event, the idea of a moral community is "ill defined." Brennan acknowledges only once that the suppression of obscenity can be linked to specific consequences, and this consequence (shaping the content of an individual's thoughts) is intangible. Specificity in this instance is no justification because, according to Brennan, the state does not have a legitimate interest in mind control.

These aspects of Brennan's opinion assume that the state's important moral interests involve "real" consequences and specific behavior. At one level, this argument is simply inapposite. Obscene material is tangible, and its absence in public places is a specific objective, not different in this sense from the objective of reducing the number of psychologically impaired children or the range of official intrusions into private lives of adults. It might be objected that, although the absence of obscenity is a tangible purpose, the moral value being sought is something different and more abstract than this physical absence. This is true, but it is also true of such "legitimate" values as psychological health and personal privacy, which involve values that are different from (and more abstract than) the mere absence of impairment or intrusion.

Even assuming Brennan were right that the public purposes to which he would assign a higher value are "harder" or more measurable than the governmental interest behind suppressing obscenity, why would he believe that "unfocused" moral interests are unimportant? Everyone can immediately think of obviously important moral purposes—such as enhancing individuals' self-respect, training vigorous and responsible citizens, or creating beautiful cities—that are intangible, vague, or unprovable. Moreover, everyone can think of public purposes—such as mending potholes—that are not so obviously important but are tangible, specific, and certain. Indeed, it is possible to find increased significance in these superficially unimportant goals by recasting them in more generalized and uncertain terms. (Mending potholes can be viewed as an effort to prevent accidents and even to enhance the everyday quality of life.) There are plain and intrinsic reasons for these relationships. Social consequences can be morally important *by virtue of* their diffuseness. Think of the many, unnameable acts of kindness and usefulness that flow from the inculcation in a single individual of character traits like tolerance, responsibility, and self-assurance. Moreover, it can be *because* a social consequence is morally important that the uncertainty of its realization may not matter decisively. Everyone knows this who has supported controversial programs to eradicate poverty, to achieve racial equality, or, indeed, make almost any major change in society. And, surely, profound moral issues, such as when human life begins or whether the death penalty is ever justified, tend to involve great controversy and uncertainty partly *as a result of* their moral significance.

Whether Brennan's idea is that "unfocused" interests involve unprovable moral values or diffuse and uncertain social consequences, his position is so implausible that it is tempting to state it as follows: "Perhaps 'unfocused' interests can be morally significant. But in the case of regulating obscenity, the achievement of those morally significant interests depends upon controlling individuals' minds and such control is repugnant to the principles of free speech." Brennan comes close to resting on this argument, but strong reliance on it would have required major changes in his opinion. He could not, for example, have so confidently distinguished compulsory public education laws and civil rights laws from obscenity laws. Moreover, he would have had to alter or elaborate considerably his position on the nature of obscenity. It was Justice Brennan himself who in 1957 wrote *Roth v. United States,* which affirmed that "obscenity" constitutes a category of ideas and communications that is outside the scope of first amendment protection. The reason given in *Roth* was that material appealing to the prurient interest, unlike even hateful ideas, is "utterly without redeeming social importance." Sixteen years later in *Paris Adult Theatre,* Brennan was not yet ready to abandon this position. He devoted several pages to a rehash of the bases for his stand in *Roth;* moreover, while admitting a need to reconsider *Roth,* he endorsed only the idea that there is a right to receive information *even if* the information has no social worth. And his proposal to permit the suppression of obscenity for certain "focused" purposes itself depends on the assumption that a separate and identifiable category of obscene communications exists.

On the whole, then, Brennan's opinion clings to the assumption that there is a set of ideas that has no redeeming social value at all. This being so, Brennan might have explained why it should be inconsistent with the first amendment to keep those ideas from becoming part of the content of an individual's thoughts. How could it interfere with "the moral content of a person's thoughts" to suppress ideas that have no redeeming social value? Put another way, if obscenity is relevant to the moral content of a person's thinking, the cleanest conclusion would have been that obscenity must have some redeeming social value. Because this is not a step that Brennan was willing to take, he cannot very convincingly be understood to be arguing that the state's interest in mind control is simply illegitimate. Perhaps it was for such reasons that in the end he leaves open the possibility that a sufficiently important state interest might justify regulations that shape character and intellect. Therefore, despite his reference to the argument against governmental mind control, it remains crucial to Brennan's position to explain why "unfocused" interests are morally inadequate.

Although no doubt Justice Brennan used the term *unfocused state interests* as a way of grading the importance of state interests, the phrase makes sense only if understood in quite a different way. Brennan could have fully acknowledged that the interests credited by the majority were morally important. Suppose he had written: "Although the connection between obscenity and rape is unproven, the prevention of rape is a high moral purpose and justifies uncertain efforts; phrases like 'the tone of the society' are vague but refer to cherished objectives, including the moral stake we all rightly have in what goes on around us and in the quality of the community that we are a part of; the destructive connection between obscenity and the 'sensitive relationships that lie at the heart of family life and human development' is unclear, and the behavioral consequences alluded to are diffuse, but these interests are too significant to be doubted." If Brennan had made all these concessions, the heart of his argument could still have been preserved. To see why, it is necessary to remember what occasioned Brennan's effort to minimize the importance of the asserted state interests in moral regulation.

Brennan decided to "scrutinize with care" the state's objectives because of "the inevitable side effects" of suppressing obscenity. Brennan pointed to three problems: lack of fair notice to defendants, the chilling effect on protected speech, and stress on judicial machinery. He urged that these problems infected both the old *Roth* standard that he had authored and also the Court's new definition of obscenity. It was because of these costs on individuals and society that Brennan turned his attention to evaluating the moral importance of the state interests in suppressing obscenity. Indeed, the word *unfocused,* when used to belittle these interests, almost seems an unconscious restatement of the fundamental difficulty that Brennan saw in the legal category "obscenity," for it was the vagueness of the term that Brennan thought produced each of the unacceptable side effects.

Now, if Brennan had conceded the moral importance of the regulatory purposes asserted in *Paris Adult Theatre,* could he have explained his conclusion that those purposes were not as significant as the side effects of the suppression? Could he have explained why the side effects were more unacceptable than the obscenity?

The concession that I have attributed to Justice Brennan undermines the usual answers to this question. He could have said (in fact, he did pretty much say) that he had surveyed society for the sixteen years following *Roth* and that his evaluation was that the side effects were simply "intolerable"—presumably, worse than anything that providing obscenity to willing adults could possibly do. This straightforward position has some obvious appeal, in that no one doubts that the side effects indicated by Brennan are grave. However, under my hypothesis Brennan could not have doubted that permitting obscenity to be available would also entail grave consequences (or, at least, that governments are justified in believing this to be so).

Of course, it is possible for anyone, including a judge, to claim some superior ability to distinguish among morally grave consequences. Such a claim might be dignified, although certainly not explained, by alluding to a "balancing" process. Perhaps Brennan could have convincingly fleshed out his moral balance. He would have had to explain why we should have less concern about loss of pride and self-respect for those living in a community that tolerates obscenity than we have about the anxiety of purveyors puzzling over risks created by vague obscenity standards. For Brennan in *Paris Adult Theatre,* this sort of direct moral assertion would have been more than usually awkward. He would have had to explain not only the superiority of his "balance" in comparison to that of other decisionmakers but also his concession that there might be another set of state interests (of which he more highly approved) that could outweigh those same side effects. He would have had to explain, for example, why adult privacy, which might justify suppression, is more important than adult self-respect, which would not.

Unvarnished claims to superior moral sensitivity are still, despite much academic commentary aimed at undergirding them, doubtful bases for judicial decisions. But Brennan, of course, purports to be applying preexisting legal standards; he says the side effects are inconsistent with "the fundamental principle of the First and Fourteenth Amendments." This characterization, however, turns out to be just a restatement of the moral balance that is at issue.

One of the side effects, in fact, is not even described as having constitutional status. Stress on the judiciary, as Brennan says, does present a "set of problems," including the burden of having to resolve constitutional questions of "exceptional difficulty" and the personal discomfort of having to review "the miserable stuff." And Brennan refers to the "appearance of arbitrary acts" created by the Court's reliance on brief *per curiam* opinions and its unexplained refusal to take certain cases. However, there is no constitutional guarantee either that the task of appellate review be easy or that the Court act without any appearance of arbitrariness. Brennan's inclusion of the problem of institutional stress along with the "problems arising from lack of fair notice [and] from the chill on protected expression" creates at least some initial doubt about how much it matters to his analysis whether the intolerable side effects amount to constitutional violations.

This doubt is increased by the nature of Brennan's argument about vagueness. He says not only that past and present obscenity standards are too vague but also that no definition, "no matter how precisely or narrowly drawn," could satisfy his constitutional standard. Moreover, by leaving open the possibility that obscenity can be regulated for purposes like child welfare, he necessarily leaves open the possibility that defendants will not have adequate notice and that potential publishers will be chilled. After all, to potential targets of regulation, it does not matter that the governmental purpose is "focused" if the legal standard is vague.

Perhaps his idea is that unconstitutional side effects created by vagueness might be outweighed by state interests that also have weight under the federal Constitution. The states' police power has some constitutional status (under the tenth amendment), and so perhaps diminution of this regulatory authority must be balanced against the "side effects." Although a phrase here and there in Brennan's dissent is suggestive of this position, it is an unlikely argument to attribute to him because it would cut against the strongly nationalistic tendencies in his thinking. At any rate, if the state's regulatory authority does have constitutional status, no obvious reason exists for limiting that status to the pursuit of "focused" objectives as long as "unfocused" objectives can serve serious moral values. Then again, if the state's regulatory authority does not have constitutional status, Brennan's proposal that obscenity regulation might be approved for "focused" purposes is inconsistent with the idea that the side effects he identifies have constitutional significance. In short, conceiving of the side effects as "unconstitutional" in a strict sense creates serious tensions and puzzles within Brennan's opinion.

It was not necessary, however, for Brennan to question either the moral or the legal importance of the unfocused state interests asserted in *Paris Adult Theatre.* Independent of such arguments, there is a possible explanation for his conclusion that the side effects of obscenity regulation are worse than the effects of obscenity. Consider this position: "Both the suppression of obscenity and obscenity itself entail profoundly bad consequences. However, when the justifications for suppressing obscenity are 'unfocused,' the side effects of suppression threaten to become widespread and to engulf us as a society. This is because the kinds of state interests asserted for suppressing obscenity can always or almost always be asserted. The advantage of 'focused' interests is simply that, by definition, they can convincingly be asserted only sometimes. Not every obscenity regulation, for instance, is designed to protect children. But every suppression of obscenity (indeed, every suppression of any offensive communication) can be justified on the basis of 'the moral character of the community.'"

It is, I think, this familiar argument against "boundless" justifications that gives force to Brennan's use of the word *unfocused*. But what sorts of judgments lie beneath the urge to reject boundless governmental purposes? The most obvious objection to such purposes is that they disable courts from invalidating legislation; however, unless the exercise of judicial power (like the exercise of a muscle) is desirable, this in itself is no objection. Under the logic of Brennan's dissent, judicial invalidation of obscenity regulations is desirable because, as those regulations become more prevalent, the side effects become more onerous. It is possible to extrapolate from Brennan's depiction of the side effects created by prosecutions under the *Roth* standard to a nightmare image of widespread timidity and arbitrary prosecutions, where valuable ideas and information about sexuality never see the light of day. If, however, obscenity regulation is permitted only when interests in privacy or child welfare are demonstrable, pervasive suppression, along with its nightmarish consequences, becomes less likely. The advantage of "focused" justifications, then, is not their moral superiority but their infrequency. The side effects of obscenity regulation are more unacceptable than the effects of obscenity, not because these side effects in themselves are worse morally, but because they are likely to expand to unacceptable proportions.

As congenial and common as such a prediction might be, it is important to ask on what it could be based.[6] It is possible that, as a psychological matter, the inclination to suppress is strong and can always be expected to expand to the limits defined by the courts. Perhaps specific political and institutional characteristics of our time make widening suppressions likely. Possibly, a perceptive eye can see in our society indications that suppression is already unexpectedly common. Even if suppression is still acceptably contained, a clairvoyant insight might reveal that soon society will undergo a sharp change of direction toward general suppression. Such descriptions, theories, and predictions are often found as aspects of legal theories,[7] but there is nothing especially legal about them. They are, in the best sense of the term, political. They involve fundamental questions of politics, the stuff of ideology and statesmanship: Of all of the things that are going wrong or might go wrong, of all the immoralities present or possible, which are worth attention and energy?

Under the dry word *unfocused,* then, we can barely make out an intimidatingly large form, a fearful image of an arbitrary and sterile society. Many besides Justice Brennan see such a society taking shape around us, and for such people Brennan's dissent in *Paris Adult Theatre* will seem compelling. The power in his argument depends, however, not on the words or the doctrines but on an animating vision that is only suggested.

Given the terms of Brennan's argument, this vision had to be kept obscure for the simple reason that it amounts to the assertion of an unfocused interest.[8] Just as there is no conclusive proof of a causal connection between obscenity and sex crimes, there is no firm proof that the *Roth* standard resulted in any significant blockage of the flow of sexual information to the public, much less that loosening the *Roth* standard would unleash any frightful wave of obscenity prosecutions.[9] The presumed timidity of potential publishers is intangible in the same sense that the effects of obscenity on family relationships and individuals' self-respect are intangible. And the precise contours of any predicted general repression are necessarily undefined for the same reasons that the damage done by obscenity to the moral character of a community is, as Brennan argued, only vaguely defined. Indeed, the grim society that Justice Brennan sought to avert by confining the states' authority to regulate obscenity might as well be described as a different version of a society without moral character—listless (as opposed to prurient), cautious (rather than reckless), repressed (instead of libertine). Put affirmatively, Brennan's position was fashioned to improve the moral character of the community by building a vigorous, experimental, individualistic ethos among its people.

As morally attractive as this purpose is, it is boundless. A society that is permitted to suppress obscenity only for the sake of adult privacy and children's welfare could be engulfed by prurient materials. A person fearful of this possibility might imagine obscenity appearing not only in downtown commercial theaters but in outdoor drive-in theaters, on bumper stickers, in municipal parks, in public libraries, on late-night television, in popular recorded music—virtually everywhere that unpleasant speech might be anticipated or from which the eye could be averted.[10] What might underlie such a prediction? As a psychological matter, it might be supposed that sexuality is an enormously powerful force that can be expected to generate a limitless market. There may be cultural and institutional weaknesses specific to our time that make commercial exploitation of obscenity especially lucrative. A perceptive eye (one, perhaps, that had watched Anita Hill make her allegations against Clarence Thomas) might already see in our society indications that sexually explicit material is disturbingly prevalent. Even if our present culture is largely free of obscenity, some prophetic insight might accurately predict a sudden and pervasive change.

It may be that such fears are far off base and that a community moved by them is exhibiting a neurotic overreaction. However, it may also be that the sorts of fears animating the position taken by Justice Brennan are seriously off base and that an institution moved by them would be suffering from elitist paranoia. Then again, there surely are plenty of signs of both obscenity and censorship in our society; perhaps both fears are reasonable. At any rate, the operative effect of using the word *unfocused* was, paradoxically, to hint at the diffuse visions that animated and gave force to Brennan's position while simultaneously discrediting the "unfocused" objectives underlying the state's position. If Brennan's language had been more powerfully expressive, it would have been clearer that two competing sets of hopes and fears were at stake: differing images of potential calamities and of virtuous communities.

Flag Burning and Political Ethos

It may seem that the preceding discussion sets up a false symmetry between the interests asserted by the state on behalf of regulating obscenity and the interests asserted in the Brennan dissent on behalf of limiting that regulation. I have said that both positions are driven by "unfocused" images of a good society and that, as a consequence, they are potentially boundless; this means that both positions threaten some potential moral disaster and, indeed, that these two versions of social calamity are reciprocal to one another, one being the end point of pervasive suppression and the other of excessive protection. Even if all this is accurate, it might be that Justice Brennan's image of a virtuous community at least has constitutional sanction. As we are used to saying, the Constitution requires that certain kinds of costs be accepted and that some risks be tolerated. We are also used to saying that the free speech clause demands that our society be "uninhibited, robust, and wide-open." Unfocused or not, this shining image is one that we are committed to by our fundamental charter, or so we often say.

As I have already indicated, *Paris Adult Theatre* is not a convincing illustration of this objection. Brennan's position was not that obscenity is constitutionally protected speech but that certain side effects of suppressing obscenity should be minimized. The connection between the justice's image of a virtuous society and a specific constitutional right, therefore, was attenuated. I propose to evaluate the objection by turning to a case where Justice Brennan spoke for the Court rather than in dissent and where the constitutional status of his conclusions was unequivocally identified and fully explained. In the famous flag-burning case, *Texas v. Johnson*,[11] the constitutional authoritativeness of the Court's imagery can be more directly assessed.

Most of this opinion is devoted to convincing the reader that invalidation of the Texas flag desecration statute was required by the prosaic application of legal doctrine rather than by any grand social vision. The Court's analysis begins by asking whether burning a flag as part of a political protest constitutes "expressive conduct." Because, under principles extracted from the relevant precedents, flag burning does fall into this category, the next question is whether "the State's regulation is related to the suppression of free expression." If there is no such relationship, "the less stringent standard we announced in *United States v. O'Brien* for regulation of noncommunicative conduct controls." If there is a relationship between the state's purpose and suppression, however, the state's purpose must be evaluated "under a more demanding standard."

All this evokes, if only from habit, nodding assent from knowledgeable lawyers, for the propositions are accurately stated and familiar. But how much do these words really convey? The Court interprets the case law to say that conduct is "expressive" if it is both intended and understood to be communicative. But it seems unlikely that *all* such conduct is protected as "speech." How is flag burning to be distinguished from all those other expressive acts (like fistfighting during a political demonstration) that are highly expressive but presumably unprotected? In any event, what might it mean for a state's regulation of expressive conduct to be unrelated to expression, and how exactly does this matter? Even under the less stringent standard, the state must demonstrate "an important or substantial" interest, and the incidental impact on free expression can be "no greater than essential to furtherance of that interest." So, if the state's purpose *is* related to expression, how much "more demanding" can the Court's standard be? These questions, as well as many others that are possible, are not carping. They are elementary efforts to get a concrete sense of what all those words might mean.

Two straightforward (but limited) propositions do emerge from the doctrinal labyrinths: (1) Many forms of expressive conduct are immune from state regulation unless some sufficient public interest justifies their regulation, but (2) no expression, no matter how clearly protected by the first amendment, is entirely immune from state regulation if the regulation serves a sufficiently important interest. In short, almost everything depends on how the state's interest in protecting the American flag is evaluated.

The State of Texas asserted that in protecting the flag from offensive acts of disrespect its purpose was to preserve the flag "as a symbol of nationhood and national unity." Now, it would be easy to misunderstand the Court's decision as holding that this purpose is illegitimate as an effort to suppress speech that is disrespectful of our nationhood. The opinion does describe the state's purpose as "content-based" and repeatedly invokes the principle that government "may not prohibit expression simply because it disagrees with its message."[12] However, none of this is used to establish that Texas's objective was improper. Rather, the Court concludes only that the asserted interest must be subject to "the most exacting scrutiny" and that it must involve some consideration other than "simply" protecting society from offensive or disagreeable ideas. The promotion of nationhood, obviously, is an objective that goes far beyond protecting the public's sensibilities from distasteful or dissenting views, and the Court itself describes this objective as legitimate.[13] Why, then, was the Texas law not constitutional?

At this point in his analysis, Justice Brennan's dilemma is parallel to the dilemma he faced years earlier on the obscenity issue. In both instances, he conceded that the conduct involved can be regulated by the state if "exacting scrutiny" reveals a sufficiently important public interest, and in both he described the asserted public interest as legitimate. His route out in *Texas v. Johnson* is over the same path he marked in *Paris Adult Theatre*. Notice that although the word does not appear in the decision, Texas was asserting an "unfocused" interest. Like the moral character of a community, nationhood is an abstraction, a self-perception, a pervasive sense. It does not consist of acts but of the meaning attributed to acts; it is not a program but an identity based on history, imagination, and sentiment. Nationhood, of course, does have tangible consequences, but they are diffuse, diverse, and uncertain. National unity, therefore, is a boundless justification. It could be promoted by protecting the flag, but (as Justice Brennan points out) it could also be promoted by sanctifying the presidential seal or copies of the Constitution. The image that looms at the end of this slide is ominous indeed; it is the image of totalitarian orthodoxy. If we can be forced to treat a flag with respect, we can be forced to express false agreement with public policies and false homage to government leaders.

Against this depressing image, the Court sets its own vision of self-assurance and tolerance. "The way to preserve the flag's special role is not to punish those who feel differently. . . . It is to persuade them that they are wrong." The flag represents "resilience, not rigidity." Appealing to "courageous, self-reliant men," the Court could imagine "no more appropriate response to burning a flag than waving one's own, no better way to counter a flag-burner's message than by saluting the flag that burns."

This vision of a tolerant society is appealing. Like the image of a society brave enough (or licentious enough) to risk having obscenity nearly everywhere, however, this objective is unfocused. Its boundless possibilities are unwittingly evoked by the image of citizens' saluting while their country symbolically burns in the street. The people are instructed to wave their flags back and forth as they watch the emblem of their common heritage being burned—or (presumably) walked over or urinated on. "Self-confidence," as much as "unity," is an answer that can always be given; as unity at the extreme turns to totalitarian force, resilience at its extreme turns to entropy. It would seem, then, that again we can have a choice of nightmares: a society without tolerance and variety, or a society without commonality and self-respect.

Just as in *Paris Adult Theatre,* however, Justice Brennan insists that the interests he prefers are focused: "We do not consecrate the flag by punishing its desecration, for in doing so we dilute the freedom that this cherished emblem represents." The state's interest, then, involves only an emblem or a representation while the Court's interest involves substantive "principles of freedom." The state's interest in flag protection is symbolic; the Court's interest is the reality behind the symbol. Thus, the state's unfocused interest in symbolism directly undermines tangible interests that have the highest legal status, constitutional freedoms.

This argument, I think, breaks down at every level. Of course, the right to burn a flag is tangible in the sense that it involves physical action. The governmental interest in preventing flag desecration is tangible in precisely the same way because it involves protecting the physical integrity of the flag. In any event, as the Court itself demonstrates, the important value in the right to burn a flag does not reside in the physical act but in the communicative power of the act. This value, however, is symbolic in the same way that the state's interest in protecting the flag is symbolic. Certainly it would be odd for anyone who believes in the importance of expression to assert that the state's interest is unimportant on the grounds that it involves "only" communicative symbolism. In short, by distinguishing "freedom" from its emblems, Justice Brennan deprecates the state's interest in symbolic communication at the same moment that he reaffirms the importance of that interest when asserted by individuals. Whatever might underlie this position, it cannot be explained on the basis of a distinction between substance and symbolism.

Even if it is admitted that the individual's interest and the state's interest are equivalently "symbolic," Justice Brennan might still be right that only the former interest has constitutional status. However, the question in the case is *whether* the individual's interest should have constitutional protection, and that question cannot be answered by assuming the substantive freedom at issue. Under the Court's reasoning, the answer depends on whether the state has a sufficiently important interest in protecting the flag. It is here that Justice Brennan is most revealing, for he plainly conceives of the Court's opinion itself as a substitute for the symbolism of the flag: "*Our decision is a reaffirmation of the principle* of freedom and inclusiveness *that the flag best reflects* . . . and it is that resilience [represented by the flag surviving the bombardment at Fort McHenry] *that we reassert* today." This is to say that national unity, correctly understood, is symbolized and protected by the Court's opinion in *Texas v. Johnson.* The reason that the free speech clause should be interpreted to create a substantive right to burn the flag is that the state's interest is inadequate, and the reason for that inadequacy is that national unity can be sufficiently protected by the Court's claims about our political heritage.

The Court, in short, presents its "reaffirmation" as an alternative to flag desecration laws. For the visual symbolism, the emotional connotations, and the historical associations of the flag, the Court would substitute its teachings—its discussion of precedent, its doctrinal analysis, and its claims about self-confidence and resilience. This means, among other things, that the interest of the State of Texas could not have been inadequate or illegitimate because it was "unfocused" or symbolic. If it were insufficient on this ground, under the Court's view of the purpose of its own opinion, that opinion also would have to be unimportant or improper.

The distinction in *Texas v. Johnson* between substantive principles of freedom and the symbols that represent those freedoms is the same distinction that Justice Brennan made in *Paris Adult Theatre* when he contrasted "strong and legitimate" state interests with "unfocused" moral objectives. In both cases, however, his opinions end up asserting a judicial version of an unfocused interest. Indeed, in the later case, Brennan's opinion for the Court substitutes an intellectualized version of a national mythology for a visual one and thus audaciously pursues symbolic interests that are identical to those of the State of Texas. Texas demanded obeisance to its symbolism by coercing conforming behavior from individuals directly; the Court demanded obeisance to its symbolism by coercing conformity from officials (and thus from individuals indirectly). The most obvious difference between the two positions is that the orthodoxy imposed by Texas was emotional and vague—the orthodoxy of attachment—whereas the orthodoxy imposed by the Court was intellectual and specific—the orthodoxy of civil libertarianism.

The important point for present purposes is that in evaluating the state's interest in protecting the flag, the Court did not demonstrate that the state's interest was unimportant; in fact, the Court explicitly conceded the significance of public symbolism and simply substituted its own. Because demonstrating the insufficiency of the state's interest was crucial to the Court's reasoning about whether a constitutional freedom had been abridged, it was question-begging to conclude that the individual's communicative interest had constitutional status. This can be put another way: The Court's position is that the promotion of nationhood is a perfectly permissible objective but that its own method of pursuing that objective is superior to the method chosen by Texas; however, the Court's method is *legally* superior only if it is assumed that there is a constitutional right to burn the flag. Without this assumption, flag desecration statutes cannot be said to be inferior to the Court's alternative on the ground that this alternative is more protective of the substance of the Constitution (or less symbolic).

National unity built on a shining vision of tolerant, flag-waving people is both possible and attractive. But it is also possible, as Bork wrote at the end of *The Tempting of America,* that unity (including vigorous commitment to individual freedom) depends less on reason than on sentiment, less on doctrine than on history.[14] If so, Brennan's vision at its end might convert a political ethos that is vigorous and proud into one that is feckless and empty. The choice between such hopes and fears is probably a matter of class, personality, and faith. It is not a matter, if the explanation in *Texas v. Johnson* is an adequate guide, of the constitutional status of the image that captivated the justices who invalidated flag desecration laws.

Boundlessness and Adjudication

I can now state in more general terms the propositions that are illustrated by Justice Brennan's opinions in *Paris Adult Theatre* and *Texas v. Johnson.*

Viewing constitutional cases as struggles between competing social images, rather than merely as arguments about principle and doctrine, can restore some sense of authenticity and significance. However, by emphasizing the extent to which the Court's decisions serve controversial aspirations and fears, this perspective forces attention to an important equivalence between judicial and other governmental interests. To the extent that both sets of interests are "unfocused," both are boundless justifications. This means that both involve potentially serious risks; moreover, to the extent that the constitutional status of the judicial interest depends on the alleged insufficiency of the competing governmental interest, the boundlessness of the judicial interest undercuts any special claims it might have to legal authoritativeness.

None of this means that judicial interests necessarily are unimportant, excessively risky, or unconnected to constitutional values. (Nor are unfocused legislative interests.) It does, however, direct attention past the Court's doctrinal rhetoric to two issues: (1) Are the asserted judicial interests legally authoritative for some reason that is independent of any characterization of the competing governmental interest as "unfocused"? (2) Is there some convincing reason why the apparent boundlessness of the judicial interest in fact involves less risk than that of the competing interest? Without an answer to one of these questions, the equivalence between the objectives pursued by the judicial and political branches presents serious problems for any priority given the judicial choice.

As I have tried to demonstrate, Brennan's two opinions do not convincingly address either of these issues. Instead, his strategy in each case is to deny the equivalence between his preferred interests and those of the government. To the extent that the Court adopts this strategy when it declares a governmental interest to be vague and potentially boundless, the judiciary is vulnerable on the very charge that it directs at the political branches. Indeed, in some ways the judiciary is more vulnerable. Not only are the Court's justifications (if they were fully expressed) patently boundless in theory but also judicial opinions almost necessarily betray a tendency to apply them to excess in practice.

To see why, consider the consequences of an assertion by the Court that its imagery has authoritative status. Given our assumptions about the Constitution as supreme law, constitutional prescriptions must apply uniformly across the nation and must subordinate all other interests. To the extent that an objective has authoritative constitutional status, judges are required to realize that objective everywhere and at all costs. As a justification it is boundless. By contrast, to the extent that putatively subordinate considerations prevail even in part, there is pressure toward concluding that the limited or defeated constitutional objectives must not have true constitutional status. In short, the more convincing a judicial opinion is in establishing that the Court's imagery is legally authoritative, the more likely the vision is to be applied as a boundless justification; conversely, the less the risk of boundless application, the less likely the Court's imagery is to be thought of as legally authoritative.

This definitional relationship has force but, of course, in the real world it does not have inevitability. Constitutional interests are never entirely boundless; as articulated, they are often riddled with exceptions and qualifications, and even so they are imperfectly realized. But through the years, the federal courts have made massive changes in our society; they have risked economic disaster, crime in the streets, presidential defiance, violence against schoolchildren, the breakdown of authority within prisons, and much more—all for the sake of what the supreme law is said "to require." Surely the intellectual pressure for full actualization that is inherent in claims of constitutional authority played a significant part in this remarkable history. On the other hand, although exceptions do not always lead to abandonment of constitutional status, there are significant instances where principles have ceased to be called "constitutional" if other interests continue to be found more important in application.[15] Outraged objections to the recent cases limiting the scope of the right to abortion are a testament to the common recognition that authoritative status becomes increasingly fragile as nonconstitutional interests begin to prevail even at the margin.

Judicial opinions that bestow constitutional stature on various images of society, then, start with a natural disadvantage on the question of likelihood of boundless application. However, the images that are in contention beneath the surface of Supreme Court decisions sometimes involve large calamities of a kind unlikely to be triggered by any single cause, including the force contained in the idea of fundamental law. Disasters can be caused by pushing ideas to their end points, but this requires (among other things) that the ideas be held with dogmatic fervor. And ideological zealotry is not normally associated with judicial review.

No doubt, most federal judges most of the time are the opposite of fanatical; they are usually moderate, thoughtful, and tolerant. Does this mean that the unfocused interests pursued by the courts should never be expected to present a realistic threat of boundless application? Most citizens most of the time are not fanatics, but the American body politic is not entirely immune from excessive zeal and pathological moods. There is no reason to think that jurists, especially when fired by the conviction that they are performing an inescapable duty, should be any different. Moreover, the issue is not simply what judges might accomplish on their own. If society should become pervaded by cheapened forms of sexuality or if heedless, habitual dissension should begin to drive out even an elementary sense of nationhood, it is only necessary for the courts to preclude the political branches from instituting adjustments and correctives. Plodding, unwavering functionaries have from time to time helped to bring on catastrophes.

There are, I submit, disquieting aspects to the way even the best judges think about even the best constitutional images. A striking illustration is one of the most important passages in American jurisprudence, a passage that is especially relevant because it provides an explicit and powerful basis for the vision that moved Justice Brennan on both the obscenity and flag-burning issues. Here is Justice Louis Brandeis's inspiring evocation of a confident, tolerant people:

> Those who won our independence believed that the final end of the State was to make men free to develop their faculties; and that in its government the deliberative forces should prevail over the arbitrary. They valued liberty both as an end and as a means. They believed liberty to be the secret of happiness and courage to be the secret of liberty. They believed that freedom to think as you will and to speak as you think are means indispensable to the discovery and spread of political truth; that without free speech and assembly discussion would be futile; that with them, discussion affords ordinarily adequate protection against the dissemination of noxious doctrine; that the greatest menace to the freedom is an inert people; that public discussion is a political duty; and that this should be a fundamental principle of the American government. They recognized the risks to which all human institutions are subject. But they knew that order cannot be secured merely through fear of punishment for its infraction; that it is hazardous to discourage thought, hope and imagination; that fear breeds repression; that repression breeds hate; that hate menaces stable government; that the path of safety lies in the opportunity to discuss freely supposed grievances and proposed remedies; and that the fitting remedy for evil counsels is good ones. Believing in the power of reason as applied through public discussion, they eschewed silence coerced by law—the argument of force in its worst form.[16]

This depiction is much admired,[17] but it is as troubling as it is beautiful.

The account is offered as descriptive and factual. This people—the "they" repeatedly referred to—was, according to Brandeis, those who won American independence and who adopted the first amendment. Yet Brandeis offers almost no historical evidence and, thus, suggests that the truth of his claims is self-evident and beyond debate.[18] He does not qualify or complicate his picture of the dispositions of our forefathers to take account even of well-known facts, for example, that some patriots ran in mobs beating their political opponents in the streets, and that prosecutions for seditious libel occurred into the nineteenth century.[19] It is not necessary to be sympathetic to either thuggery or suppression to recognize that not all the people Brandeis referred to were as tolerant as he says or even to wonder whether any of them were. There is something more than exaggeration and simplification at work here. By associating his own unqualified position on tolerance and self-confidence with those who created the nation, Brandeis implies that anyone who takes a more cautious or restrained position is outside American traditions. Thus, a passage that extols inclusiveness and magnanimity paradoxically generates hostility and intolerance toward opposing views. A passage that approves of open-mindedness is itself overly certain and dogmatic. A poetic endorsement of rationality and the search for truth is cavalier of facts and designed to establish a political mythology. For Brandeis, history is malleable according to aspiration. His words inspire fervor on behalf of liberty as they manipulate and delude.

The underside of Brandeis's lyricism proves little, of course, about the propensities of judges generally, but many of its characteristics are recognizable in less eloquent opinions, including those of Justice Brennan.[20] Brandeis's passage, then, does raise questions that should be assessed openly and carefully. To what extent might the stubborn reasonableness and the highly intellectualized fervor of our judges cover over signs of a more sinister potential? Under what circumstances are they, like others in power, capable of obduracy and even, in their own way, of fanaticism? Might they push—have they pushed—their boundless justifications to end points where pleasing images dissolve into painful excesses?

I myself do not think that disasters wait at the end of most judicial efforts. But, then, I do not think that the populace at large is as prone to boundlessness as the courts sometimes assume. What is disquieting is the customary stance of the judiciary and its supporting institutions (especially the legal academy). That stance, as exemplified by the harsh certainty of mainstream scholars like Laurence Tribe and Ronald Dworkin, is to deny confidently and often angrily that our political heritage is complex and that simplified constitutional ideals can be pushed too far.[21] The society that Justice Brennan would create is thought by many to be not only morally attractive but legally imperative. In that imagined society, virtually all acts expressing defiance are protected as "speech"; people revel in, hide from, or are inured to the clamor of offensive communications and sexually explicit materials; church and state are separated by a high and (mostly) impregnable wall; gender differentiation has been eliminated; abortion is freely available; sexual freedoms have been extended to minors and to the unmarried; the institution of marriage has withered into legal insignificance; and death itself is a liberty protected by the Constitution. For many judges and legal academics, this world, or something like it, marks the limit of imagination and tolerance. In this there is a dogmatism that the law dignifies and obscures.

Some danger attends all unfocused governmental interests, especially when pursued with strong intellectual self-assurance. Recognizing this should affect how we react during periods of retrenchment, such as the one we have experienced for roughly two decades, when the Court slows what otherwise would have been its own pursuit of boundless images. Given the reasons to expect rigidity and intolerance among our judges, it ought to be reassuring that the massive power exercised by the federal judiciary can, at least over the course of decades, be qualified and redirected through political checks. Then again, perhaps the current, relatively conservative Court has or will deprecate progressive legislative objectives as potentially boundless while obscuring its own agenda of unfocused interests. This would occur under a number of circumstances, the most obvious being the possibility that the asymmetrical evaluation of public purposes is a method of institutional or ideological aggrandizement.[22] It could also occur on other assumptions, for example: that conservative justices will be captive to the instrumentalist assumptions of liberal individualism, or that the tradition of doctrinal justification will remain strong and will itself tend to suppress the articulation of animating visions, or that there are inherent aspects of the judicial function that discourage candid communication.

Whatever the future may hold for the brand of legalism that Justice Brennan did so much to shape, the modern record of the Court has been characterized by an intellectually powerful form of moral evasiveness. This misdirection presents the Court's objectives as limited and safe while it dismisses competing public purposes as treacherously uncontainable and illegitimate. The effect, like the eyes-averted stance toward affirmative action described in Chapter 2, is to obscure the risky and imponderable nature of our collective moral decisions. It may be said, perhaps, that our political culture demands some such alchemy from the judiciary, that our disputes must be reduced and domesticated somehow or they will overwhelm us. If this is true, it demonstrates how much the institution of judicial review is aimed at protecting us from ourselves. Moreover, constitutional law, viewed this way, is a form of self-delusion that is sometimes accomplished—as I shall explain next—by censorship.

7

Correcting the Political:
Interpretation as Mind Control

As Justice Brennan's arguments in *Paris Adult Theatre* and *Texas v. Johnson* reveal, it is intensely uncomfortable to recognize the extent to which we have a common interest in the attitudes, beliefs, and character traits of our fellow citizens. But this interest is a fact, and it is as unavoidable as it is dangerous. Many, like Brennan, who deny that it matters much whether society is permeated with pornographic materials believe that it is crucial for our culture to be suffused with courage and tolerance. Others, often on university campuses, deny the importance of a shared core of affection and respect for our country but propose "hate codes" and various forms of "sensitivity training" to assure that we all possess enlightened views about race, gender, disability, or sexual preference. To admit as a general principle that we do have a significant stake in the moral character of the community opens each of us to the possibility of domination by groups whose values and objectives we distrust. However, in pursuing our own moral visions, we necessarily attempt to inflict on others the very types of controls that we tend to think would be illegitimate if inflicted by others on us.

Our own aspirations, then, commit us to a principle that we find frightening. This fear can be escaped or reduced through a number of stratagems. In constitutional law, as I observed in the preceding chapter, a major one is the asymmetrical characterization of objectives. In society at large, a prevalent technique is to convince ourselves that efforts to shape moral climate are exceptional (and specially justified) or recent (and alarming). Thus, for example, "political correctness" is often discussed as if it were not a part of a long history of formal and informal efforts to enforce various orthodoxies on university campuses.[1] The purpose of this chapter is to examine a range of constitutional decisions to see how ordinary and deeply embedded are our efforts to shape the mental states of those with whom we must live.

Regulating Sexist Speech

In 1973, the year that Justice Brennan dissented in *Paris Adult Theatre* and eighteen years before Anita Hill testified at the Thomas hearings, it might still have been possible to find a newspaper here or there that organized its want ads according to the fast-fading presumption that men and women tend to have different interests. There might have been columns labeled "Male Help Wanted" or "Jobs—Female Interest." But in that year, the Court helped to put an end to this practice. The decision was *Pittsburgh Press Co. v. Pittsburgh Commission on Human Relations.*[2] Justice Brennan, who was occupied in worrying about whether loosening constitutional protections for obscenity would suppress too much sexual information, was less concerned about the availability of sexist information, and he joined the majority opinion.

The gist of that opinion is that no important free-speech principle was at stake. The legal question was framed as if it were simple and limited. Under the precedents then in effect, advertisements that propose a transaction, such as a possible employment relationship, were considered "commercial speech," a category—like obscenity—of unprotected speech. The Court saw in the gender-specific headings no "position on whether, as a matter of social policy, certain positions ought to be filled by members of one or the other sex. . . ." The headings, therefore, amounted to no more than commercial speech and could be regulated by the states.

The Court's discussion did go on to consider a further possibility. If the doctrine of "commercial speech" allowed governmental regulation of editorial decisions of the sort involved in selecting and using gender-specific headings, should legal precedent be revised to provide at least some first amendment protections for commercial speech? While reserving judgment on the broader aspects of this question, the majority quickly concluded that *this* kind of commercial advertisement did not deserve constitutional protection. After all, "[d]iscrimination in employment is not only commercial activity, it is *illegal* commercial activity. . . ." Thus, newspapers may be prohibited from using gender-specific headings in the same way that they can be prohibited from titling a column "Narcotics for Sale." Sensing, perhaps, that this analogy was less than precise, the Court went on to note that it was illegal in Pennsylvania to "aid . . . in the doing of any act declared to be an unlawful employment practice. . . ." Because the column headings "signaled that the advertisers were likely to show an illegal sex preference in their hiring decisions," the ads were themselves illegal and deserved no first amendment protection.

The apparently straightforward decision in *Pittsburgh Press* did not cause much stir in academia. For the most part, it seemed to involve no novel principle. Indeed, years later when civil libertarians succeeded in extending free speech protections to commercial advertisements, the Court even then said that states could prohibit ads proposing illegal activities.[3]

The simplicity of the Court's reasoning and the casualness with which it was received, however, obscure questions of considerable importance. I doubt that the result in *Pittsburgh Press* can be justified on anything less than the highly controversial proposition (denied by Justice Brennan in both the obscenity and flag-burning cases) that the government may control information in an effort to purify our minds.

To see why this is so, let us reexamine the steps in the Court's reasoning. Is it true, first of all, that the newspaper's layout communicated no position on the question of whether certain jobs ought to be filled by one sex or the other? The headings, certainly, conveyed very little substance. But many brief, contentless messages take positions, even strong positions. As early as 1971, well before deciding the *Pittsburgh Press* case, the Court had noted that the words "Fuck the Draft" can convey important information and an emphatic opinion.[4] Years later, you will recall, the Court had no trouble in concluding that acts devoid of all verbal content, acts such as burning the flag, often send messages effectively. The idea conveyed by "Jobs—Male Interest" is milder, but mild positions are still positions. The newspaper, plainly, was communicating to its readers certain presumptions about their likely vocational interests and, in doing so, implicitly confirmed that different interests were a fact and an acceptable fact.

The message conveyed by the newspaper's employment headings was potentially persuasive (perhaps dangerous) because of its brevity. Gender differences were assumed, not argued. This assumption was put forward as a shared and uncontroversial aspect of our understandings; it was built into the arrangement of the paper in the same way that underlying beliefs and stereotypes about sexual differences are built into the unexamined assumptions of our social and personal lives. The ad presented gender differences as an ordinary part of life. Thus, when the Court "emphasize[d]" that nothing in its decision allows the government to prevent a newspaper from publishing an advertisement "commenting on the . . . propriety of sex preferences in employment[,]" it was not guaranteeing that the newspaper could print the *same* substantive message as the one communicated by the sex-specific headings. Indeed, the permitted messages would be in some ways weaker, because "commenting" necessarily involves conceding more than the self-assured, complacent headings do.

The ads' terseness also undermines the Court's claims that the headings either proposed illegal behavior or were likely to lead to illegal acts. An ad placed under the heading "Narcotics for Sale" does propose an illegal transaction. In the same way, a heading that said "Only Men May Apply" would propose illegal employment practices. But an ad placed under the heading "Jobs—Female Interest" does not propose that the employer will hire only women; it presumes a certain perspective or set of inclinations among readers. It was not illegal under the Pennsylvania Human Relations Act for women to prefer—or even to believe they should prefer—certain types of jobs. Neither the potential employer nor the newspaper was committing an illegal act by believing and announcing that women and men have their own stereotypical interests.

Is it, nevertheless, *likely* that employers will make illegal hiring decisions if they believe that members of each sex have statistically different employment interests? An affirmative answer to this question may seem so obvious (as it did to the Supreme Court) that it is necessary to pause to examine the matter carefully. To begin with, it is improbable that *any* informed person in 1973 believed that in general men and women had the same job preferences and skills. Those members of the Commission on Human Relations who disapproved of the newspaper's advertising layout presumably knew that employment segregation by sex was widespread and that one reason for this (and one consequence of it) was that many women and men had internalized sex-specific career aspirations. In fact, it was precisely this presumption that made the layout insidious— the sex-specific headings were all too likely to match pre-existing attitudes. (If not, the layout would be an inconvenience for readers and would eventually become an economic disadvantage to the paper.) Moreover, any enlightened employer who wanted to break down sexual stereotyping in hiring decisions would also be likely to hold the belief that such stereotypes existed in the minds of many potential employees, male and female. This would be part of the problem that such an employer would want to help to solve. In short, strong proponents of sexual equality in the workplace would have had much the same understanding of differential employment interests as is expressed in the forbidden advertising layouts. An intention to discriminate, then, cannot be inferred from a person's beliefs about statistical imbalances in employment preferences.

It is true, however, that gender egalitarians would be unlikely to approve of sex-specific ad layouts. But this does not indicate that those who do approve of such layouts (or those willing to use them) are likely to discriminate. An egalitarian would favor sexually neutral headings because such headings are an implicit argument for altering existing preference patterns. Neutral headings might cause some readers to come to believe that it is normal or expected that women and men should have the same interests and aptitudes. It is perfectly possible for an employer to disagree with this reformist message (indeed, to opt for its opposite) and still have no intention of making discriminatory hiring decisions. People obey laws they disagree with every day.

Suppose, however, that the column headings had gone much further than they did. Imagine that the ads had said this:

> We emphatically disagree with the policies of the Human Relations Commission. We believe that men and women are generally happier at and better suited for different kinds of jobs because they have different abilities and interests. This newspaper advocates that both employers and potential employees take gender into account when making hiring decisions.

This hypothetical advertisement would be different from the ones prohibited under *Pittsburgh Press* in that the real ads merely presumed certain preferences among the newspaper's readers and the imagined one advocates illegal employment decisions. Nevertheless, because the actual headings were so opaque, it is perhaps possible to see a similar message of advocacy in them. Even on this extreme reading, however, it does not follow that advertisers are likely (in any legally recognizable way) to make illegal employment decisions.

One of the established principles of free-speech law is that the government may not suppress speech on the assumption that those who advocate illegality are themselves going to commit illegal acts. Compare, for example, the column headings forbidden in *Pittsburgh Press* with these far more lurid and ominous facts: Members of the Ku Klux Klan invite a reporter and a cameraman to a nighttime rally, where twelve hooded figures brandish weapons and burn a cross. One speaker refers to the possibility that federal government might continue "to suppress the white, Caucasian race" and concludes that "there might have to be some revengence taken." There was also talk to the effect that "the nigger should be returned to Africa, the Jew returned to Israel." These individuals were charged with advocating the "propriety of crime . . . violence or . . . unlawful methods of terrorism as a means of accomplishing . . . political reform." In its famous, much-praised decision in *Brandenburg v. Ohio,* the Court held that

> the constitutional guarantees of free speech . . . do not permit a State to forbid or proscribe advocacy of the use of force or of law violation except where such advocacy is directed to inciting or producing imminent lawless action and is likely to incite or produce such action. . . . "[T]he mere abstract teaching . . . of the moral propriety or even moral necessity for a resort to force and violence, is not the same as preparing a group for violent action and steeling it to such action." A statute which fails to draw this distinction impermissibly intrudes upon the freedoms guaranteed by the First and Fourteenth Amendments.[5]

In short, mere advocacy (even of violent action) is to be distinguished from incitement to imminent lawless action.

If angry speeches about "revengence" uttered by armed men burning a cross is not "incitement," it would seem rather clear that a newspaper's staid column heading, even if interpreted to contain a message of advocacy, cannot amount to incitement of employers. Some lawless employment decisions will be made at some point after the publication of the want ads, but they are certainly not "imminent"—unless ordinary employers advertising in newspapers are to be thought closer to illegal actions than are those hooded men gathered on a rural farm late in the night.

Whether sex-specific want ads reflect employers' beliefs about sex differences or amount to advocacy of illegal conduct, it miscasts the issue to say that employers who utilize such a layout are likely to make discriminatory decisions. The format did "aid" the discriminatory plans of some employers, but in quite a different and more direct way. Undoubtedly, the immediate effect of the headings was to discourage some women from seeking "male" jobs and some men from seeking "female" jobs. As I earlier suggested, the ads would have this effect for readers who gave in to the implied social pressure. It would also have this effect on those who wrongly presumed that the headings represented strict, legally enforceable prerequisites or who calculated that employment opportunities would be bleak given the employer's attitudes. In any event, dissuading these applicants would tend to relieve those employers who intended to discriminate from the necessity of doing so.

If the commission's objective was to prevent this kind of "aid," the aim of the censorship was to protect readers from their own evaluation of information. What "aids" the employer who intends to discriminate is the effect the advertising format has on the intellectual and emotional reflexes of the readers. It is true that job seekers of both sexes might be more audacious in their pursuit of nontraditional jobs if they were ignorant of the beliefs of some employers and of many in the community generally. As Justice Ginsburg wrote before she was appointed to the Court, because the "overriding objective must be an end to role delineation by gender," what is required is "conduct . . . in the job market, signalling that in all fields of endeavor females are welcomed as enthusiastically as males are."[6] The Human Relation Commission's effort to generate these signals amounted to a governmental attempt to control communication in order to correct the attitudes and inclinations of those in the labor force. In fact, potential applicants can be persuaded—either by keeping them ignorant or by the implicit argumentation of socially approved sex-neutral advertising—to react differently and more boldly. Whether these new, improved applicants are thought of as more courageous or more heedless, it is their creation that was the object of the commission's order. The object of the Court's misleadingly simplistic discussion was to obscure this plain but disconcerting fact.

The Court and Consciousness Raising

Although the Court saw little at stake in *Pittsburgh Press,* the underlying issue can be stated in very far-reaching terms. May a government agency censor the editorial decisions of a newspaper because those decisions are thought to be subverting the kinds of attitudes that, if common in the population, would help the government achieve its preferred outcomes without coercion? Can the government control information to shape a people who want what the government wants for them?

We like to believe, and the courts often tell us, that the answer to this question is: usually not. There are, of course, special circumstances (normally involving children) where censorship for the purpose of mind control or character formation is necessary. Nearly everyone, for instance, concedes that inculcation of certain civic and intellectual values is among the purposes of mandatory education laws.[7] The content of courses and the books that comprise public school libraries, therefore, must be selected purposefully. Similarly, most people concede that the state has a broad interest in seeing that children are raised properly. During their impressionable years, the government may act (within limits) to protect them from harmful verbal abuse, pornography, and so on. But what is occasionally necessary for children is, we assure ourselves, inappropriate with adults.

Even with adults, however, exceptions can be found. The state can prevent us from purchasing obscenity because (so say judges and some legal theorists) obscenity has no artistic or social value at all. When restrictions go beyond the limits of such tightly defined categories, we expect the courts to protect us from official overreaching. If, as in *Pittsburgh Press,* the judiciary fails us, we sometimes find a way to minimize the significance of the decision ("The ad was itself illegal!" or "Commercial speech gets less protection!"). If this is unconvincing, we can admit the Court made a mistake but console ourselves with the hope that the failing was aberrational. If necessary, we can resort to outrage. In a notorious 1991 case popularly referred to as the "gag-rule" decision, the Court upheld a broad authority in federal regulators to condition family planning funds on compliance with rules strictly limiting communications with patients on the subject of abortion.[8] Many in academia and in the general public reacted with disbelief and anger. Outrage, too, preserves the reassuring sense that it is possible (if only the Court would do its job) to avoid governmental efforts to mold our thinking through the manipulation of information.

Neither law nor courts can, however, be expected to protect us from our collective efforts to shape one another, to create a moral climate. Indeed, not only does the Supreme Court sometimes permit agencies to censor information for purposes of mind control but also in important areas the Court itself acts as the censor. This claim, I recognize, seems extreme and perverse. However, a straightforward examination of three decisions, each concerning a different and significant area of constitutional law, shows it to be true. Through the judiciary, too, we try to bend our neighbors' behavior to our will by controlling what they know.

Prayer

In 1984 the State of Alabama enacted a statute providing as follows:

> At the commencement of the first class of each day in all grades of all public schools the teacher in charge of the room in which each class is held may announce that a period of silence not to exceed one minute . . . shall be observed for meditation or voluntary prayer. . . .

Although we do not always regard legislative enactments as communications, they are, obviously, just that. Even laws that require or restrict speech are themselves expressive acts.[9] The Alabama provision was an official authorization addressed directly to public school teachers and secondarily to administrators and students. It controlled behavior (by allocating to teachers the decision about whether to have a moment of silence), but it also expressed a moral position on the importance of individual meditation and prayer. Because this position reflected the formal judgment of the representatives of the people of the state, it carried the weight of a community's shared belief (in the same way as, but more forcefully than, a newspaper's informal judgment that its readers were likely to have gender-differentiated employment interests). Viewed as a communication, the "moment of silence" statute conveyed important information about the values prevalent in a political community.

For the reasons I described in Chapter 5, the Supreme Court invalidated Alabama's statute as a violation of the establishment clause of the first amendment.[10] Although we do not usually regard the exercise of the power of judicial review as censorship, the invalidation of statutes, obviously, has just that effect. *Wallace v. Jaffree* means that Alabama citizens may not receive a certain message from their state government.

Was this censorship aimed at mind control? Recall, the Pittsburgh Commission on Human Relations characterized the purpose of its censorship as the prevention of violation of antidiscrimination laws. In the same way, the Court in *Wallace* claimed that its purpose was to prevent a constitutional violation. The Court had previously announced the relevant legal standard: Government programs that aid religions must have a secular purpose. If the "actual purpose is to endorse or disapprove of religion[,]" the government's objective is not secular. In *Wallace,* the Court found that the legislature's actual intent had been not merely to protect the right of students to engage in voluntary prayer, but "to return prayer to the public schools." By the Court's account, then, it can be said that the only "mind control" involved is a kind necessitated by the Constitution, which itself prohibits public officials from acting with a certain purpose or mental state.

I noted in Chapter 5 that it is unclear why this motivation is illegal. The words *or voluntary prayer* that were added to the statute do not themselves endorse religion, and the mental state that supposedly accompanied the enactment of the statute was not communicated to students or teachers and so could not have altered the literal meaning of those words. It is possible that the mental state of the legislators could have increased the likelihood of subsequent acts actually accomplishing an establishment of religion. But the intention to undermine or subvert the Court's prior school prayer decisions is not eliminated by invalidating the moment of silence statute; indeed, that motivation could accompany a statute allowing meditation and never mentioning prayer. To take the example a step further, it is even possible for a legislature to continue to fund an entirely secular public school with the hope and intention that someday official prayers would be reintroduced there. Indeed, it is possible that thousands of schools across the country are funded with something like this mind-set.[11] It seems unlikely that the Court could be pursuing a program of eliminating in legislators an unconstitutional mental state by invalidating statutes that, although legal in effect, were partly the product of that mental state.

If the censorship in *Wallace* was not aimed at controlling the minds of the legislators, what was its objective? The answer is suggested by the stark paradox presented by the Court's decision. It is constitutional for schools to permit students to pray silently, and it is constitutional for legislatures to authorize this practice. Under *Wallace v. Jaffree,* however, the Alabama legislature is not permitted to say—in specific terms—that it is authorizing the practice. The words *or voluntary prayer* could not be used.

As in *Pittsburgh Press,* it is possible to imagine a realistic and convincing explanation for this act of censorship. Just as it is reasonable to believe that sexist attitudes are widespread among potential employees, it is reasonable to believe that many schoolchildren in Alabama have been raised to think that they *should* pray. Such children, if told to meditate or pray silently for a moment, might be inclined to pray or, at least, to pretend to pray. This expected pattern would be partly a result of internalized values and partly of the social pressure created by the apparent decisions of other children. For a statute or a teacher to say to these students that they may "meditate or pray" would be to trigger much prayer. This, like reflexive compliance with the implicit message of want ad headings, would be a consequence of the beliefs and instincts of the students.

These students might, of course, be less inclined to pray if they were told only that they could "meditate" for a moment. Some might not share the understanding of the justices of the Supreme Court that meditation necessarily subsumes prayer; some might conjure up only various exotic modes of self-awareness or relaxation; some might have no specific associations at all for the word *meditate.* In any event, dropping the reference to prayer makes it less likely that students will understand that they may pray or will decide to pray. This, in turn, will change the character of their mental life. If the Supreme Court would prefer that fewer students pray during their moment of silence, keeping the words *or voluntary prayer* from them is surely one potentially effective method. And there may be some idea of a desirable community according to which this judicial censorship is justified. Perhaps pluralism or intellectual independence will flourish in schools where fewer pray. However, because the forbidden words were chosen by the political representatives of the parents of Alabama's school students, the Court was imposing its aspirations not only on children but also on adult citizens who held to a different moral vision.

Abortion

Nine years after the Supreme Court established a constitutional right to abortion in *Roe v. Wade*, the Commonwealth of Pennsylvania enacted an "informed consent" law. Like many other statutes promulgated through the years, this was an act of recalcitrance and reflected profound disagreement with the moral balance struck by the Court in *Roe*. Pennsylvania's law required that physicians provide: (1) the name of the person who was going to perform the abortion; (2) the fact that detrimental physical and psychological effects might occur and were not accurately foreseeable; (3) the medical risks associated with the procedure to be employed; (4) the probable gestational age of the fetus; (5) the medical risks associated with carrying the child to term; (6) the fact that medical assistance benefits might be available if the fetus were carried to term; (7) the fact that the father was required to assist with child support; and (8) that printed information from the commonwealth was available describing the fetus and listing agencies that offered alternatives to abortion.

This law required communication and was itself a communication. Insofar as its effect was to provide information to women who were considering abortion, the law was (in a way) perversely consistent with *Roe*. That decision created a right to decide to terminate a pregnancy, and the provision of accurate information could have been seen as helping to assure knowing, voluntary decisions.[12] Insofar as the effect was to convey the sense that the authorities in Pennsylvania were seeking to discourage abortion, the provision was arguably consistent with the case law that followed *Roe*. The Court, while extending the right to abortion against a wide range of restrictions, had upheld the authority of both the states and the national government to allocate public medical funding to childbirth rather than abortion.[13] These decisions reasoned from the proposition that it is legitimate for the government to prefer childbirth over abortion.

In *Thornburgh v. American College of Obstetricians*, however, the Court invalidated the "informed consent" provision.[14] Until it was reversed in 1992,[15] this decision made less likely the receipt by female patients of information potentially relevant to their decision, and it prevented receipt of the moral message implicit in the statute itself. Why did the Court, once again, act as censor? The opinion gave two reasons. First, the information was designed to dissuade rather than to inform. Second, the rules inflexibly applied to all patients irrespective of their individualized needs and thus intruded on the discretion of the physician.

These "reasons" have an immediate ring of plausibility because they are an accurate description of the statute. However, a description of a law is not an explanation for its invalidation. Of course, the rules were an effort to discourage abortion; the question was why the state may not advocate in this way. Of course, the discretion of physicians to withhold information was abridged; the question was why the state may not require medical doctors to provide information that some patients might find relevant. Censors, no doubt, often believe that information is danger-ous because it is potentially persuasive and that people should be relieved of the burden of deciding whether to be persuaded. It is sign of how far the justices were from recognizing their role as censors that, intending to justify suppression, they could simply and unashamedly describe the nature of the impulse to suppress.

I do not mean to suggest that the Supreme Court had no good rea-son for its decision in *Thornburgh*. It was pursuing a familiar ideal, the kind of climate that exists within a therapeutic relationship. This climate—consisting of trust, receptiveness, and the nonjudgmental pursuit of physical health—has its attractive side. Indeed, as Robert Bellah and his co-authors have shown, it is one of the major moral paradigms available in our culture.[16]

A patient who heard what the Commonwealth of Pennsylvania had to say on abortion might well have suffered an altered relationship with her physician. As the Court said, the mandated description of fetal devel-opment "no matter how objective . . . may serve only to confuse and punish [the patient] and to heighten her anxiety, contrary to accepted medical practice."[17] To tell a patient that medical assistance may be avail-able for a live birth or that the father may be responsible for support "may be cruel as well as destructive of the physician-patient relationship." To recite possible physical and psychological risks may "increase the patient's anxiety, and intrude upon the physician's exercise of proper professional judgment." All this is true. The patient might become uncer-tain and conflicted. She might resist professional advice. She might sub-ordinate her own best medical interests for the sake of moral consider-ations external to the therapeutic relationship.

The patterns of interaction and the implicit morality of the doctor-patient relationship are attractive but not insuperably so. Just as many school children in Alabama were raised to be receptive to the state's suggestion of prayer, many pregnant females—by instinct or accultura-tion—were, no doubt, highly receptive to reasons for giving birth. The Court's repeated and somewhat patronizing emphasis on patients' anxi-ety was, perhaps, an implicit recognition of this strong receptivity. The problem, then, was the patient. She could not be required to react ap-propriately; she would not be made to accept her physician's advice. But patients can be helped to want what the Court cannot mandate. If medical doctors, rather than the state, control the information available to the patient during certain crucial moments, rival moralities can be kept within their place. Pregnant patients, that is, can be protected from their own minds and inclinations. They can be shaped to behave properly.

Racial Integration

Aided by Congress and the executive branch, over the past forty years the federal courts have struggled to implement the principle that racially segregated public schools deny the right to equal protection of the laws. This has been an uneven effort—sometimes heroic, sometimes politically pragmatic, and sometimes obdurate. It has generated many legal and moral paradoxes. Chief among them is this: The constitutional right is to admission "on a racially nondiscriminatory basis," but (generally speaking) segregation may not be remedied by simply allowing parents to choose the school their children will attend.

The legal inadequacy of "freedom of choice" plans was established in *Green v. County School Board of New Kent County*, which was decided in 1968, some eighteen years after the original desegregation decision.[18] The consequence of this ruling has been that previously segregated districts across the country are required to achieve a significant degree of racial balance in their schools. This, in turn, has engendered detailed judicial control over educational decisionmaking, massive expenditures, and angry political opposition. This heavy price has been exacted as the initial legal paradox has widened into a powerful and troubling question. If (as the Court has said repeatedly[19]) racially imbalanced attendance patterns are not per se unconstitutional—that is, if the right is to nondiscriminatory admission rather than to a racially mixed result—why must formerly segregated systems achieve balance? Much sophisticated and fervent theorizing has gone into answering this question. Here I want only to develop the point that *Green* and its massive ramifications can be understood as another judicial effort to build a moral community by shaping the minds of the citizenry.

The "freedom of choice" plan presented in *Green* was a complex communication to students and their parents. Literally, it informed them that they could decide to attend either of the district's two schools, but this message existed and had meaning in a specific social context. Between 1902 and 1954, the school district had operated racially segregated schools in accordance with Virginia law. In the face of the Supreme Court's decision invalidating such laws, various state statutes continued to authorize segregation until 1965, the year the district adopted its freedom of choice plan. This plan was enacted despite the existence of other, potentially effective methods for achieving desegregation; for example, because the area was integrated residentially, the placement of students according to geographic proximity would have resulted in racially mixed schools at low cost. These facts—unlike the legislative history of Alabama's "moment of silence" statute—were known to all and supplemented the effective meaning of the district's plan. At a minimum, the decision to allocate attendance decisions to parents must have been seen to reflect an official reluctance to mix the races. More realistically, it probably was understood as embodying a strongly held desire for racial separation to continue.

It is one thing to suggest (as I did in the preceding section) that it is not necessarily illegitimate for the government to try to persuade pregnant women to avoid abortion. It is a different question whether school districts may officially communicate a preference for racial separation. The core of the reasoning in *Brown v. Board of Education* was that segregating students on the basis of race "generates a feeling of inferiority as to their status in the community that may affect their hearts and minds in a way unlikely ever to be undone." If state statutes can stigmatize schoolchildren in this way, it is certainly possible that official efforts to discourage or avoid racial mixing could as well, at least to the extent that those efforts are understood by students as being based on racist motivations. In short, invalidation of the freedom of choice plan in *Green* might have been explained on the ground that the evident intention of the school officials generated feelings of racial inferiority and, therefore, made the plan itself unconstitutional.[20] Some later decisions do extend the reasoning in *Brown* in this direction, although these do not demonstrate a connection between the officials' segregative motivations and students' perceptions and thus do not, strictly speaking, apply *Brown*'s conception of equal protection.[21]

In *Green* the Court did not go this far. It held, not that the defendants had committed a new constitutional violation, but that they had failed in their obligation to remedy their past violation. The Court announced that the obligation on a district that had been segregated by law was "to take whatever steps might be necessary to convert to a unitary system in which racial discrimination [is] eliminated root and branch." A plan must promise "realistically to work, and . . . to work *now.*" The New Kent County freedom of choice plan failed to meet this standard:

> In three years of operation not a single white child has chosen to attend [the school formerly designated for blacks] and although 115 Negro children enrolled in [the formerly all-white school] . . . 85% of the Negro children in the system still attend the all-Negro . . . school.

The primary deficiency in the freedom of choice plan, then, was not that it communicated an official preference for racial separation. The plan was inadequate because it did not work; it did not work in the sense that it did not produce adequate levels of racial balance. The Court did note that the plan "operated . . . to burden children and their parents [with the school attendance decision]," but this is as close as *Green* comes to suggesting that the plan, in context, was an effort to persuade blacks and whites to go to school separately.

If even in the circumstances of the *Green* case "freedom of choice" is not unconstitutional because of its communicative impact, why should it have been thought an inadequate remedy for past segregation? Why, that is, was the district obligated to achieve a racially balanced result? It is true that in general defendants must rectify the consequences of their illegal conduct, and the *Green* Court appeared to be applying this maxim by insisting that the district convert its dual system into a unitary one. But a "unitary" (or racially balanced) system does not necessarily correct the consequences of the old segregated system. The psychological and educational deficits of segregation are, as the Court said originally, "unlikely ever to be undone."[22] Certainly there is no reason to assume that racial mixing, if it is known by all to have been coerced by judicial decree, will dispel the accumulated sense of inferiority. Conversely, it is at least possible that the exercise of choice, even in a highly imperfect setting, can help to establish self-respect. In any event, the removal for all races of legal barriers to school attendance means that the system is "unitary" in the sense that it is nondiscriminatory.

What is striking about cases like *Green* is their extraordinary emphasis on external statistical outcomes when the constitutional harm to be corrected is personal and developmental. The fixation on attendance configurations diverts attention from the direct remedial implication of the initial holding in *Brown.* If segregation damaged the hearts and minds of generations of minority school students, then the government must correct that damage. It must correct those minds. If this is the government's remedial obligation, the difficulty with freedom of choice plans is that they assume that black parents have the very kind of competence and self-concept that *Brown* denies they can have. Under this view, the relevance of the fact that only 15 percent of the black children in New Kent County were attending school with whites was not that their education was being harmed by the substantial separation of the races. (After all, if there has been no history of school segregation, schools that are entirely black are not thought to result in unequal education.) The relevance of the attendance configuration was that it demonstrated the extent to which the attitudes of black parents had not yet been corrected. To put this point in its most unattractive light, the reason why choice was (as the Court phrased it) a "burden" on minority parents was that, under the logic of *Brown*, they were not yet whole persons. The Court prevented the school district from addressing them as if they were.

This explanation for *Green* can be framed in a less offensive way. Paul Gewirtz, for instance, argues eloquently that what was at stake in *Green* and in many subsequent cases is the "corrective ideal."[23] He writes, "When discrimination has occurred, choices are not free in the way that the corrective conception requires. . . ." He notes that both schools in New Kent County continued to carry their old racial identity, even to the point that the "black school" was named for a local black pastor and school principal. Moreover, the "attitudes, tastes, and perceptions" of all parents had been shaped by the history of legal discrimination. In making their decisions, black parents had to face hostility and possible retaliation. They may even have internalized "the segregationists' conception of . . . place." Gewirtz concludes that it "would not be plausible to explain the segregated pattern [that resulted from the freedom of choice plan] as a product of autonomous choices that were independent of discriminatory forces."[24]

Gewirtz, of course, does not describe *Green* as an act of censorship. For him, the decision has to do with remedying the consequences of legal wrongs. To require racial balance is a "transition." Broadened and fortified by the experience of attending integrated schools, both blacks and whites will eventually be ready for choice. Thus, the massive effort over the past several decades to achieve integrated results can be conceived of in a way that does not forfeit our usual happy belief that censorship for purposes of mind control is exceptional.

But can *Green* be limited in this way? The censorship involved in each of the other cases discussed in this chapter was in part a reaction to prior illegality. Newspaper readers were likely to be influenced by the implicit message of sex-specific want ads because of familiar employment patterns set up by years of illegal sexual discrimination. Alabama schoolchildren might have been quick to pray because of a culture created by years of mandatory Bible reading and prayer in public schools. Pregnant women were susceptible to the argumentation contained in Pennsylvania's "informed consent" provision because of attitudes formed during the many years when abortion was a criminal offense. In none of these cases, however, was the government's (and the Court's) censorship directed only at the specific class that had been subject to illegal treatment.

In *Green*, the Court held that a previously segregated school district could not speak to black parents as if they were autonomous. The decision mandated certain education choices, but it also censored the expression of an important point of view. The purposes of this suppression went far beyond the parties to the lawsuit. It helped to build, for better or worse, a moral climate. As Gewirtz himself says:

> [T]he corrective enterprise . . . may be as much a viewpoint as an analytic tool. . . . [I]t insists upon an imagery and locates a source of commitment. The images are rooted in the past—the awful, deliberate wrongs inflicted on black people for so long, the brutal sweep of continuity between past deeds and present life. From that image of wrong comes the commitment to correction. . . . The corrective idea insists that racial justice not be assimilated to other distributive objectives. It affirms that, because of the past, the claims of black Americans are unique and uniquely just.[25]

This "way of thinking" (as Gerwitz calls it) may be morally compelling or historically inescapable. No doubt, something like it has driven decades of Supreme Court decisions. It is a strong animating vision but only one of many. Its disadvantage is that it begins by denying full respect and dignity to black Americans.

Mind Control and Censorship

It is one thing to acknowledge that we all have a strong and legitimate interest in the mental states of our fellow citizens. It is another to view censorship as a normal or acceptable way to assert that interest. Yet as the cases discussed in this chapter demonstrate, censorship does seem more common than we usually like to admit; although labeled differently, its substance even appears in the decisions of the most respected branch of government. Moreover, just as the exercise of the power of judicial review can amount to censorship, other aspects of our everyday political and personal lives, if examined, can also be seen to entail suppression.

Even in academic discourse, which is supposedly where ideas are examined with utmost tolerance and curiosity, arguments are often framed not only to supplement or rebut the position of another scholar, but to discredit that position altogether.[26] A sufficiently powerful reply might, if successful, blow an idea or line of inquiry right off the map—inhibiting further elaboration of the idea and discouraging others from considering it. In any conversation, the line between effective engagement and bullying, between refutation and suppression, appears and disappears like a river in dry country.

Along these shifting banks it is difficult to know who is suppressing whom. In my university a prominent official (in fact, a football coach, who perhaps might be forgiven for not appreciating all the fine points of academic freedom) took a strong public position in favor of an anti-gay rights initiative. This initiative will be described in the next chapter. For present purposes, the important point is the nature of the coach's statement.[27] He quoted the Bible, calling homosexuality an "abomination." Was this a part of fierce but appropriate moral debate or an effort to silence the increasingly vocal gay rights groups on campus? The university's president (who presumably did understand intellectual exchange) decided that it was suppression. She instructed the coach that he was not to identify himself as a university employee if he were to vent his views as a part of external political debate and that on campus he was not to express his opinions about the issue at all. She explained that, while a university is a place "where all ideas are welcome . . . and where all have a right to free expression[,]" it was the coach who threatened these values.[28] The university as a forum "belongs to all of us, and it should be captured by no one, for such action makes a mockery of freedom of expression." Worse, the coach had "dominate[d] the exchange of ideas" in a way that left segments of the university community "feeling unwelcome and unvalued. . . ."

Like most decisions made under the press of events, the president's position was not fully worked out. She did not comment, for example, on whether her action might leave the small minority of the students who are Biblical literalists feeling unwelcome or unvalued. Nevertheless, her stance is a graphic illustration of a widespread contemporary phenomenon: the use of censorship to achieve intellectual diversity.[29] The censorship was clear, for the president enjoined all those in positions of "authority, influence, or power—whether chancellor, professor, counselor, or coach"—from expressing certain unacceptable views on campus and from identifying their employment when stating those views to the general public. The stated goal of this censorship was to protect the mental state of gays on the campus so that they could participate in the intellectual life of the university.

Although the self-consciously radical ideas of feminists and critical race theorists can be seen at play in this episode,[30] as well as in many other similar contemporary events, it should be obvious that administrators who censor for the sake of diversity are not necessarily political or intellectual radicals. They are acting in line with well-established academic traditions that have, perhaps inevitably, straddled the shifting line between open debate and oppressive orthodoxy. They are, moreover, acting in line with other public authorities, including the Supreme Court, which have long tried to control minds in the name of progressive change.

There is a crucial similarity between the university president's decision to censor the coach and the constitutional decisions described earlier in this chapter. In each case a public official censored in order to protect the sensibilities of a group thought to be in need of improvement. If women are to enter nonconventional jobs, they need to be protected from the implicit argumentation of sexist want ads. If female patients are to feel free "enough" about abortions, they must be protected from information that might interfere with therapeutic values. If Alabama school students in sufficient numbers are to overcome their upbringing and decide to meditate rather than pray, they must not hear the words *or pray* from the state. If southern blacks, who have suffered from a heritage of segregation, are to be made whole, they must not hear the loaded message of choice from local school boards. And gays, whose behavior has been criminalized and scorned, might not respect themselves if they are permitted to hear an authority figure quote Scripture.

Change (or progress, if you will) is most difficult when it cuts against the understandings and instincts established by the visceral experiences of those to be improved. In these circumstances, competing messages are especially dangerous, for the beneficiary class cannot be trusted to hear such messages until after progress has been accomplished. In these circumstances, the natural instinct of reformers is to try to purge the campus, to purify the law, to dominate the language.

8

Arguing with Enemies:
Interpretation as Invective

The Bible-quoting football coach described in the last chapter might have had enough authoritarian instincts of his own to sympathize, at least a little, with the university president's censorship of his antigay opinions. But he must have been stunned to hear her depictions of his behavior. The president claimed that he had made "a mockery of freedom of expression" and that he had threatened "the value and dignity of other human beings." Thus, for having made a brief and literal reference to a revered book, the coach was cast as a dangerous, evil man. He no doubt believed that his statement had been an exercise of free speech, not an attack on that principle, and that his Christian concepts of sinfulness are compatible with human dignity. Even on the assumption that there was some truth in the charges, they represent a commonly observed contemporary phenomenon—the degeneration of public debate into exaggeration and invective.

Name-calling, obviously, serves many of the same functions as outright censorship. As a threat, it frightens some people into silence. Moreover, it discredits what the brave (or foolhardy) do say. As the coach's experience demonstrates, it defines moral disputes as settled when in fact they are still underway. In these ways, it protects the beneficiary class—the people who are thought to be in need of improvement—from having to consider opinions that the leadership thinks they are not able to handle for themselves.

Name-calling has deep roots in electoral politics, where it is refined into the artform of caricature and systematized into the science of propaganda. But one reason "political correctness" has received so much recent attention is that name-calling is now an accepted part of life in supposedly polite settings; words like *racist, sexist,* and *homophobic* are normal terms, for example, in many educational settings. As we have seen, even those time-honored practitioners of harmlessly empty public rhetoric, university presidents, sometimes traffic casually in harsh and extreme insults.

The degeneration of discourse in polite institutions is dismaying because it undermines our belief that self-control and personal moderation can be effective constraints in public debate. If intention, training, and role cannot civilize, what can? Such doubts are sufficiently troubling that there is a natural tendency to see the behavior of the various educated elites in the best possible light and to minimize incontrovertible excesses as aberrations. Hence, for example, name-calling within the universities is often regarded as remarkable, as a contemporary anomaly. But, once again, a straightforward examination of the judiciary's record indicates that our failings are deep-seated. Indeed, the disappointing consequences of judicial restraint as a guide for modern judges suggests that, at least under circumstances of significant cultural division, even strongly held philosophies of moderation will not civilize either our vocabulary or our decisions.

Name-Calling in the Courts

In the winter of 1993, the District Court for the City and County of Denver, Colorado, was asked to issue a preliminary injunction against enforcement of a state constitutional amendment that had just been enacted by a vote of the people.[1] The provision, called "Amendment 2," prohibits the state and its subdivisions from enacting or enforcing any law "whereby homosexual, lesbian or bisexual orientation, conduct, practices or relationships shall constitute or otherwise be the basis of . . . [any] claim . . . [of] minority status, quota preferences, protected status or claim of discrimination." This law, needless to say, had been vigorously debated among the thousands of Colorado voters; indeed, it continues to be the focus of intense political and economic pressures involving groups from across the country. In our system, however, it fell to a solitary municipal judge to decide the issue, at least as a preliminary matter, and it eventually will fall to a few other state and federal judges to resolve it on a more permanent basis.[2]

This case involves, obviously, intense and profound differences of opinion about morality, human nature, and political justice. On the one hand, opponents invoke important values such as personal autonomy, equality, and procedural fairness. Supporters of the amendment, on the other hand, have concerns about the growing list of groups receiving special protection under various civil rights laws; they are anxious about the viability of the institution of marriage (which, after all, has historically been premised on the assumption that society can favor heterosexual relationships); and they are profoundly uncertain about egalitarian experimentation on policies having consequences for such a sensitive and mysterious matter as sexual identity. It is to the judicial system that many people look for careful, fair treatment of both sides of such difficult conflicts.

From the very outset of the lawsuit, however, those challenging the amendment insisted that it had no legitimate purpose at all.[3] Their legal argument begins with a description not only of the defendants and the plaintiffs but also of "the proponents" of Amendment 2. They note that the amendment was drafted and promoted by a nonprofit group called Colorado for Family Values (CFV). They assert that CFV was assisted by the National Legal Foundation, which is described as "an organization founded by the Reverend Pat Robertson." After summarizing various statements made by CFV in support of its position on the amendment, the challengers assert that CFV's campaign is an effort by the religious right "to legislate discrimination against gays, lesbians, and bisexuals." Next they helpfully (but without revealing any source) define the "religious right" as being characterized by ". . . a belief that the Bible should be interpreted literally, opposition to a set of values labelled 'secular humanism,' and an evangelical commitment to convert and to limit the influence of Satan, liberalism, socialism, and communism." Painting now with a broad brush, the argument asserts that in the early 1980s the "'New Right' political movement incorporated the religious right . . ." and that the "approach developed by the 'New Right' . . . to promote anti-homosexuality measures . . . is akin to Hitler's appeals to traditional German family values." This discussion ends with a list of organizations—"Paul Weyrich's Free Congress Foundation, Beverly LeHaye's Concerned Women of America, Jerry Fallwell's Moral Majority, Robert G. Grant's Christian Voice, Phyllis Schlafly's Eagle Forum, Paul Cameron's Family Research Institute, Pat Robertson's Christian Coalition . . ."—and with the assertion that these organizations provided support for "what appeared to be local, grassroots efforts to defeat 'homosexual privilege proposals.'" It is unclear whether the challengers mean that all or any of these organizations were behind local support for the Colorado amendment. They do note darkly that "[a]t least two national religious right organizations are based in Colorado Springs [where, as the brief had noted earlier, CFV is also located]." To close the point, they assert that "several" employees of James Dobson's Focus on the Family "sit on Colorado for Family Values advisory boards."

To what is this sinister description of "the proponents" relevant? Although the specific logical connections are largely left to the reader's imagination, the challengers are quite clear about the general significance of the information.[4] They use it to support the argument that the purposes of those who voted for Amendment 2 were illegitimate. Those purposes are described as a "desire to harm a politically unpopular group" and as an expression of "prejudice," "fear," and "antipathy." The amendment's true and sole purpose was "to encourage and support discrimination." The proponents' "purportedly neutral rationale" was used to "mask their campaign of hatred."

Now, the issue of gay rights evokes powerful ideological and moral loyalties, but these can be put aside long enough to acknowledge that the argument I have described is conspiratorial and ugly in its own way. Its circles of moral condemnation shift and merge until they envelop the voters of an entire state. Although aimed at progressive objectives, this absolute rhetoric and these loose generalizations have a disconcerting resemblance to the reactionary propaganda of, say, the John Birch Society.

Our electoral campaigns give full expression to deep fears, flimsy theories, and harsh accusations. (The debate that preceded enactment of Amendment 2—the debate in which my university's football coach tried to play a part—evidenced much of it on both sides of the issue.) In our political life some of this is unavoidable and even useful, but how did it come to pass that in our ordinary courts of law it is thought appropriate and useful to characterize the official decisions of our fellow citizens in crude and extreme ways?

It is possible, of course, to answer this question by asserting that realism and accuracy sometimes require the public's motivations to be described in completely negative terms. Those who see Colorado voters as prejudiced and hate-filled will be inclined to this view.[5] But such an answer only moves my question: How did it come to pass that the educated people who give this answer (including careful lawyers) can so confidently and severely condemn the thinking and the motivations of hundreds of thousands of people? This question is especially troubling in the circumstances of Amendment 2, where the decision being judged involved sensitive and elusive issues that, while profoundly important to us all, are not fully understood by any of us.

I have been describing a single argument made in a single case. Even if my characterization of that argument is accurate, neither the case nor the argument is necessarily typical of discourse in the courts. Much theorizing about the judicial function and many popular attitudes toward the courts assume just the opposite.

Actually, however, the shrill and simplistic depiction of public purposes has become a common feature of our constitutional jurisprudence. It is such a frequent part of the work of even Supreme Court justices (let alone everyday lawyers advocating their causes) that we are hardly conscious of it. At least, we are not usually surprised or offended by the harshness of the judgments that are so routinely passed. Accordingly, it is worth reviewing some of the well-known constitutional opinions that contain insulting descriptions of the objectives of public decisions, not to count them up or analyze them but simply to try to see their language for what it is.

The place to start is race. I realize that in both political debate and in academic commentary, charges of "racism" are now endemic. Nevertheless, it is striking how free judges have felt to make the charge against other public officials and even, on occasion, against whole electorates. They have done so appropriately with respect to laws that are plainly intended to separate and stigmatize, but they have also made the accusation in more complicated and subtle circumstances. For example, school board decisions that fail to achieve prescribed levels of racial balance are termed "intentionally segregative acts," even when the goal of balance was in competition with other legitimate public objectives, such as neighborhood schooling or funding for educational quality.[6] It is less frequent, but courts have also made similar charges where the official action was facially neutral, nondiscriminatory in its immediate effect, and unrelated to any injunctive regime. Thus, a state constitutional affirmation of the absolute right of any person to sell private property was found to involve the state in private racial discrimination and to "encourage" such discrimination.[7] In any of these situations, the local authorities or voters may well have been wrong for one reason or another, but it surely is untrue to the complexity of what many of them were trying to do to portray their purposes as "segregative" or "discriminatory."

Given the central place that racism undoubtedly holds in our history, it may be that suspicions about official motivations and purposes in this area are specially justifiable or, at least, defensible. But the justices have made analogous charges in a number of nonracial cases. They described the public's objective in providing (but not requiring) separate nursing education for women as perpetuating nursing "as an exclusively woman's job."[8] The Court concluded that a city ordinance singling out group homes for the mentally retarded reflected an "irrational prejudice."[9] An eligibility requirement for food stamps that excluded households containing unrelated members was said to be based on "a bare congressional desire to harm a politically unpopular group."[10] The justices insisted that a prohibition on the distribution of contraceptives that distinguished between married and unmarried persons was wholly "irrational."[11]

To describe public objectives as prejudiced and irrational and as being aimed only at doing harm to specific groups—this is a strikingly condemning stance that on a wide range of issues our judges seem neither reluctant nor surprised to take. But the cases I have alluded to do not at all complete the bleak picture that the Supreme Court draws of the rest of us. In a variety of settings, justices have described public officials as being intent on nothing less than the subversion of the Constitution itself. For example, the Court recently invalidated an ordinance that made it illegal "to unnecessarily kill, torment, torture, or mutilate an animal" on the grounds that city officials "did not understand, failed to perceive, or chose to ignore . . . the Nation's essential commitment to religious freedom."[12] Recall that the Alabama law authorizing public school students to have a moment of silent meditation "or voluntary prayer" was, according to the Court, intended to endorse prayer and even to return official prayers to the schools.[13] (This conclusion was largely based on what one legislative supporter had said.) Similarly, a law requiring "balanced treatment" of evolution and creation science in public schools was "clearly" intended to advance the creationists' religious viewpoint.[14] (The Court treated one legislator's statement that evolution was "contrary to his family's religious beliefs" as evidence for this conclusion.[15] In an earlier case, the justices had based a similar conclusion about the influence of "fundamentalist sectarian conviction" in part on the content of newspaper advertisements and letters to the editor.[16]) When Congress enacted the Flag Protection Act of 1989, it was not giving voice to legitimate concerns about the importance of the flag as a symbol of national unity. It was, according to the justices, only providing further proof of the "popular" inclination to stifle dissenting viewpoints.[17] The Pennsylvania statute that required women seeking abortions to be provided with certain truthful but troubling information was not merely misguided on a morally complex issue; it was seeking to "intimidate women," to create the "opposite" of informed consent, and to defy the lawful authority of the Court in much the same way that southern rioters tried to block school integration.[18]

It is possible that every law struck down by the Supreme Court using words like *irrational, prejudiced, invidious, suppressive,* and *defiant* were, on the whole, bad laws. Some of the motivations that went into their enactment may have been—probably were—regrettable or even reprehensible.

Still, the justices' extreme rhetoric (as well as the "findings" and legal analysis that it expresses) is inaccurate in that it does not leave enough room for the difficulty of the judgments involved, the ambiguity of human motivations, and the complex nature of public decisionmaking.

Every Supreme Court decision that condemns a public enactment as being an expression of prejudice, irrationality, or invidiousness invites untold numbers of legal arguments of the sort used to attack Amendment 2 in Colorado. Every such argument urges another of the thousands of state and lower federal courts to label some product of our political institutions as wholly unjustifiable (or worse). In short, to a remarkable extent our courts have become places where the name-calling and exaggeration that mark the lower depths of our political debate are simply given a more acceptable, authoritative form. The mainstream in legal academia has been so busy applauding the judiciary's theoretical capacity for elevated dialogue and sensitive moral decisionmaking that it has not much noticed the tenor of much of what the judges have actually had to say. Their condemnations are seldom directed at the elite in the legal profession. Moreover, we professors and lawyers are safe in assuming that the fears, animosities, guesses, and hopes that animate our own political agendas are unlikely—after all, since we produce the judges—to be crushed under the weight of words like *prejudice.*

There are many reasons why the discourse of our public law has sunk so low. To begin with, the vocabulary of the law necessarily reflects the larger culture, and our society (we increasingly fear) lacks the capacity for moral debate. There are also more specific factors at work. The adversary system, which honors argument more than discernment, tends to promote caricature; the adjudicatory system, dealing as it does with winners and losers, leaves little room for ambiguity; legal education is easier and more fun if it promotes forms of analysis that are both simple and self-serving; and so on. However, one especially disheartening factor is this: The dominant version of judicial restraint, a philosophy of moderation that might have been expected to civilize the vocabulary of legal discourse, has not worked.

Judicial Restraint and Moral Heroism

It is only a slight overstatement to say that in modern times there has been just one intellectually respectable version of judicial restraint. Neither rigorous textualism nor serious historicism has been practiced by the Supreme Court, and piles of academic commentary have posed very significant questions about whether either approach is possible or would (in any event) result in a restrained judiciary. The banishment of these forms of legal traditionalism has been personalized in the Senate's rejection of Robert Bork's nomination to the Court and in the flood of harsh criticism spawned by his subsequent book. By way of contrast, the reputation of the common law methodology of Justice John Marshall Harlan has solid foundations in the work of eminent scholars like Alexander Bickel,[19] and it continues to grow. Recently, Harlan has been the subject of considerable and respectful academic interest.[20] His jurisprudence is held up as a model of responsible restraint even in popular journals.[21] Conservative justices, including Sandra Day O'Connor, David Souter, and Anthony Kennedy, find themselves being rehabilitated by mainstream commentators who find Harlan-like tendencies in their work.[22] From the other end of the political spectrum, the liberal jurist Ruth Bader Ginsburg was pronounced acceptable during her confirmation hearings by conservatives who were impressed by her cautiously incremental, lawyerlike style.

Harlan's approach is highly regarded for good reason. He understood constitutional issues to involve, not the "narrow" or "literal" issues of text and history, but the grand and practical issues of political life. To these issues, however, he brought intellectual rigor rather than emotion or abstraction. He understood the need to defer to wisdom expressed in the political process. He was restrained both in his formulation of the issues and in his willingness to let the meaning of initial decisions be elaborated on a case-by-case basis. Moreover, Harlan saw the judiciary's task of interpretation as an aspect of its duty to adjudicate specific disputes. He stood, in short, for civilized moderation.

Harlan's methods are rooted generally in ancient common law traditions and specifically in a constitutional theory that goes back at least to Professor James B. Thayer, who made his seminal contribution in 1893.[23] The central proposition in Thayer's argument is that courts should declare a legislative act unconstitutional only when the law was "not merely a mistake, but . . . a very clear one—so clear that it is not open to rational question."[24] One of the major purposes of this rule, according to Thayer, was to promote a proper degree of respect for legislative judgments. He emphasized how constitutional questions can "seem unconstitutional to one man, or body of men, [and] may reasonably not seem so to another. . . ." He described the judicial decision as secondary, both in sequence and in importance. He said that constitutional questions properly involve issues of practicality in which legislatures can be expected to have expertise; in addition, he repeatedly warned against traditional legalistic methods as "pedantic," "narrow," and "literal." He wanted it to be "studiously remembered" that the courts should always assume "virtue, sense, and competent knowledge" in the legislature.

As restrained and respectful as Thayer's proposed method was intended to be, his clear error rule does anticipate that sometimes courts will hold a legislature's constitutional judgment to be irrational. Thus Thayer's formulation seems to require courts to engage in at least some of the harsh terminology that I have described as a significant part of our modern constitutional discourse. His rule, however, contemplates that the charge of irrationality will be rare and will be made in a way that is consistent with appropriate judicial humility.

Indeed, it is logically possible for a court operating under Thayer's rule to disregard statutes infrequently and even then to express high regard for the enactors' motivations and knowledge. For instance, legislators might decide to ignore a very specific and profoundly immoral constitutional provision—such as a requirement, which was once a part of our fundamental charter, that each state deliver up escaped slaves. The resulting statute might be unconstitutional in a way "not open to rational question" and yet the legislators' action could be described as valiant, moral, and enlightened. Even the decision to violate a legal obligation to uphold the Constitution might be praiseworthy from many perspectives. Judges presumably would be faced with such statutes on few occasions and would invalidate them reluctantly—only because no rational view of the Constitution permitted judicial enforcement. Such a judge could express admiration for the ideas underlying the statute while "disregarding" it as a legal matter.

Although Thayer intended for the clear error rule to be applied in a way that is respectful of legislatures and although even when it leads to the invalidation of a statute the rule is logically compatible with such application, the seeds of the opposite result lie throughout his essay. Indeed, as a realistic matter Thayer's formulation is a recipe for creating a self-deluding and intolerant judiciary.

The self-image of judges employing the clear error rule will be profoundly complacent. They must feel and announce great reluctance before invalidating a statute. Even when on a "just and true construction" a law seems unconstitutional, they are to exercise restraint. Naturally, these judges will be motivated to believe that they are highly selective in voiding legislation and that, when they do, their judgments are specially justified. Moreover, because Thayerian judges have had to reach "the really momentous question" raised by the clear error rule, they have entered the realm of statesmanship. Their role goes far beyond that of mere lawyer. In constitutional cases they act as a kind of safety net, protecting the fundamental law against the worst violations, intervening only where (even given the widest range for "the great, complex, ever-unfolding exigencies of government") there is but a single rational conclusion. Their judgments necessarily involve some of the most vital and imponderable political issues, yet their conclusions are finally a matter of inescapable legal duty. Respectful and restrained, intellectually capacious and yet rigorous, called to act only in the most extreme circumstance, these judges are, in brief, quiet heroes.

The view from the heroic perspective is a fine one, but what is to prevent heroic judges from running amok? The range of their decisions is not restricted to those few cases in which a literal reading of the text or some other "pedantic" analysis can authoritatively decide the issue. Moreover, the sense of complacency and elevation encouraged by the clear error rule might reduce actual self-restraint even as it induces the conviction that discipline has been exercised. In particular, the heroic judge can be expected to brook no opposition or dissent after a determination of unconstitutionality. The disputed governmental policy, after all, was illegal in a way "not open to rational question." Political disagreement in this circumstance will tend to be perceived as illegitimate defiance, not as potentially useful information. In short, Thayer's methodology relies on judicial self-restraint in a way that greatly reduces the potential for external checks. Yet it is precisely the ambitions of leaders who see themselves as heroic that stand in greatest need of limits imposed from the outside.

Thayer, of course, did not think that his rule of restraint would have the perverse consequence of producing morally imperious judges. He believed that legislatures would not often make irrational constitutional judgments and that courts—if properly instructed about the need to presume good sense in legislators—would confine their power to those extraordinary occasions. This presupposes the happy circumstance that judges and political representatives have common criteria for "rational" constitutional decisions even when these decisions involve the evaluation of a wide assortment of practical considerations. Without this assumption, there is no reason why conscientious legislators (working from their criteria) might not frequently come to conclusions that (from the radically different perspective of a judge) appear clearly irrational. If this should occur, we would expect Thayer's judges, the most eminent of which was Justice Harlan, to intervene often, to be unaware of the scope of the power they are exercising, and to be impervious to criticism.

The Ideal of Moderation in a Divided Society

To what extent do judges and political decisionmakers hold the same criteria for rational constitutional judgment? It is possible that a society

exists where lawyers and general citizens fully share a general intellectual culture and a specific decisionmaking methodology. This could hap-
pen where lawyers exercise great power and thus shape the terms of
public dialogue.[25] It would also seem likely where lawyers are subject to
the influence of the wider culture—where, for example, legal training is
not highly differentiated from other education, where the adjudicatory
function is not isolated or specialized, and where lawyers do not constitute an identifiable economic and social class.

In our society the intellectual methods employed by lawyers are no
doubt used by virtually all other groups at least to a limited extent, and
these methods overlap significantly with the problem-solving instincts of
many in the educated, professional classes. However, American society
is varied enough and lawyering is specialized enough that the judgmental standards common to the law are at least somewhat foreign to almost
all nonlawyers, and they probably are downright alien to some groups.[26]
The happy circumstance presupposed by Thayer's formulation—that
political representatives and judges will agree on standards for rational
constitutional judgment—certainly cannot be assumed to exist. If the
specific issue is one that evokes differential standards even from groups
normally sympathetic to legal methods or if political influence has been
exerted by groups for whom legalistic criteria are alien, the clear error
rule will not serve as a constraint.

As an illustration of competing standards of rationality in operation,
consider again the issue of flag burning. Akhil Amar has called *Texas v.
Johnson* "plainly right, and even easy—indeed as right and easy a case in
modern constitutional law as any I know."[27] This sprightly description is
probably accurate if it means that the Court's decision was consistent
with cases and principles that are much admired within the legal profession (and especially by law professors such as Amar). Legal academics
generally approve of how the *Johnson* Court construed "speech" function-
ally to protect communicative conduct that is useful in political debate.
They approve of its application of a strong principle against "content
discrimination" because they agree with the justices that "offensiveness"
as a justification for suppressing an idea is dangerously boundless. The
mainstream concedes that the Court had to acknowledge (as modern,
realistic judges almost always do) that a sufficiently important public
objective would nevertheless justify the statute. The Court made one final
claim—that its own ruling, as a symbol of our common commitment to
tolerance, would provide a satisfactory alternative way to sustain our
sense of nationhood. This assumption of the centrality and efficacy of
the judicial role probably sums up the general attitude that has pervaded
free-speech law for decades. Amar is right, I think, that all this is self-

evident to many lawyers, so clear as to be beyond reasonable disagreement.[28]

As it happened, of course, neither the Court's conclusion nor its reasoning seemed ineluctable to large segments of the American public. The Congress reacted to *Texas v. Johnson* by quickly enacting the national Flag Protection Act of 1989, which the Court also invalidated, giving the same self-evident reasons. As I have already indicated, the justices dismissed the "groundswell" that prompted Congress and the president to act as further evidence of the populace's inclination to suppress ideas with which it disagreed.

It is true that the urge to suppress had something to do with the political interpretation of the Constitution that the Court disregarded in *United States v. Eichman*. But, if lawyers' intellectual standards can be set aside for a moment, it is the Court that can be viewed as irrational. Obviously, a functional definition of "speech" has potential ramifications that could obliterate the distinction between speech and conduct. Lawyers and judges may think that they can be trusted to avoid absurd extensions of functionalism, but the outcome in *Johnson* itself could be thought by the general public to undermine this assurance. After all, despite the fact that burning the flag is expressive, in our history this behavior has not been commonly viewed as protected "speech" any more than urinating on the flag has been.[29] Justices capable of taking leave of such long-established understandings might sensibly be thought capable of eventually dissolving the basic distinction upon which the free speech clause depends.

Similarly, the "principle" against content discrimination is a plain sign of irrationality to someone operating on the basis of practical knowledge rather than conceptualism. To claim that the government can or should treat all ideas as equally valuable is almost literally crazy for the simple reason that some ideas are worthless or harmful. Of course, legal theorists know this but tend to believe that there is an extreme danger in permitting official judgments based on content. Again, why should an experientially minded public regard this danger as real? Flag desecration laws had long existed in many states, and they had shown no sign of the kind of cancerous growth feared by the Court.[30]

Finally, the notion that judicially announced principles of tolerance can serve the same unifying purposes as the flag is suggestive of the sort of self-importance that in private lives precedes civil commitment. It assumes that nationhood is built entirely on the basis of ideas—indeed, specifically on certain civil libertarian ideas that have had great influence on the courts over the last seven decades—to the exclusion of emotional and symbolic bases. This assumption is at odds with the observed behavior of societies throughout history.

In sum, the flag-burning controversy presents us with a vivid illustration of how on a crucial constitutional issue the legal profession and much of the general public possess profoundly different judgmental criteria. Lawyers tend to honor abstract theory, conceptualism, and intellectualism generally; segments of the public rely more on historical sense, practicality, and visceral experience. From each perspective, the other looks irrational. Is this intellectual divide long enough and wide enough to turn practitioners of judicial restraint into the kind of self-deluding juggernaut that I have suggested is theoretically possible? A review of the record of the federal judiciary over the past four decades is instructive. In many respects that record displays exactly what would be predicted if the clear error rule were to be applied in circumstances of significant cultural division.

There have been, as I indicated in Chapter 2, innumerable judicial decisions invalidating political determinations. These decisions have touched virtually every topic of public concern, but they are concentrated and most spectacular in two kinds of areas. The first involves issues, such as freedom of speech and criminal procedure, where lawyers' thinking is highly specialized and, therefore, counterintuitive to a broad range of the public. The second involves issues like abortion, school desegregation, and religion, in which public policies have been influenced by social classes that are educationally and socially distinct from the class occupied by elite lawyers. These judicial decisions cannot be explained as manifestations of straightforward partisan differences. They have continued despite considerable changes in the political complexion of the bench. They appear, that is, to represent cultural disagreements.

This extraordinary array of decisions has not been accompanied by proportionate signs of self-awareness on the part of the judges exercising power. Many audacious constitutional opinions actually emphasize the courts' responsibility to defer to majoritarian preferences and painfully examine the record for any sign of good sense. Indeed, even while ordering the redesign of a state's entire prison system or the reorganization of a city's program of public education, jurists profess great reluctance and humility. They seem genuinely regretful that the political decisionmakers did not face up to their responsibility to decide the issues in the way that the judges believe would have been correct. Only this unfortunate and rather inexplicable obduracy, the decisions say, forces judicial intervention.[31]

Ostensibly respectful attitudes, however, tend to dissolve when political decisionmakers either defy or are thought likely to defy a judicial ruling. As I explained in Chapter 5, in such circumstances the courts have freely expanded the scope of constitutional protections—by way of prophylactic rules, elaborate doctrines, and so on—in order to forestall not only outright defiance but also more shaded forms of disagreement.[32] On certain memorable occasions, the Supreme Court has used the specter of defiance to assert astonishingly large claims for its own authority. Lower courts in similar settings can be more direct; not uncommonly, they react by taking over more administrative or legislative functions and sometimes even by abridging the constitutional rights of those who express disagreement.[33]

All this is precisely what would be expected of judges possessing the self-image of reluctant hero that is a natural outgrowth of Thayer's version of judicial restraint. Of course, the mentality of the clear error rule is only one of many possible causes of the intolerant cultural imperialism that has characterized modern judicial power. Naive textualism, simplistic historicism, rampant pragmatism, arrogant rationalism, clanky doctrinalism—any of these can and do explain aspects of the phenomenon. Even if it is theoretically (and perversely) possible that judicial restraint helped to build the contemporary judicial machine, why believe that it in fact did so or that it was a significant factor?

Restraint and the Judicial Machine

Although Thayer is the main source for the most respected modern version of judicial restraint, Justice Harlan is—as I have already indicated—its most important practitioner. Today Harlan is admired for his philosophy of restraint, but I think he is also admired because in actual operation his moderate judicial philosophy led him to the role of quiet hero. In fact, his work set the stage for much of the cultural imperialism that is the record of the Court in the second half of this century.

The flag-burning decision, for example, is directly traceable to *Cohen v. California,* a much admired and influential opinion written by Justice Harlan.[34] In upholding the right to wear a now-famous "scurrilous epithet" sewn to a jacket, *Cohen* used virtually the same logic as the Court later employed in *Johnson.* In style, however, Harlan's opinion displays all the appealing attributes of a rigorous common law decision. It defines the legal issue with great precision; it carefully and deferentially examines all the arguments for permitting suppression; its conclusion is painstakingly restricted to circumstances in which the government has not shown "a more particularized and compelling reason for its actions. . . ." Yet behind all this thoughtfulness and caution can be heard the voice of the hero.

Harlan dismisses the notion that the display of the words *fuck the draft* was inherently likely to cause a violent reaction as "plainly untenable . . . reflecting an 'undifferentiated fear or apprehension. . . . '"[35] As for the claim that suppression served the purpose of maintaining a "suitable level of discourse within the body politic," Harlan invokes "examination and reflection." He is confident that the sensibilities of passersby could be adequately protected if they would just (why didn't the local officials think of it!) avert their eyes. By contrast, what is at stake in protecting this "trifling and annoying instance of . . . distasteful abuse of a privilege" is, if only enough thought is applied, momentous. Protecting individual freedom here will serve to "produce a more capable citizenry and more perfect polity. . . ." In fact, "no other approach would comport with the premise of individual dignity and choice upon which our political system rests."[36] Plainly, the officials of California had made an enormous error; the moral underpinnings of our political system were at risk; only the measured reflections of a few justices lay between us and eventual calamity. This was a small decision, reluctantly and carefully arrived at, but it would serve the highest, not to say the most grandiose, purposes.

Some citizens who are not blessed with a legal education may plausibly wonder about the rationality of the Court's continuing claim that "the premise of individual dignity and choice upon which our political system rests" requires ordinary people to walk around with their eyes averted against what in some places has become a virtual onslaught of crude, offensive messages. Be that as it may, a second line of modern cases is, if anything, an even clearer example of the Court's cultural imperialism. These are the decisions that establish and elaborate the right to privacy, especially as this right applies to sexual conduct and to abortion.[37] This line descends directly from the contraceptive case, *Griswold v. Connecticut,* with which Senator Biden skewered Judge Bork. This decision in turn grew directly from Justice Harlan's famous dissenting opinion in a case called *Poe v. Ullman.*[38]

The *Ullman* dissent is, in most respects, vintage Thayerism. Harlan begins by arguing that the Court should not avoid deciding the constitutional question raised by a state's rule against the use of contraceptives. Like Thayer, Harlan emphasizes that the power of judicial review arises from the Court's "duty to decide . . . the particular controversies which come to it. . . ." On the merits of the issue, Harlan departs somewhat from Thayer by attempting to justify the imposition of a nondeferential standard for evaluating the state's purpose. Despite this, much of his analysis remains consistent with the clear error rule. He asserts that the Court should view the Constitution as a "basic charter of our society" rather than as a text to be taken literally, and that the due process clause has become a general bulwark "against arbitrary legislation." The con-

straints on judges in this endeavor are their own "judgment and restraint."
He acknowledges the controversial nature of the moral decisions that
are involved in regulating human sexuality and notes that this alone
requires the judge "to hesitate long before concluding that the Constitution precluded Connecticut from choosing as it has among these views."
Having expressed his reluctance and humility, Harlan is freed to explain
his conclusion, which is sufficiently convincing to most people today that
there is a danger of passing too quickly over his excited phrasing. He
says that the application of the criminal prohibitions in the statute to
married couples "is an intolerable and unjustifiable invasion of privacy
in the conduct of the most intimate concerns of an individual's life." The
state, Harlan asserts, has not "even remotely suggest[ed] a justification
for the obnoxiously intrusive means it has chosen. . . ." What is at stake
for the individual, however, is "the very essence of constitutional liberty
and security."[39]

Again, while Harlan describes the constitutional interest in terms of
the most timeless aspects of civilization and the governmental action as
both aberrational and utterly unjustifiable, he is still careful to limit the
reach of the decision that he is urging on the Court. For example, he
says his reasoning would not apply to intrusions required to enforce laws
against adultery and fornication. The restrained judge remains secure
in the knowledge that his intervention has been exceptional and small.
But, given the terms of Harlan's own opinion, these assurances ring
hollow. Those terms make Harlan the protector of society's most basic
and valuable principles against forces that are mindless and profoundly
dangerous; that is to say, Harlan establishes a role that is sure to be irre-
sistible to the later judges who would actually determine the ultimate
implications of the "modest" decision at hand.

In addition to continuing activism in the areas of free speech and
privacy, I have said that the record of the Court in recent decades has
been marked by large claims about the judiciary's institutional role. These
claims are manifest in the largely unfettered prerogative of lower courts
to assume administrative and legislative powers when faced with local
recalcitrance and in the Court's self-important descriptions of its own
function. The most extravagant expression of this hubris was the assertion by several justices in *Planned Parenthood v. Casey* that at least on the
most socially destructive and morally profound issues, such as abortion,
it is the Supreme Court's job to call "the contending sides of a national
controversy to end their national division."[40] This language was authored
by three justices (O'Connor, Souter, and Kennedy) who no doubt view
themselves as careful judicial moderates. Moreover, the groundwork was
laid by that earlier embodiment of judicial modesty, Justice John Marshall

Harlan. In 1958, Harlan signed *Cooper v. Aaron,* which asked the American public "to recall some basic constitutional propositions which are settled doctrine."[41] These included a reiteration of the familiar assertion that the federal judiciary is "supreme in the exposition of the law of the Constitution," a claim that the justices described as "respected by . . . the Country as a permanent and indispensable feature of our constitutional system [ever since *Marbury v. Madison*]." This proposition presumably not being open to rational question, the Court went on to say that the Court's decisions themselves are the "supreme law of the land" and that, accordingly, every state officer is obligated to support these decisions.[42]

Nothing seems further than the distance between the modest Thayeristic assumption that the power of judicial review arises from a legal duty to decide cases and the exasperated pronouncement in *Cooper v. Aaron* that all officials must obey the "supreme" expositor. It might be thought, therefore, that this specific idea should not be attributed to Harlan. He was only one of the justices who signed the opinion, and the circumstances of the case, which involved violent resistance to the Little Rock desegregation decree, were extraordinary. The lineage of the expansive claims of *Cooper,* however, does go back to Harlan himself. It was this proponent of judicial restraint who had insisted that the following sentence be included in the first of the important decisions implementing *Brown v. Board of Education:* "[I]t should go without saying that the vitality of these constitutional principles cannot be allowed to yield simply because of disagreement with them."[43] This was the strongest language in the decision, and it is clear enough, I think, why Harlan would favor it—and why he would later sign *Cooper v. Aaron.* The rigorous and restrained analysis in his opinions was in significant instances only a prelude to overwrought characterizations of the societal interests to be served by the justices' decisions. Dissent that threatens such decisions threatens those lofty interests; it threatens the authority of judges who already believe they have done the minimum necessary to protect us from policies that, without any possible justification, threaten the social fabric. Under this view, disagreement is intolerable. Thus, from a restrained view of the judge's duties emerges the overweening claim that the Court has authority to terminate fundamental moral conflicts.

Harlan's form of judicial restraint, of course, is not necessarily or entirely responsible for the kind of cultural imperialism that has characterized the judicial record for the past several decades. The clear error rule can restrain judges, and Harlan was often restrained.[44] However, given enough cultural separation between jurists and the general public, Thayer's ideas in operation can be expected to—and did—produce a great deal of disrespectful, intolerant, and expansive judicial decision-making; that is, his prescription, applied in our circumstances, led to what it was intended to avoid.

In our society today there are many cultivated voices that deal in exaggeration, insult, and intolerance. These voices belong to people (judges, university presidents, and law professors like Dworkin and Bork) who sincerely aspire to highly civilized standards. But criticisms that are felt to be reluctant and specially justified can turn out in fact to be frequent and harsh. In a fragmented culture the line between modesty and self-righteousness is easily and imperceptibly crossed. When it is crossed, well-intentioned citizens not only stifle specific debates but also contribute to the general sense of moral degeneration that itself intensifies this urge to censor ourselves.

9

Censoring Ourselves

The words *censorship* and *vilification* conjure up ominous historical associations. We think, for instance, of the wholesale effort to keep abolitionist materials out of the antebellum South or the ugly name-calling by Senator Joseph McCarthy. Efforts to prevent change by the suppression of destabilizing messages have often had a grave and systematic character. It is odd, then, that a prevalent reaction when these tactics are used to induce change is humor. The attempts of progressive censors to sanitize the minutiae of our public vocabulary are so targeted and detailed as to verge on the frivolous.[1] Even the ever-lengthening list of words of opprobrium (*ageist, Eurocentrist, logocentrist*) seems to be too mechanical to convey real condemnation. Political correctness verges on self-parody. Its practitioners, although resolutely humorless while going about the endless task of improving the rest of us, are the source of considerable amounts of somewhat nervous comedy.

There are some solid reasons for the nervousness in our laughter. I suggested in the last two chapters that both suppression and name-calling are much more common than is often assumed. These are not devices used only by right-wing authoritarians and hypersensitive campus reformers. These tactics are built into contemporary life; they are practiced where we do not notice—by highly trained administrators, elite scholars, and moderate judges. A second reason for nervousness is that progressive intolerance is more likely to gain official status when powerful groups view others as imperfect, weak, and in need of correction. Viewed this way, the beneficiaries of reform cannot be trusted to improve themselves unless they are first protected from themselves. The tendency for elites to see the recalcitrance of others as a sign of personal deficiencies will be great in times, like our own, of acute cultural self-doubt. As the Thomas hearings reminded us, in such times we see each other as self-deluding, weak, and indulgent. To reformers this reinforces the sense that people are unworthy (and in need of improvement). By the same token, some of those subject to reform will feel uneasy or even guilty about themselves and, thus, will be inclined to submit.[2] Moreover, to the extent that various factions believe that they are part of a culture that is characterized by moralistic opportunism, they will perceive their opponents as dangerously unrestrained.[3] Moral and legal inhibitions against engaging in mind control then break down, as groups compete to impose their visions on others before it is done to them.

Cultural self-doubt encourages censorship in other ways as well. In a weak society, it is not merely individuals or groups that are thought to be deficient; the ethos that defines us as an ongoing civilization itself seems doubtful. In such a setting any specific problem can seem potentially catastrophic. Thus demands for reform are likely to be far-reaching and urgent.[4] Naturally, backsliding is less tolerable to the extent that improvement must be drastic and immediate. There is no time to persuade the reluctant or the ignorant. Ready or not, they must be changed.

Although cultural reform measures are likely to be ambitious (or, perhaps, desperate), the prospects for success are likely to seem low. Society, after all, is comprised of members who do not believe that their fellows can even face up to problems honestly, let alone exercise the civic-spirited discipline necessary to solve them. This low confidence is too diffuse and disabling to be tolerable. It means that nothing important is likely to be improved and that there is no available lever for reestablishing a sense of control and competence. This creates a brooding fear of potential disaster that can easily be converted into concrete images of calamity. In our time we see evidence of this deep anxiety about the future in specifications (down to the day and hour) of biblical prophecies of doom, diverse and conflicting environmental alarms, exaggerated forebodings about economic collapse, obsessive worries about personal health, and despairing visions regarding crime or racial division. Such concerns, I recognize, are certainly not baseless. But, as we know only too well from our occasional "red scares," when diffuse anxieties are poured into sharply formed images, there is an intensity that can lead to strong demands for censorship. Once the intractable cultural problems of character and confidence have been reduced to specific disasters, the next step is to demand some immediate sign of control.

Superficial mind control measures can be quickly undertaken, but they tend to increase the very kinds of anxieties and doubts that gave rise to the initial urge to censor. The reformers' self-conscious regulation of cultural symbols thus feeds on itself. This occurs because the regulation of public discourse creates a gap between vocabulary and experience. It is possible to define the beneficiaries of affirmative action programs as equal or qualified, but the difficulties they face on the job, in the school, or—for that matter—at the confirmation hearing cannot be changed as quickly as legal terminology. Sexist want ads can be eliminated, and traditionalist presumptions and sensibilities can be purged from the law. But stereotypical beliefs about gender differences persist and find continual reinforcement in everyday life. State legislatures can be enjoined from uttering the word *prayer,* but students know that the authorities do not regard prayer and meditation as moral equivalents. The Court could decree that statutes must say abortion is only a medical procedure, but most pregnant women would continue to regard it as something quite different and more complicated. The word *abomination* could be effectively banished from every campus, but gay students would know that the overwhelmingly normal and accepted "life-style" involves heterosexual relationships and procreation. The gap between vocabulary and experience can be viewed as an injustice and a frustration; its size, however, depends not on what morality might be thought to require, but on how deeply set existing beliefs or behaviors are and how superficial change has been.

To the extent the gap is significant, the reformer is driven to exercise more complete control over public discourse. This is because the reformer's case is constantly being undermined; as vocabulary separates from experience, the regulator's position becomes more insecure. And we all know that—in conversation or in politics—people tend to shout the loudest when they are least sure that their answers will persuade. Thus, when we pursue our visions in a culture of profound self-doubt, we will tend to resort quickly, and then increasingly, to censorship.

I said at the outset of this book that claims about general cultural degeneration are highly speculative. Collective self-doubts of the kind raised by the Thomas-Hill confrontation can be delusions themselves. Pessimistic conjecture about the dangers posed by contemporary tactics of suppression is, accordingly, dubious too. In Chapter 2, I suggested that the Supreme Court's modern record provides us one angle from which to check our fears. That record gives some reason to be worried about our culture generally as well as to be concerned about progressive censorship. Indeed, the Court not only occasionally exemplifies our inclinations toward mind control but also in a larger sense embodies our need to escape ourselves. The degree to which in modern times we increasingly and unshakably are dependent on this institution is a sign of how much we want to censor ourselves.

Principle Ascendant

If love is affection strong enough to survive disappointment, we Americans love judicial review. Political liberals in academia and elsewhere continued to be devoted to it despite the fact that before the election of President Clinton conservative appointees dominated the federal courts for more than twenty years. Indeed, while facing what appeared to be a likely prospect of decades more of conservative hegemony, most liberals were indefatigable; they strategized about how to maximize their eventual reemergence two or more decades hence, and they energetically analyzed theory and doctrine in an effort to salvage what they could in the short run.[5]

Conservatives might have been expected to relish judicial power during this period, but in fact they experienced one profound disappointment after another.[6] With the beginning of the "Burger Court" around 1971, race-conscious remedies were approved for school desegregation decrees, and most public aid to parochial schools was declared unconstitutional. In subsequent years, the Court created the right to abortion, extended free speech protections to areas like exotic dancing and flag burning, permitted judicial control over prison reform in a majority of the states, and approved such innovations as the judicial power to raise taxes. Meanwhile, the Court advanced conservative causes (such as the protection of property rights and the elimination of affirmative action) only cautiously. Nevertheless, conservative lawyers continued to grind out new theories and arguments, ever hopeful.

The devotion to judicial power of liberals, like Tribe, and conservatives, like Bork, is all the more surprising in light of the failure of any theory to justify the current practice of judicial review. Although the Bork hearings, as well as innumerable Supreme Court decisions, strongly suggest that we have a consensus to the effect that the courts should create nonenumerated rights out of our traditions, no one has proposed a generally accepted theory that explains this practice, and, indeed, virtually everyone bitterly criticizes the practice when it results in decisions that they think are unwise, which is often. With judicial power thus unexplained as a matter of theory and severely questioned as a matter of pragmatic outcomes,[7] commentators and citizens alike nevertheless march ahead, serene in their attachment to the Court's right to "speak before all others" on the meaning of the Constitution.

What hope continually renews this devotion? There is, at least, a "mainstream" answer to this question. A broad array of elite theorists, as well as other educated observers, believe that the legal culture improves on politically expressed values because of something called *principle,* which both Bork and his critics treat as the opposite of *fiat* or *lawlessness.* Both wings of the mainstream even seem to mean roughly the same thing in their use of these words. The hope on all sides is that reliance on "principle" enables judges to escape the personal.

According to Bork, the key tactic in modern, lawless constitutional interpretation is exemplified by *Griswold v. Connecticut:* the expansion of a limited or partial right that is protected by specific language (such as the fourth amendment's protection from unreasonable searches) into a general value that is not (such as the "right to privacy").[8] He sees this technique not only in the contraceptive and abortion cases, but also in John Hart Ely's famous "representation-reinforcement model," in Tribe's "antisubjugation principle," in Dworkin's distinction between concepts and conceptions, in Justice Brennan's ideal of "human dignity," and elsewhere. Bork makes the powerful point that because the framers' decision where to stop is as important and as entitled to respect as their decision where to go, such expansions are illegitimate expressions of personal preference.

For his part, when Ronald Dworkin pronounced Bork "a constitutional radical who rejects a requirement of the rule of law . . ." he was not referring to Bork's emphasis on the framers' intent as a guide to interpretation. In fact, Dworkin, like Bork, would look to evidence about that intent.[9] According to Dworkin, the problem is that, although Bork acknowledges that the framers' intent must be thought of as a "general principle," he has no explanation for the level of generality at which he chooses to define that principle. For example, Bork would construe the equal protection clause to prohibit racial discrimination but does not explain why he would not construe it to prohibit all discrimination based on prejudice. The failure to explain his preference for an intermediate level of generality means, according to Dworkin, that Bork's philosophy is "not just impoverished and unattractive but no philosophy at all."[10]

Apparently, then, the legal requirement that "all sides" had agreed upon before Bork was that the framers' intent should be set at a high level of generality:

> Judges in the mainstream of our constitutional practice are much more
> respectful of the framers' intentions, understood as a matter of prin-

ciple, than Bork is. They accept the responsibility . . . to develop legal
principles of moral breadth. . . .[11]

Under Dworkin's version of respect for the framers' intentions, the
Constitution prohibits not only racial discrimination but also discrimination against homosexuals because of a "principle" against "appealing
to the majority's preferences about . . . what sorts of lives their fellow
citizens should lead. . . ."[12] Although Chairman Biden used a different
illustration, Dworkin's point is one that the senator made more pithily
during the Bork hearings: Why should privacy (and other constitutional
principles) not be conceived more generally so as to prohibit a broad
range of offensive governmental actions?

Perhaps Judge Bork has never provided a satisfactory answer to this
question. Yet what is striking about Dworkin's critique is that his position is plainly deficient in the same way that Bork's position is deficient.
Dworkin says his equal protection principle prevents appeals to majoritarian moral preferences only when those judgments relate to the "culture that . . . [the behavior of fellow citizens] generates[.]"[13] But why
should the principle stop there? As I tried to show in Chapter 6, broad,
"unfocused" public purposes can be more significant than tangible purposes. If sexual freedom is sufficiently important to prevail over diffuse
cultural objectives, why not over concrete purposes? Similarly, Biden's
concept of "privacy" need not stop at the bedroom door. The protection of private sexual conduct might be thought valuable because of an
asserted value in uninhibited physical pleasure. Nothing in Dworkin's
self-assured critique (or in Biden's incredulous questions) convincingly
explains their more general but still intermediate levels of generality.[14]
The "mainstream," then, shares an ideal of impersonality in constitutional
interpretation, yet that ideal remains radically incomplete. Although
certainly redolent of judicial work and of the superiority of mentality over
emotionality, the use of "principle" does not explain specific moral
choices. Dworkin's principles are a highly intellectualized patch that
covers, but does not essentially change, the kind of heartfelt desires that
animate Biden's political affirmations.

Much sophisticated effort has been devoted to trying to explicate the
nature of principled decisionmaking and its special advantages. I will leave
these mysteries to others. Here I want only to develop a simple observation about legal principles: They are invoked to exclude, not political
pressures generally, but influence of an identifiable kind. Indeed, judicial
use of "principle" can be seen as a reflection of a prejudice or impulse
widely seen among the intellectual elite—an unexamined bias against the
inarticulate. I can develop this observation by examining a case that

involved a factual backdrop so confused and forlorn as to call into question the justices' basic attitudes toward progress and decay in American society.

Principle, "Progress," and the Tradition of the Family

Its facts are highly personal, but the case bears a strangely anonymous name, *Michael H. v. Gerald D.*[15] A child (Victoria D.) was born to Carol in 1981, while she was married to Gerald. Carol, however, had had an affair with Michael and believed him to be the father, a possibility that appeared to be confirmed by a blood test voluntarily undergone in 1981. During the next three years, Carol and her child lived in a "variety of quasi-family units," including Michael's home at various times and occasionally with Gerald. Eventually, Michael sued to establish his paternity and visitation rights. In 1984, Carol stipulated that Michael was Victoria's father, but a few months later she reconciled with Gerald, with whom she subsequently lived and by whom she had two children. Michael's efforts to gain visitation rights were cut short in 1985 when Gerald's motion for summary judgment was granted on the basis of a California statute providing that "the issue of a wife cohabiting with her husband, who is not impotent or sterile, is conclusively presumed to be a child of the marriage." During the course of this litigation, Carol had variously supported and opposed Michael's claims, as she moved from household to household. At the time of the summary judgment motion, Carol was with Gerald and had withdrawn her earlier stipulation as to Victoria's paternity; she did not (as she could have under the law) allow the presumption to be refuted by moving for a new blood test.

Like so many other aspects of American life, this chronicle of high living, indecision, and tenuous attachments ended as a constitutional issue before the Supreme Court. The central question was whether an unmarried putative father has a due process right to prove paternity against the wishes of the married mother and her husband. This was a serious legal claim because of the Supreme Court's earlier decisions establishing a constitutional right to privacy that included the right to bear and raise children. More specifically, in several cases the Court has held that a biological father's established and substantial relationship with his children creates a protected privacy interest despite the absence of a "legal relationship" with the mother.[16] Justice Scalia's opinion, in which only a plurality of the Court joined, limited these cases by excluding from the right to privacy the ties of a "natural father of a child conceived within and born into an extant marital union that wishes to embrace the child."

When the distinctions and nuances of the concurring opinions are factored in, *Michael H. v. Gerald D.* has a more restricted and uncertain meaning than emerges from the Scalia opinion. (One concurring opinion joined the plurality opinion "in all but [footnote] 6.") But the wider importance of the case arises from the sustained confrontation between Scalia's plurality opinion and Justice Brennan's dissent. This dissent is a typically capable and thorough rendition of the sort of thinking that has dominated much of constitutional law in modern times. The plurality opinion, however, does not merely depart from this thinking; it methodically and pointedly disputes each of the major arguments raised by Justice Brennan. The two opinions are so different in their basic assumptions and orientations that the result is less like an argument than a conversation carried on in different languages.

The modern mind-set typified in the Brennan dissent is insistently reductionist and morally nonjudgmental. Thus, the Court has frequently emphasized biological and natural relationships rather than legal and normative ones. Justice Brennan once declared that the right to access to contraceptives must be the same for married and unmarried alike: "[i]f the right of privacy means anything, it is the right of the *individual*, married or single, to be free . . . to bear or beget a child."[17] Accordingly, in *Michael H.*, Brennan describes the relationship of Michael, Victoria, and Carol as "a family."[18] After all, they lived together at times, Michael contributed to the child's support, and "Victoria called Michael 'Daddy.'" In fact, Brennan compares this family to the married unit of Carol, Gerald, and Victoria by saying, "The only difference between these two sets of relationships . . . is the fact of marriage." To give constitutional significance to the legal status of marriage is "pinched." For Brennan, it is an open question whether "'family' and 'parenthood' are part of the good life [but in any event] it is absurd to assume that we can agree on the content of those items. . . ."

In contrast, Scalia's opinion describes the relationship between Michael and Carol as "an adulterous affair."[19] A family is not, he says, a "relationship established between a married woman, her lover, and their child, during a 3-month sojourn in St. Thomas, or during a subsequent 8-month period when, if he happened to be in Los Angeles, he stayed with her and the child." Plainly, for Scalia, the legal status of a couple has moral significance, while for Brennan it is almost irrelevant. For Scalia natural relationships can be important, but judgments can be made about their relative moral quality.

Brennan's apparent tolerance is partly a consequence of another major characteristic of conventional enlightened thinking—fatalism about the future. His dissent emphasizes, as so many of his writings have through the years, that the Constitution is a "living charter" and that "times change." Indeed, the pressure of change is so intense that the future has already arrived: "The situation confronting us here . . . repeat[s] itself every day in every corner of the country." The imminence and inevitability of social change makes judgments about its desirability futile. Policies aimed at preserving some aspect of the past—policies to encourage the integrity of married families and the legitimization of children—are "out of place in a world in which the fact of illegitimacy no longer plays the burdensome and stigmatizing role it once did." Brennan is charmed by the idea of change and for him *old* is a pejorative word; to protect old values is to be "stagnant, archaic, hidebound . . . steeped in the prejudices and superstitions of a time long past." In short, newness is good, or at least the future is too close to question.

This resolutely progressive stance has been a theme of constitutional decisions for many years in areas like privacy, sex discrimination, and free speech. Scalia's opinion in *Michael H.* is an exuberant affirmation that change can be opposed and that the Constitution is a link to the past rather than a slide into the future. The purpose of the Constitution, he says without embarrassment, "is to prevent future generations from lightly casting aside important traditional values—not to enable this Court to invent new ones." This means, he says, that political institutions should be given latitude to shape the future even when that involves clinging to aspects of the past. (Brennan treats this as a matter of legal precedent: "We [the justices] have declined to respect a State's notion, as manifested in its allocation of privileges and burdens, of what the family should be.") According to Scalia, it also means that when constitutional interpretation does confine political discretion, it should do so by appealing to the accumulated political wisdom represented by tradition. Thus, in determining the scope of the right to privacy, Scalia urges that the Constitution should protect only fundamental interests "traditionally protected by our society." Indeed, he goes further to argue that the tradition should be understood at "the most specific level at which a relevant tradition . . . can be identified." The legal standards and political practices relevant to the case at hand, then, were those "regarding the rights of the natural father of a child adulterously conceived. . . ."

Brennan, by contrast, argues that "parenthood" is the interest that has been traditionally revered. Here we have use of the relatively abstract characterization of a principle that Bork correctly described as central to modern constitutional arguments and decisions. The Brennan dissent, consequently, can rely on considerable legal authority in explaining his more generalized version of our traditions. Scalia's opinion, however, challenges this fundamental aspect of the modern mind-set. He argues that the more abstractly the tradition is defined, the more unconstrained judicial power is. Making the same point that I previously noted, he argues that preference for abstraction would require ever wider conceptualizations. "Why should the relevant category not be even more general— perhaps . . . 'personal relationships' or even 'emotional attachments' . . . ?" Justice Brennan (sounding much like Dworkin) replies that the issue is whether to be "generous." However, unless it is true that our political or moral traditions are generous (a word that begs the question whether broadly defined rights are morally preferable), it would be wrong to appeal to those traditions as a basis for Justice Brennan's moral preference or conclusion. If judges use "principle" to find impersonal authority, the issue is not whether to be generous, but how to be accurate.

These two opinions carry on an extraordinary debate about whether recent trends in our culture represent progress or decay. At the heart of this argument is the issue at the heart of our society's extraordinary devotion to judicial power: What does it mean to use "principle" in interpreting our political and moral traditions? In *Michael H.*, Justice Brennan speaks for many of our most sophisticated theorists and judges when he claims that it is principled to define our traditions as relatively abstract statements. What does he accomplish by doing this?

He achieves transcendence by way of inaccuracy. Notice how Brennan's account of our "generous" traditions leaves out crucial facts. His argument is that our traditions have honored the privacy interests of unmarried putative fathers even where the assertion of their parental interests would, at least potentially, interfere with established and formalized marriages. A major obstacle to this argument is the long-established legal rules presuming that paternity lies in the married father. Brennan answers that the putative father's interests have been respected even if not legally protected. This response glosses over the fact that, for the most part, it has not occurred to people to enact legislation protecting the relationship that they supposedly respect. Brennan also claims that parenthood (including unmarried parents living with their children as informal families) has in fact received legal protections. This claim ignores what is implicit in the limitations on those protections; they have not, for the most part, been extended to adulterous relationships.

Finally, Brennan insists that the received tradition of protecting formalized marriage is "crumbling." He notes, for instance, that in a few jurisdictions, proof of paternity is allowed even as against the child of a married couple. Brennan thus diverts attention from the large number of jurisdictions that have not changed their rules, as well as from the fact that even where the rules have begun to change, those changes have not yet gone so far as to grant parental rights. He also sees the received tradition "crumbling" in that its often-asserted basis—the need to protect children from illegitimacy—is of decreasing importance due to changes in the legal and social status of illegitimacy. In this, Brennan denigrates those imperfectly understood or expressed values that continue to underlie the rule. In short, whatever can be said in favor of Justice Brennan's version of our moral traditions, it cannot be said to be a fully accurate description.

These inaccuracies have a function. The effect of Brennan's opinion (had it attracted a majority of the justices) would have been, obviously, to move our laws beyond what they are or have been. This effect, whether viewed as progress or degeneration, means that Brennan's account of our traditions transcends those traditions. Conversely, Scalia's opinion shows that a full and objective account of our traditions inevitably describes what we have been. To appeal to tradition in the more complete way that Scalia does is to appeal to the past. Needless to say, the past does hold the seeds of change, but the direction of that change is precisely what has not yet been determined, and this is what Scalia's opinion, too, leaves open, for his position allows people in the various states to decide on the legal rights of unmarried putative fathers. Principle, then, enables us to describe ourselves in a new way by overlooking something about ourselves. The progressive judge or theorist believes that some aspect of our heritage is best forgotten or obliterated. To appeal to the relative generality of "principle" is to argue from this belief.

Principle as Suppression

What does principle leave out? Is there some identifiable aspect of our history that judges censor when they invoke principle? Of course the specific answer varies, but there is a commonality. It is captured by the distinction between what I call "mute behavior" and "articulate pressure." Articulate pressures include most of what we normally think of as political influence and argument—not only marches down Constitution Avenue and mail to the justices but also the great political mobilization that resulted in the New Deal and the small mobilization that occurs when a judge has tea in the Yale faculty lounge and learns what professors smirk at and what they take seriously. In each instance, some person or group has considered some issue and attempts to bring an opinion or preference before the judge. Mute behavior is the opposite. It exists when it has not occurred to anyone to articulate an opinion, let alone bring that opinion to bear on a judge. If, for example, in two hundred years almost no one has thought to abolish or dramatically alter the states as governmental organizations, the resulting institutional patterns are what I mean by mute behavior. If for many generations it never dawns on anyone to use humiliation in the stocks as punishment, the absence of that form of punishment is a mute behavior. If until about 1970 no one imagined that the Constitution protected a right to abortion, that also is a mute behavior.

It should be obvious that mute behaviors, like articulate pressures, are a form of political influence.[20] When people do not ask for a change, when they remain silent, they can affect governmental decisionmaking. The issue presented by the modern penchant for relatively generalized values—"principles"—is, then, whether there is some reason for judges generally to pay attention when people want something but to ignore people when they take things for granted, are uninterested, or are content.

By their nature, mute behaviors are not announced or even clearly understood. If the consequences of governmental action or inaction are acceptable, especially over a long time, the resulting state of affairs will seem normal and may not even be noticed. Similarly, if the government is urged to undertake some action, the limits established for action may not be consciously understood, for those limits represent an implicit consensus about what is tolerable or even desirable in the existing state of affairs. Mute behaviors, like articulate pressures, reflect human experience. They can, therefore, be either attractive or repellent; they can represent deep wisdom or intractable prejudice. Perhaps most often they embody less dramatic values such as caution and prudence.

Should judges be influenced by mute behaviors? The mainstream of modern constitutional theory assumes that they should not be. When Ronald Dworkin argues that the equal protection clause should be interpreted to invalidate discrimination against homosexual conduct, he is arguing that certain reasons given for adopting the fourteenth amendment should count more than the fact that the enactors never imagined that they were changing any laws regarding homosexuality or, indeed, regarding any kind of sexual behavior.[21] When Bruce Ackerman grounds the right to use contraceptives partly in the New Deal's transformation of our concept of property, he is arguing that affirmative political argument and pressure regarding centralized economic regulation should count more than the fact that those reforms were not precipitated by any concern about restrictions on sexuality.[22] When Justice Brennan claims that our traditions protect the privacy interests of unmarried putative fathers, he can point to various articulate voices for "progress" but he must ignore the implicit decisions about where progress should stop. The normal interpretive practices of our judges systematically ignore or downplay significant mute behaviors. All the innovations that we have become so accustomed to—from the Court's discovery that sexual privacy is a right independent of the institution of marriage to its conclusion that flag burning is a protected form of expression—involve a decision to disregard the weight of established behaviors and implicit understandings.

One possible justification for crediting affirmative pressures but not mute behaviors is that affirmative pressures represent conscious thought and active decisionmaking rather than reflex. To some degree this contrast is a false one. Individual people can decide not to raise an issue or propose a change on the basis of private reflection. If many people—virtually everyone—had long decided not to push for something (or even to talk about it) so that an issue had not become public, the resulting inactivity would seem to reflect an emphatic kind of collective decision. To some degree, however, the contrast is accurate, because nonaction can sometimes represent lack of thought or concern or imagination. If conditions or events are not unsatisfactory enough even to inspire thought, however, the absence of conscious consideration has strong significance because the resulting inactivity might be a powerful endorsement of the way things are.

There is a deeper problem with the claim that affirmative pressures should be preferred because they represent conscious thought and active decisionmaking. When jurists and legal theorists focus on the principle inherent in active politics and ignore what was not considered, they are not honoring conscious thought in any realistic sense. Indeed, the whole effect of their "principles" is to get around the inconvenient fact that, for example, recent legal changes do not go so far as to protect the rights of putative fathers in Michael H.'s position, or that Reconstruction and the New Deal did not involve consideration of homosexuality or contraceptives. The *point* of "principle" is to push legal protections beyond what people have considered, proposed, and enacted. Assuming that conscious thought is an advantage, the only way to know what was consciously thought about is to pay attention to mute behaviors.

A second possible justification for crediting affirmative pressures is that, while mute behavior can represent intellectual activity, it cannot (by definition) represent dialogue. Under this view, what has not been talked about is not worthy of the judges' attention. As trendy as this justification is,[23] it is hard to understand. Mute behaviors do not represent verbal interchange among people or groups but they do represent other forms of communication and interaction. The prolonged nonrepeal of statutes, the subtle coordination of expectations whereby a group senses that they have gone far enough in establishing a new rule, or the implicit message of approval communicated by satisfied inattention to an issue—these are all forms of interaction. They are important even if not verbal. The quiet flow of human conduct is not necessarily less eloquent than the excited noise of public debate.

A third objection is that attention to mute behaviors would make the judges' task impossibly complicated. It would require them to take account of virtually our whole political and social history; they would have to arbitrate not only profoundly conflicting demands but also among those demands and countervailing silences. This is true, but it is a consequence of the ambitious moral and political role of the judiciary that is already a fact. If judges are to interpret our traditions, if they are to help establish our values by interpreting our political history, then presumably they should interpret our whole history, not only what has been desired and said but also what has been accepted and left unspoken.

The reason for our persistent slighting of mute behavior has to do, not with complexity, but with fear. To the extent that rights are defined according to a complete account of our politics, then for better or worse we are thrown back on ourselves and on the strength of our culture. We all know and expect, as the Bork hearings and a realistic examination of Supreme Court opinions demonstrate, that politics will shape law. Through the metaphysics of principled analysis, however, one side of our political culture can be significantly disabled in the process. Through generalization, the influence of mute behaviors can be weakened and sometimes eliminated. As a result, an additional advantage in public decisionmaking goes to groups adept at abstract theorizing and forceful verbalization.

This advantage does not, of course, completely protect the mainstream from anxiety; it is a source of unease to recognize the impact on law of the character of ideological competitors within the educated classes. Tribe must contend with Bork. Still, the elite can drive out its own heretics and then return to the larger project of ensuring that the fundamental law is not directly shaped (and limited) by the whole culture. Progress, as defined by a self-assured but small segment of society, becomes possible. The visions that are currently dominant in the articulate classes—unqualified by the varied experiences of the many kinds of people whose lives constitute the whole nation—become the official visions of the whole nation. Principled argument, if it works, suppresses the rest. To the extent that society at large harbors doubts about itself and its past, it participates willingly in its own censorship. We not only put up with judicial review, we demand more.

Principle and Cultural Decline

Despite the brave front that Justice Brennan put on them, the facts of *Michael H.* display many of the reasons why people worry about the health of our culture. Like the allegations made during the Thomas-Hill confrontation, this is a saga of deception, pleasure, privatization, and opportunism. That the legal issue revolved around a child emphasizes an additional and distressing fact—that the weight of our weaknesses and confusion is leaving its imprint on the future in ways that we cannot now comprehend.

Using a "principled" interpretation of our traditions to resolve such a morass is superficially reassuring but provides no real escape from the cultural deficiencies that we fear. To abstract from our legal history a principle that our society respects "parenthood" is to appeal to the past in order to escape from it. It is to tell us that we have always been a certain way, not because we have been, but in order to make us that way. This is another self-deception in a culture already afraid that it is too dependent on euphemism and evasion.

Invoking principle, perhaps, allows us to feel that Justice Brennan's interpretation is at least cerebral; it will help protect us, one might think, from our capacity for self-indulgence and privatization. But used this way, intellect only establishes another individual right. It would enable Michael H. to assert his own interests against the security of a "family" as defined by many states over many years in an effort to serve the public good. The discipline of intellect, utilized this way, authorizes and dignifies self-interested behavior and separates all of us further from the aspiration of civic responsibility.

Law, especially constitutional law, is supposed to protect us from opportunism. It requires us to decide according an enduring standard, rather than according to some immediate calculation of benefit. But Michael H.'s claim of a constitutional right is itself an example of simplistic moralism—indeed, an embodiment of Senator Biden's childlike infatuation with "privacy" and of Senator Metzenbaum's impatience for results. Such constitutional claims push "progress" faster than what has resulted from the lawful procedures of a federal, democratic system. In the name of what seems morally right and urgent at the time, these kinds of claims short-circuit legitimate decisionmaking processes.

An anxious society will turn to its judges, trying at once to escape and silence itself. This resort to the courts, however, only reenacts our weaknesses. Constitutional interpretation, as it is now practiced, is an exercise in misdirection, individual self-assertion, and impatience. The peculiar institution called judicial review, although laced with pretensions about legal values, has become a collective expression of those deficiencies of character that cause us to doubt that our culture has the capacity to sustain the rule of law.

American society has historically been extraordinarily self-confident and free, but underneath the strong sounds of energy and optimism has always been a background hum, a disturbing sense of distrust in ourselves and a fear of disintegration. One recurring manifestation of this self-doubt has been our dependence on courts. It should be a source of serious concern that in recent decades this dependence has become more pervasive and more entrenched. In the years ahead, those who are uneasy about the possibility of cultural decline, including enforced orthodoxy, can gauge the danger in part by carefully watching how we use judicial power. They should especially fear the great decision, the "landmark" case. The more we demand this protection, the stronger is our need for all the less noticed deceptions and excesses and suppressions that make up so much of modern constitutional politics. Those who hope for renewal should look for it where it has to begin, in our democratic institutions and in ourselves.

Notes

Chapter 1

1. Robert A. Dahl, "Decision-Making in a Democracy: The Supreme Court as a National Policy-Maker," 6 *J. Pub. L.* 279 (1957). Later work suggests that in some respects Dahl underestimated the Court's power, but his essential insight remains persuasive. *See, e.g.*, Jonathan D. Casper, "The Supreme Court and National Policy Making," 70 *Am. Pol. L. Rev.* 50 (1976).

2. On abortion, see Kristin Luker, *Abortion and the Politics of Motherhood* (University of California Press, 1984). More generally, see Gerald N. Rosenberg, *The Hollow Hope: Can Courts Bring About Social Change?* (University of Chicago Press, 1991).

Chapter 2

1. One indication that anxiety about moral decline is widespread is the general popularity of books such as *How Should We Then Live?* (Fleming H. Revell, 1976) by Francis A. Schaeffer and *The Closing of the American Mind* (Simon & Schuster, 1987) by Allan Bloom. Among academics it is evidenced by the intense interest in, for example, *After Virtue: A Study in Moral Theory* (University of Notre Dame Press, 1981) by Alasdair MacIntyre. See generally Richard John Neuhaus, *The Naked Public Square: Religion and Democracy in America* 75, 140 (2d ed., Eerdmans, 1986). At least one legal scholar has made the distressing connection between the Thomas hearings and general cultural deficiency. John Hart Ely, "On Giving Lies for Professional Reasons," 9 *Const. Comm.* 1 (1992).

2. For a thoughtful discussion about the possibilities that affirmative action benefits establishment institutions and that it does not much assist the underclass, see Stephen L. Carter, *Reflections of an Affirmative Action Baby* 20, 71, 80 (Basic Books, 1991). *See also* Shelby Steele, *The Content of Our Character* 6, 77–87, 118 (Harper Perennial, 1991).

3. *Id.* at 47–69, 86.

4. 438 U.S. 265 (1978).

5. *See, e.g.*, Carter, *supra* note 2 at 73–75; Steele, *supra* note 2 at 14, 28–29, 33, 102, 137.

6. Of course, there were subtle interconnections between the racial and sexual aspects of the hearings. *See, e.g.*, "The Ongoing Struggle over Clarence Thomas," 1 *Reconstruction* 58 (1992).

7. The classic formulation is Cohen v. California, 403 U.S. 15 (1971). Recent and important extensions of this point of view can be found in Hustler Magazine v. Falwell, 485 U.S. 46 (1988), and Texas v. Johnson, 491 U.S. 397 (1989).

8. Meritor Sav. Bank v. Vinson, 477 U.S. 57 (1986). The Court has since expanded the right. See Harris v. Forklift Systems, Inc., 114 S. Ct. 367 (1993).

9. Craig v. Boren, 429 U.S. 190 (1976).

10. 410 U.S. 113, 153 (1973).

11. Kristin Luker, *Abortion and the Politics of Motherhood* (University of California Press, 1984).

12. Michael M. v. Superior Court of Sonoma County, 450 U.S. 464 (1981).

13. *Nomination of Clarence Thomas to Be Associate Justice of the Supreme Court of the United States: Hearings before the Senate Comm. on the Judiciary*, 102d Congress part 4, at 40 (1991) [statement of Anita Hill].

14. *Id.* at 288 [testimony of Susan Hoerchner].

15. Bates v. State Bar of Arizona, 433 U.S. 350 (1977).

16. Elrod v. Burns, 427 U.S. 347 (1976). *See also* Branti v. Finkel, 445 U.S. 507 (1977); Rutan v. Republican Party of Illinois, 497 U.S. 62 (1990).

17. United States v. Nixon, 418 U.S. 683 (1974). *See* Gerald Gunther, "Judicial Hegemony and Legislative Autonomy: The *Nixon* Case and the Impeachment Process," 22 *UCLA L. Rev.* 30 (1974).

18. Morrison v. Olson, 487 U.S. 654 (1988). As of this writing, the act is now expired and its future is uncertain.

19. Thomas Hearings, *supra* note 13, at 302.

Chapter 3

1. Robert H. Bork, *The Tempting of America: The Political Seduction of the Law* (Free Press, 1990).

2. *Nomination of Robert H. Bork to Be Associate Justice of the Supreme Court of the United States, Hearings before the Comm. on the Judiciary*, 100th Cong., 1st Sess. 114–16 (1987) (hereinafter cited as *Bork Hearings*).

3. *Id.* at 259, 262, 578, 683.

4. *Id.* at 682.

5. *Bork Hearings, supra* note 2, at 1278–81.

6. Ronald Dworkin, "The Bork Nomination," *New York Review of Books*, Aug. 13, 1987, at 3.

7. Ronald Dworkin, "Reagan's Justice," *New York Review of Books*, Nov. 8, 1984, at 27, 31.

8. Kenneth B. Noble, "Bork Panel Ends Hearings," *N.Y. Times*, Oct. 1, 1987, at B9; *Bork Hearings, supra* note 2, at 1899.

9. In response to Justice Douglas's comment that *Reynolds v. Sims* "is founded not on what we think government policy should be, but on what the Equal Protection Clause requires," Bork writes, "Douglas must have enjoyed that line." Robert H. Bork, *The Tempting of America: The Political Seduction of the Law* 90 (Free Press, 1990). He adds: "The practice of stating emphatically that the Court was not doing precisely what the Court was doing was common in the years of the Warren Court" (p. 91). More generally, he claims that law schools "regularly" teach a view of the judicial process that is "profoundly cynical" (p. 71). He repeatedly asserts that jurists and scholars use constitutional doctrine as fabrications to cover their political objectives and thus to thwart the will of the people (pp. 6, 7, 10, 135, 136, 199, 200, 215, 245, 262). He includes scholars in his charge that opponents of his confirmation knowingly misrepresented facts about him (pp. 312, 323, 336, 337).

10. In 1981, Bork testified that *Roe v. Wade* was "an unconstitutional decision, a serious and wholly unjustified usurpation. . . ." He added, "I also think that *Roe v. Wade* is by no means the only example of such unconstitutional behavior by the Supreme Court." He said the Human Life Bill (which would have deemed human life to exist from conception for purposes of the due process clause) would alter "the constitutional function of the courts as we have known it since *Marbury v. Madison*" but described this change as "no more drastic than that which the judiciary has accomplished over the past 25 years." *Hearings on S. 158 before the Subcomm. on Separation of Powers of the Comm. on the Judiciary*, 97th Cong., 1st Sess. 310–11 (1981).

11. For example, in voicing his opposition to the Human Life Bill (which is described in note 10, *supra*), Tribe referred to a letter of opposition signed by eighteen distinguished scholars and public servants and asked why the bill "should have called forth such an unprecedented unison of voices." He then suggested that the "most likely reason . . . is that virtually all careful students of the Constitution—those who write and teach about it, as well as those sworn to enforce it" agreed with his position. *Human Life Hearings* at 255–56 (cited in note 10).

The Human Life Bill involved difficult interpretive issues arising out of both *Roe v. Wade* and the various cases defining Congress's power to enforce section 5 of the fourteenth amendment. Nevertheless, Tribe claimed that no "*truly reasonable basis*" existed to support the constitutionality of the bill—that "invalidity . . . is *the only plausible verdict* to which a considered analysis can lead. . . ." *Human Life Hearings* at 256 (cited in note 10) (emphases in original). Well, perhaps the Human Life Bill did present unusually clear issues? Here is Professor Tribe on the Religious Speech Protection Act: "H.R. 4996 is a clearly, and I underline the word 'clearly' constitutional exercise of Congress power." (He acknowledged a bit later that "it is true" that the U.S. Supreme Court had not yet spoken directly on the issue.) *Religious Speech Protection Act: Hearing before a Subcomm. on Elementary, Secondary, and Vocational Education of the House Comm. on Education and Labor*, 98th Cong., 2d Sess. 46–47 (1984). Similarly, Tribe co-authored a letter to Senator Edward Kennedy on the constitutionality of the "line-item veto." The letter concludes that "any attempt to exercise such a 'line-item veto' would clearly be unconstitutional." 135 *Cong. Rec.* S14387 (daily ed. Oct. 31, 1989). A thoughtful explanation of the actual complexities of this issue can be found in J. Gregory Sidak and Thomas A. Smith, "Four Faces of the Item Veto: A Reply to Tribe and Kurland," 84 *Nw. U. L. Rev.* 437 (1990). Tribe was also overly certain in his evaluation of state limitations on federal congressional terms. *See* Roderick M. Hills, Jr., "A Defense of State Constitutional Limits on Federal Congressional Terms," 53 *U. Pitt. L. Rev.* 97, 99 (1991).

12. Dworkin, *supra* note 6, at 10.

13. John Hart Ely, "On Discovering Fundamental Values," 92 *Harv. L. Rev.* 5 (1978).

14. Michael J. Perry, *The Constitution, the Courts, and Human Rights* 11, 24, 91 (Yale University Press, 1982).

15. Mark Tushnet, *Red, White, and Blue: A Critical Analysis of Constitutional Law* (Harvard University Press, 1988).

16. In fact, a basic theme was (with somewhat different emphasis) the same as Bork's—that the Burger Court imposed middle-class values. *E.g.*, Mark Tushnet, ". . . And Only Wealth Will Buy You Justice—Some Notes on the Supreme Court 1972 Term," 1974 *Wis. L. Rev.* 177, 180 (justices' real agenda was to promote interests of "their wives and friends"). To take an extreme example, Professor Catharine MacKinnon's attacks on privacy and free speech cases, in the opinion of one reviewer, are "pathological" and "obsessively enraged." *See* Michael Levin, "Book Review," 5 *Const. Comm.* 201, 207–14 (1988). The Rehnquist Court, according to a perfectly sane mainstream writer, is causing the Constitution to "vanish." Erwin Chemerinsky, "The Vanishing Constitution," 103 *Harv. L. Rev.* 44 (1989).

17. Quoted by Bork at p. 202.

18. The quoted phrase comes from Alexander M. Bickel, *The Supreme Court and the Idea of Progress* 181 (Harper & Row, 1970). The other references are to Michael J. Perry, *The Constitution, the Courts, and Human Rights* (Yale University Press, 1982) (prophets); Ronald Dworkin, *Law's Empire* (Harvard University Press, 1986) (Hercules); John Hart Ely, *Democracy and Distrust: A Theory of Judicial Review* (Harvard University Press, 1980) (democracy); Robert A. Burt, "Constitutional Law and the Teaching of the Parables," 93 *Yale L.J.* 455 (1984) (parables).

19. Richard A. Wasserstrom, "Racism and Sexism," *in* John H. Garvey and T. Alexander Aleinikoff, *Modern Constitutional Theory: A Reader* 360 (West, 1989).

20. On *Brown*, see *The Tempting of America* at p. 82; on sexual distinctions, p. 150; on reapportionment, p. 86; on commerce, p. 306.

21. Bork's praise of these rulings emphasizes, as does most scholarly commentary, the brilliance of Marshall's arguments from text and structure (pp. 21–

28). But he does not comment on Marshall's failure to review evidence on the framers' intentions regarding either the power of judicial review or congressional power to incorporate banks. On Bork's interpretive methods, see pp. 5, 150, 163, 167–69, 189, 254.

22. He refers to the "actual Constitution" (pp. 130, 270) and to meaning that "does not come out of the Constitution but is forced into it" (p. 114).

23. Douglas Laycock has shown that serious interpretation of this general description is quite capable of generating virtually all modern constitutional doctrines, including the right to abortion and the various levels of equal protection review. Book Review, "Taking Constitutions Seriously: A Theory of Judicial Review," 59 *Tex. L. Rev.* 343 (1981). Mark Tushnet argues that it could generate his own socialist agenda. "Does Constitutional Theory Matter? A Comment," 65 *Tex. L. Rev.* 777 (1987).

The definiteness of Tribe's assertions about the content of the law apparently arise from this same sense of intellectual seriousness, for he agrees with Bork that a judge should "interpret the law and not make it." *Bork Hearings*, *supra* note 2, at 1274. For a few of Professor Tribe's rather certain views on what the Constitution really means, see note 11, *supra*. Similarly, for all his sophistication about the idea of intent, Dworkin can write unequivocally about "the responsibility the framers imposed on [judges] to develop legal principles of moral breadth. . . ." *The Bork Nomination*, cited in note 6, *supra*. On the issue presented by *Brown v. Board of Education*, Dworkin writes, "The plaintiff school-children are being cheated of what their Constitution, properly interpreted, defines as independent and equal standing in the republic." *Law's Empire* 389 (Harvard University Press, 1986). Indeed, he generally defends definite assertions about what the law "is" against the charge that the speaker is pretending to have discovered more than what the law "should be." *Law's Empire* at 261–62. His reply is:

> . . . the grounds of law lie in integrity, in the best constructive interpretation of past legal decisions, and that law is therefore sensitive to justice. . . . So there is no way Hercules *can* report his conclusion . . . except the way that the law, as he understands it, is [as Hercules asserts it to be].

Id. at 262 (emphasis in original). As it is with Hercules, so it is with Dworkin, Tribe, and Bork.

24. Ronald Dworkin, "Bork's Jurisprudence," 57 *U. Chi. L. Rev.* 657, 658 (1990); and Dworkin, note 6, *supra*. In an early and famous essay against the idea of judicial restraint, Dworkin began by associating that position with Richard Nixon. *Taking Rights Seriously* 131 (Harvard University Press, 1977). He then adopted the McCarthyesque device of using "Nixon" to refer, "not to Nixon, but to any politicians holding the set of attitudes about the Supreme Court that he made explicit." *Id.* at 132. He explains, "There was, fortunately, only one real Nixon, but there are, in the special sense which I use the name, many Nixons." *Id.* Yes, and some were named Thomas Jefferson, Abraham Lincoln, and Franklin D. Roosevelt.

25. *Bork Hearings, supra* note 2, at 1272 (Tribe). Dworkin thought that, unlike Bork, Kennedy had adopted a tenet central to having a legal philosophy. Kennedy would demand not only "some demonstrated historical link . . . [to] the announced declarations and language of the framers" but also would look to "our ethical culture, our shared beliefs, our common vision." Ronald Dworkin, "From Bork to Kennedy," 34 *New York Review of Books*, Dec. 17, 1987, at 36. A few details of Kennedy's philosophy, however, still remained to be worked out at the time of his confirmation. He disclaimed having any "unitary theory of interpretation" and confessed to be "searching . . . for the correct balance." *Nomination of Anthony M. Kennedy to Be an Associate Justice of the United States Supreme Court before the Senate Comm. on the Judiciary*, 6 (Feb. 1, 1988). He did feel sure, nevertheless, that "[t]he Constitution *cannot be divorced* from its logic, and its language, the intention of its Framers, the precedents of the law, and the shared traditions and historic values of our people." *Id.* at 10 (emphasis added). Depending on how a judge assesses our shared traditions regarding judicial power, of course, it is quite possible that this philosophy might turn out to be much like Bork's. A hint in this direction is provided by Kennedy's assurance that

> . . . [T]his doesn't mean the Constitution changes. It just means that we
> have a better perspective of it. . . . It just means that our understanding
> of it changes.

Id. at 8. Compare Bork in *The Tempting of America* at 168. ("The world changes in which unchanging values find their application.")

26. *Bork Hearings, supra* note 2, at 2548.

27. *The Tempting of America* at 148–49.

28. *Id.* at 163.

29. *See* Bruce Ackerman, "Transformative Appointments," 101 *Harv. L. Rev.* 1106, 1178–79 (1988); Ronald Dworkin, "From Bork to Kennedy," 34 *New York Review of Books*, Dec. 17, 1987, at 36, 38–40; Laurence H. Tribe, *God Save This Honorable Court* 131 (Random House, 1985).

30. Senator Specter defended *Bolling v. Sharpe* on the basis of the justices' "feelings" about the "needs of the nation." *Bork Hearings, supra* note 2, at 262. Senator Biden argued that the right to privacy arises because humans "exist." *Id.* at 296. Regarding homosexuality, see *id.* at 88 (Senator Biden asking whether any legislative body can regulate sexual behavior of "a married couple, or anyone else"). *See also id.* at 124–25 (Bork linking right to privacy with protection of homosexual conduct and use of cocaine and asking Senator Kennedy, "Privacy to do what, Senator?"). As to obscenity, see *id.* at 256 (Senator Specter apparently criticizing Bork for having written that the first amendment does not reach pornography or obscenity). As to subversion, see *id.* at 412 (Senator Specter defending Holmes's statement that if proletarian dictatorship is "destined to be accepted by the dominant forces of the community . . . they should be given their chance and have their way.").

31. *The Tempting of America*, at 353.

32. Bork criticizes political demonstrations directed at the Court (pp. 3–4, 116) and the influence of public opinion generally (p. 313), and political confirmation hearings (pp. 313–14, 346) and congressional efforts to change judicial interpretations of the fourteenth amendment (p. 325). He writes that judges should "apply law and not emotion" (p. 62); he criticizes Justice Douglas's lyricism in *Griswold* as "incoherent" (p. 97); he calls "ordered liberty" "a splendid phrase but not a major premise" (p. 118); he condemns the idea that a liberty might be "deeply rooted in this Nation's history and tradition" as "pretty vaporous stuff" (p. 118); and Bork's retort to claims about Justice Blackmun's "passion" and "eloquence" is to note that these are "poor substitutes for judicial reasoning" (p. 120).

Chapter 4

1. Robert H. Bork, *The Tempting of America: The Political Seduction of the Law* 3 (Free Press, 1990).

2. *See, e.g.*, Marbury v. Madison, 5 U.S. (1 Cranch) 137 (1803) (fidelity to text); Herbert Wechsler, "Toward Neutral Principles of Constitutional Law," 73 *Harv. L. Rev.* 1 (1959) (neutrality); John Hart Ely, *Democracy and Distrust: A Theory of Judicial Review* (Harvard University Press, 1980) (participation); Alexander Bickel, *The Least Dangerous Branch: The Supreme Court at the Bar of Politics* (Bobbs-Merrill, 1962); and Michael Perry, *Morality, Politics, and Law* (Oxford University Press, 1988) (moral precepts).

3. It is not entirely clear what Blackmun was including as "emotion and predilection" in contrast to "constitutional measurement." His two preceding paragraphs seem to suggest that they include virtually all sources of personal beliefs about morality and policy:

> We forthwith acknowledge our awareness of the sensitive and emotional nature of the abortion controversy, of the vigorous opposing views, even among physicians, and of the deep and seemingly absolute convictions that the subject inspires. One's philosophy, one's experiences, one's exposure to the raw edges of human existence, one's religious training, one's attitudes toward life and family and their values, and the moral standards one establishes and seeks to observe, are all likely to influence and to color one's thinking and conclusions about abortion.
>
> In addition, population growth, pollution, poverty, and racial overtones tend to complicate and not to simplify the problem.

410 U.S. 113, 116 (1973).

4. Thornburgh v. American College of Obstetricians and Gynecologists, 476 U.S. 747, 771 (1986).

5. 492 U.S. 490, 535 (1989) (Scalia, J., concurring).

6. *Id.* at 537, *et seq.* (Blackmun, J., concurring and dissenting).

7. The plurality does say, "[W]e do not see why the State's interest in pro-

tecting potential human life should come into existence only at the point of viability." 492 U.S. at 519. It is, however, logically possible to deny the significance of viability and still oppose abortion limitations, including limitations in the third trimester. On the issue whether limitations should be permitted earlier than viability, the plurality says only that the mandated viability test "permissibly furthers the State's interest in protecting potential human life." 492 U.S. at 519–20. The plurality admits that the requirement increases the costs of abortions and affects the physicians' determination of viability, but notes that the tests are "reasonably designed to ensure that abortions are not performed where the fetus is viable–an end which all concede is legitimate. . . ." *Id.* at 520.

8. The plurality denies that legislative bodies "in a Nation where more than half of our population are women, will treat our decision today as an invitation to enact abortion regulation reminiscent of the dark ages. . . ." 492 U.S. at 521.

9. 491 U.S. 397, 421 (1989) (Rehnquist, C.J., dissenting).

10. *See* Rehnquist, "The Notion of a Living Constitution," 54 *Tex. L. Rev.* 693 (1976).

11. 496 U.S. 310, 318 (1990).

12. 112 S. Ct. 2791, 2815 (1992).

13. 112 S. Ct. at 2854–55.

14. When the Court repudiated *Usery*, it relied in part on the academic writings that had been critical of that decision. Garcia v. Metropolitan Transit Authority, 469 U.S. 528, 551 n.11 (1985).

15. 410 U.S. at 116–17.

16. 410 U.S. at 152 ("The Constitution does not explicitly mention any right of privacy.").

17. Even Justice Rehnquist, dissenting in *Roe*, expressed admiration for the sweep of Blackmun's opinion and countered with his own interpretation of our traditions. 410 U.S. at 171, 174–77. In a more recent case, Justice Scalia presented the most restrictive current view of constitutional authority, and his position is that political and moral traditions are relevant and appropriate to defining the right to privacy if they are conceptualized at their narrowest level of abstraction. Only Justice Rehnquist joined in this proposed limitation. Michael H. v. Gerald D., 491 U.S. at 127 n.6. *See* pp. 66–70, ch. 5.

18. At the end of the State of Missouri's oral argument in *Cruzan v. Director, Missouri Department of Health*, Justice Blackmun initiated the following exchange:

QUESTION: Mr. Presson, before you sit down, I'd like to ask a–an impertinent and perhaps an improper question. Have you ever seen a patient in a persistent vegetative state?

ANSWER: I have seen Nancy Cruzan herself.

QUESTION: You have seen Nancy?

ANSWER: Yes.

QUESTION: Any others?

ANSWER: Yes.

QUESTION: How come?

ANSWER: I was at the hospital, at Mount Vernon Rehabilitation Center.

Official Transcript, *Cruzan v. Director, Missouri Department of Health* at 44 (Dec. 6, 1989).

19. *See, e.g.*, Cass Sunstein, "Interest Groups in American Public Law," 38 *Stan. L. Rev.* 29 (1985). Ronald Dworkin has praised the Bork hearings as being "often of extremely high quality . . . and . . . sometimes . . . of academic depth and rigor . . . an extended seminar on the Constitution. . . ." "From Bork to Kennedy," 34 *New York Review of Books*, Dec. 17, 1987, at 36.

20. Bruce Ackerman, "Constitutional Politics/Constitutional Law," 99 *Yale L.J.* 453, 511–15 (1989).

21. 61 *Tulane L. Rev.* 979 (1987).

22. *See* Daniel A. Farber, "The Supreme Court and the Rule of Law: *Cooper v. Aaron* Revisited," 1982 *U. Ill. L. Rev.* 387; Sanford Levinson, "Could Meese Be Right This Time?" 61 *Tulane L. Rev.* 1071 (1987).

23. These reactions are cited and discussed in Robert F. Nagel, "A Comment on Democratic Constitutionalism," 61 *Tulane L. Rev.* 1027 (1987). *See also* Levinson, note 22, *supra*.

24. *See* R. George Wright, "Could a Constitutional Amendment Be Unconstitutional?" 22 *Loyola U. Chi. L.J.* 741 (1991). *Cf.* Geoffrey R. Stone, "Flag Burning and the Constitution," 75 *Iowa L. Rev.* 111, 124 (1989).

25. *E.g.*, Bruce Fein, "A Circumscribed Senate Confirmation Role," 102 *Harv. L. Rev.* 672 (1989).

26. As Bickel observed,

When the law summons force to its aid, it demonstrates, not its strength and stability, but its weakness and impermanence. The mob, like revolution, is an ambiguous fact. The mob is bad when it is wrong; it may be heroic when it is right. It is surely a deeply ingrained American belief that mobs of our people do not generally gather to oppose good laws, and the very fact of a mob, therefore, puts the law in question.

Alexander M. Bickel, *The Least Dangerous Branch: The Supreme Court at the Bar of Politics* 266 (Bobbs-Merrill, 1962).

27. *E.g.*, William J. Brennan, Jr., "Why Have a Bill of Rights?" 9 *Ox. J. Leg. Stud.* 425, 434–35 (1989).

28. This limitation is criticized in Grover Rees III, "Questions for Supreme Court Nominees at Confirmation Hearings: Excluding the Constitution," 17 *Ga. L. Rev.* 913, 932 (1983).

29. *Compare Nomination of Robert H. Bork to Be Associate Justice of the Supreme Court of the United States: Hearings before the Comm. on the Judiciary* 105, 100th Cong., 1st Sess. (1987) (Bork asserting that he would not commit himself "as to how [he] might vote on any particular case), with *id.* at 114, 279, 288, 327, 428, 829 (Bork committing himself).

Chapter 5

1. Planned Parenthood v. Casey, 112 S. Ct. 2791, 2815–16 (1992).

2. For a description of the "ongoing guerilla war against *Roe,*" see Albert M. Pearson & Paul M. Kurtz, "The Abortion Controversy: A Study in Law and Politics," 8 *Harv. J.L. & Pub. Pol'y* 427 (1985).

3. *See, e.g., Planned Parenthood v. Casey, supra* note 1 (trimester system abandoned as not being part of the "core" of *Roe*'s holding); Webster v. Reproductive Health Services, 492 U.S. 490 (1989) (trimester system applied flexibly); Dayton Board of Education v. Brinkman (*Dayton I*), 433 U.S. 406 (1977) ("root and branch" desegregation remedy modified by significant requirement of causality); Milliken v. Bradley (*Milliken I*), 418 U.S. 717 (1974) ("root and branch" remedy modified by need to preserve school district boundaries).

4. As I explained in Chapter 4, this possibility was one of the assumptions behind then Attorney General Edwin Meese's notorious argument for political correction of decisions that do not conform to the Constitution. "The Law of the Constitution," 61 *Tulane L. Rev.* 979 (1987). Although it is axiomatic among lawyers that judges are especially competent to examine historical materials and to parse text, this confidence may be more a function of professional bias than of the Court's actual record.

5. *See* Robert F. Nagel, "Political Law, Legalistic Politics: A Recent History of the Political Question Doctrine," 56 *U. Chi. L. Rev.* 643, 661–62 (1989).

6. *See, e.g.,* Thornburgh v. American College of Obstetricians and Gynecologists, 476 U.S. 747, 771 (1986); Powell v. McCormack, 395 U.S. 486, 549, 552 n.4 (1969); and Cooper v. Aaron, 358 U.S. 1, 19 (1958).

7. Occasionally, academic writers suggest that state actions should have some authoritative force, *e.g.,* Terrance Sandalow, "Judicial Protection of Minorities," 75 *Mich. L. Rev.* 1162, 1186–87 (1977). But most proposals single out congressional action as the appropriate way to revise the Court's decisions. Daniel O. Conkle, "Nonoriginalist Constitutional Rights and the Problem of Judicial Finality," 13 *Hast. Const. L.Q.* 9, 37 (1985); Henry P. Monaghan, "The Supreme Court, 1974 Term—Forward: Constitutional Common Law," 89 *Harv. L. Rev.* 1 (1975); John Agresto, *The Supreme Court and Constitutional Democracy* 135 (Cornell University Press, 1984); Paul R. Dimond, *The Supreme Court and Judicial Choice: The Role of Provisional Review in a Democracy* 13–20 (University of Michigan Press, 1989).

8. *See, e.g.,* Thornburg v. Gingles, 478 U.S. 30 (1986); Fullilove v. Klutznick, 448 U.S. 448 (1980); City of Rome v. United States, 446 U.S. 156 (1980).

9. An extravagant version of this argument can be found in *Planned Parenthood v. Casey, supra* note 1. There the Court asserted:

[The American people's] belief in themselves . . . as such a people [who aspire to live by the rule of law] is not readily separable from their understanding of the Court invested with the authority to . . . speak before all others for their constitutional ideals. If the Court's legitimacy should be undermined, then, so would the country be in its very ability to see itself through its constitutional ideals.

Id. at 2816. Here and in related passages the connections between closure, principle, and the appearance of imperviousness are made explicit. The Court's rather romantic claims, however, purport to be specific to *Brown* and *Roe*, where the Court supposedly called upon "the contending sides of a national controversy to end their national division. . . ." *Id.* at 2815. This limitation is, I think, unconvincing and perhaps disingenuous. The fact is that neither the Burger nor the Rehnquist Court has explicitly overruled *any* major rights decision (although, as in *Casey,* many have been whittled away). This record suggests strongly that what is at stake is generalized unwillingness to invite disagreement by appearing to have rewarded recalcitrance. In any event, it does not seem likely that the social importance of the Court's role as expositor of law is implicated in an altogether different (and lesser) way in such cases as *Miranda v. Arizona, New York Times v. Sullivan,* and *Texas v. Johnson,* than in *Roe* and *Brown.*

10. An early and influential argument for shared interpretive authority emphasized that legislative determinations precede judicial ones. James B. Thayer, "The Origin and Scope of the American Doctrine of Constitutional Law," 7 *Harv. L. Rev.* 129, 135–36 (1893).

11. *See* Dames & Moore v. Regan, 453 U.S. 654, 678–82 (1981); Youngstown Sheet & Tube Co. v. Sawyer, 343 U.S. 579, 637 (1952) (Jackson, J., concurring).

12. For an account of congressional resistance to *I.N.S. v. Chadha,* see Louis Fisher, "Separation of Powers: Interpretation outside the Courts," 18 *Pepp. L. Rev.* 57 (1990).

13. *Nomination of Robert H. Bork to Be Associate Justice of the Supreme Court of the United States: Hearings before the Senate Comm. on the Judiciary,* 100th Cong., 1st Sess. 1336 (1987) (letter to Chairman Biden and Senator Thurmond from one hundred law professors opposing Judge Bork's confirmation as Associate Justice of the Supreme Court, Sept. 22, 1987).

14. *Bork Hearings, supra* note 13, at 1278 (statement of Laurence H. Tribe).

15. Justice Blackmun (who in *Roe* examined state laws, the positions of professional organizations, and various religious and philosophical writings) has vigorously protested judicial responsiveness to political influence. *E.g.,* Thornburgh v. American College of Obstetricians & Gynecologists, 476 U.S. 747, 759, 771 (1986). Other justices, who think that political traditions are relevant, have also objected to political pressure. *E.g.,* William J. Brennan, Jr., "Why Have a Bill of Rights?" 9 *Ox. J. Leg. Stud.* 425 (1989); Antonin Scalia, "The Rule of Law as a Law of Rules," 56 *U. Chi. L. Rev.* 1175, 1179–80 (1989); William H. Rehnquist, "The Notion of a Living Constitution," 54 *Tex. L. Rev.* 693 (1976).

16. *See, e.g.,* Michael H. v. Gerald D., 491 U.S. 110, 124–25 (1989); Bowers v. Hardwick, 478 U.S. 186, 192–94 (1986); Roe v. Wade, 410 U.S. 113, 138–41 (1973).

17. Griswold v. Connecticut, 381 U.S. 479, 493–94 (Goldberg, J., concurring) (1965); Meyer v. Nebraska, 262 U.S. 390, 400–01 (1923).

18. A theme developed in Robert F. Nagel, *Constitutional Cultures: The Mentality and Consequences of Judicial Review* (University of California Press, 1989).

19. Griswold v. Connecticut, 381 U.S. 479, 493 (Goldberg, J., concurring)

(1965) ("[J]udges are not left at large to decide cases in light of their personal and private notions.").

20. For a wide-ranging description of the traditional worldview that underlies opposition to *Roe v. Wade*, see Kristin Luker, *Abortion and the Politics of Motherhood* (University of California Press, 1984).

21. *See, e.g.,* Michael H. v. Gerald D., 491 U.S. 110, 125–28 (Scalia); Roe v. Wade, 410 U.S. 113, 138–41 (Blackmun).

22. *See, e.g.,* Webster v. Reproductive Health Services, 490 U.S. 490, 538, 556–58, 560 (1988) (Blackmun, J., dissenting) and Thornburgh v. American College of Obstetricians and Gynecologists, 476 U.S. 747, 759, 771 (1986).

23. Griswold v. Connecticut, 381 U.S. 479, 486 (1965).

24. *U.S. Const.* art. I, § 4, cl. 1.

25. *U.S. Const.* art. II, § 1, cl. 2.

26. *U.S. Const.* art. IV, § 1.

27. *U.S. Const.* amend. X.

28. *See* Akhil Reed Amar, "Of Sovereignty and Federalism," 96 *Yale L.J.* 1425, 1500 (1987).

29. *U.S. Const.* amend. IX.

30. It is a more complicated question than is usually admitted how much *Brown* itself contributed to desegregation. *See* Gerald N. Rosenberg, *The Hollow Hope: Can Courts Bring About Social Change?* (University of Chicago Press, 1991). The mythology, especially within the legal profession, however, is that courageous judges gradually faced down the opposition.

31. This case apparently had a major positive impact on the Court's public image. Walter F. Murphy & Joseph Tanenhaus, "Publicity, Public Opinion, and the Court," 84 *Nw. U. L. Rev.* 985, 1006–07 (1990).

32. I developed this theme in *Constitutional Cultures, supra* note 18, at 1–4, 23, 153–55 (1989).

33. For two examples, see Bernard Schwartz, *Super Chief–Earl Warren and His Supreme Court: A Judicial Biography* (N.Y.U. Press, 1983), and Tinsley E. Yarbrough, *Judge Frank Johnson and Human Rights in Alabama* (University of Alabama Press, 1981). For one egregious effort to characterize questionable tactics as "judicial statesmanship," see Owen M. Fiss, "Dombrowski," 86 *Yale L.J.* 1103 (1977). In this regard, it is worth noting the dedication page of what is probably the most admired recent book on constitutional law:

For Earl Warren
You don't need many heroes if you choose carefully.

John Hart Ely, *Democracy and Distrust: A Theory of Judicial Review* (Harvard University Press, 1980).

34. 472 U.S. 38, 61 (1985).

35. *Id.* at 59–60.

36. The Court said:

We decline the Government's invitation to reassess this conclusion [that the public interest in "national unity" was sufficiently important to satisfy "the most exacting scrutiny"] in light of Congress' recent recognition of a purported "national consensus" favoring a prohibition on flag-burning. Even assuming such a consensus exists, any suggestion that the Government's interest . . . becomes more weighty as popular opposition to that speech grows is foreign to the First Amendment.

U.S. v. Eichman, 496 U.S. 310, 318 (1990) [citations deleted].

37. 476 U.S. 747, 759–64 (1986).

38. 443 U.S. 449, 463 (1979).

39. *Thornburgh* is over-ruled, at least for the moment. *See* Planned Parenthood v. Casey, 112 S. Ct. 2791, 2822–23 (1992).

40. 443 U.S. at 461–63.

41. *See* David A. Strauss, "The Ubiquity of Prophylactic Rules," 55 *U. Chi. L. Rev.* 190, 203 (1988) (arguing that a common feature of constitutional interpretation is to "take into account institutional limitations and propensities").

42. United States v. Calandra, 414 U.S. 338, 348 (1974) (exclusionary rule); Miranda v. Arizona, 384 U.S. 436, 467 (1966).

43. *See* Thomas S. Schrock & Robert C. Welsh, "Reconsidering the Constitutional Common Law," 91 *Harv. L. Rev.* 1117, 1118–20 (1978).

44. Miranda v. Arizona, 384 U.S. 436, 448–57 (1966).

45. *See* Monaghan, *supra* note 7.

46. The modern trend toward greater instrumental control is described in my *Constitutional Cultures, supra* note 18, ch. 7.

47. *Cf.* Monaghan, *supra* note 7, at 23.

48. There have been, for example, "major court orders" on prisons and jails in forty states. Malcolm M. Feeley & Roger A. Hanson, "The Impact of Judicial Intervention on Prisons and Jails: A Framework for Analysis and a Review of the Literature," *in* John J. DiIulio, Jr., *Courts, Corrections, and the Constitution: The Impact of Judicial Intervention on Prisons & Jails* 13 (Oxford University Press, 1990).

49. *E.g.*, Ira P. Robbins & Michael B. Buser, "Punitive Conditions of Prison Confinement: An Analysis of *Pugh v. Locke* and Federal Court Supervision of State Penal Administration Under the Eighth Amendment," 29 *Stan. L. Rev.* 893, 917–19 (1977).

50. *Id.* (on prisoners). Missouri v. Jenkins, 495 U.S. 33, 77 (1990) (Kennedy, J., concurring in part) (on schools).

51. On the relationship between expansive injunctive relief and local disagreement, see Robert F. Nagel, "Controlling the Structural Injunction," 7 *Harv. J.L. & Pub. Pol'y*, 395, 400–01 (1984), and sources cited therein.

52. One interesting exception is Paul Gewirtz, who convincingly advances the position that, at least in school desegregation, less control can sometimes lead to more compliance. "Remedies and Resistance," 92 *Yale L.J.* 585 (1983).

53. For a defense of the use of the word *vanishing,* see Erwin Chemerinsky, "The Vanishing Constitution," 103 *Harv. L.J.* 44 (1989). In 1978, Schrock and Welsh were referring to the "annihilation of rights," *supra* note 43, at 1159.

54. Planned Parenthood v. Casey, 112 S. Ct. at 2816.

55. *See* Rosenberg, *supra* note 30, at 185–89; Luker, *supra* note 20, at 137–44.

56. *Constitutional Cultures, supra* note 18, ch. 2.

Chapter 6

1. For examples, see my *Constitutional Cultures: The Mentality and Consequences of Judicial Review* 121–22, 131–55 (University of California Press, 1989). An extraordinary recent example is R.A.V. v. City of St. Paul, 112 S. Ct. 2538 (1992), where Justice Scalia was able to apply the "strict scrutiny" standard to a law that abridged "fighting words," a category of speech that had long been regarded as unprotected altogether.

2. Consider, for example, the public's interest in the Bork confirmation hearings, described in Chapter 3.

3. A discussion of the Court's tendency to demand measurable public purposes is contained in *Constitutional Cultures, supra* note 1, at chs. 4, 5, 6.

4. 413 U.S. 49, 70 (1973).

5. For an important example that seems to have influenced Justice Brennan, see Henkin, "Morals and the Constitution: The Sin of Obscenity," 63 *Colum. L. Rev.* 391 (1963). Although Professor Henkin's article is careful, its dismissive tone is unmistakable. He says, for example, that obscenity is suppressed "for the purity of the community and for the salvation . . . of the 'consumer.'" *Id.* at 395. He states flatly, "Due process of law demands that legislation have a proper public purpose; only an apparent, rational, utilitarian social purpose satisfies due process. A state may not legislate merely to preserve some traditional or prevailing view of private morality." *Id.* at 402. Moreover, he distinguishes repeatedly between promoting "social welfare" and protecting "morals." *Id.* at 405. A less restrained example of the same intellectual impulse is the work of David A. J. Richards. He has this to say in response to Alexander Bickel's observation that "what is commonly read and seen and heard and done intrudes upon us all . . .":

> [This argument] must be rejected not only because it is intellectually indefensible, but also because its conclusions are morally outrageous. It would dilute the moral force of liberty into the empty and vapid idea that people be allowed to do that to which no one has any serious objection. It would elevate every form of popular prejudice, bigotry, and intolerance, *without more*, into a moral basis for law. Majority attitudes per se . . . are merely intractable prejudices . . . .

"Free Speech and Obscenity Law," 123 *U. Pa. L. Rev.* 45, at 86–87 (1974) (citations omitted, emphasis in original). *See also* material cited in Chapter 9, note 12.

6. For an effort to unpack the kinds of judgments that underlie slippery slope arguments as well as more general tendencies to distrust governmental institutions, see Schauer, "The Calculus of Distrust," 77 *Va. L. Rev.* 653 (1991), and "Slippery Slopes," 99 *Harv. L. Rev.* 361 (1985).

7. Two important illustrations are Thomas I. Emerson, *The System of Freedom of Expression* (Vintage, 1970), and Lee C. Bollinger, *The Tolerant Society: Freedom of Speech and Extremist Speech in America* (Oxford University Press, 1986).

8. As Professor Schauer observed, "In virtually every case in which a slippery slope argument is made, the opposing party could with equal formal and linguistic logic also make a slippery slope claim." Schauer, "Slippery Slopes," *supra* note 6.

9. Despite its disapproval of the *Roth* standard, the 1970 Commission on Obscenity was vague about the number of prosecutions and their effect. Its claims were not based on measurement but on logical inferences from the subjectiveness of the existing definition of obscenity. The commission observed, for example, that because of legal indefiniteness

> persons *may* either *be unfairly convicted*—because they honestly believed they were free to distribute material later held to be obscene—or they *may*, out of fear of prosecution . . . *forbear from distributing* materials which are, in fact, constitutionally protected. . . . In either event . . . in some communities constitutionally protected material *may* simply *not be available* because of the dangers. . . .

The Report of the Commission on Obscenity and Pornography 421 (Bantam Books, 1970) (emphasis added). The report also notes that vigorous enforcement in fact had been episodic and "rare." *Id.* at 387.

When *Miller* and *Paris Adult Theatre* were decided, the fear was, of course, that the newly announced standards would make prosecutions easier and therefore more frequent. But by 1986, when the Attorney General's Commission on Pornography published its report, it was generally recognized that the content of pornography had become more explicit and violent. *See, e.g.*, Downs, "The Attorney General's Commission and the New Politics of Pornography," 4 *Am. Bar Found. Res. J.* 641, 660 (1987). The report itself found that, although in some areas aggressive prosecutions had ended "the open availability of most extremely explicit materials, . . . more commonly prosecution remains minimal, and highly explicit materials are widely available" *Attorney General's Commission on Pornography, Final Report* 248 (1986). It claimed that in the period following 1974 there had been "strikingly few actual or threatened prosecutions of material that [was] plainly not legally obscene." *Id.* at 271. The report went on to say that

> We live in a society unquestionably pervaded by sexual explicitness. In virtually every medium . . . matters relating to sex are discussed, described, and depicted with a frankness and explicitness of detail that has accelerated dramatically within a comparatively short period of time.

Id. at 277. Some critics of the second commission fell back on predictions that future repression might take the form of decentralized and informal "vigilante" actions, rather than formal prosecutions authorized under the *Miller* standard. Downs, *supra* at 671. It is not necessary to accept the findings or judgments of the *Attorney General's Report* to recognize that the likelihood of suppression does not depend only on the degree to which it is formally permitted under the terms of constitutional doctrine.

10. For Justice Brennan (and often for the Court) privacy is implicated only if the audience is somehow "captive." He has rejected the sufficiency of "privacy" justifications in a wide range of settings, and presumably his reasoning would be applicable if the speech were obscene, too. *See, e.g.,* FCC v. Pacifica Foundation, 438 U.S. 726, 762, 765 (1978) (Brennan, J., dissenting) (profane humor broadcast on daytime radio); Erznoznik v. City of Jacksonville, 422 U.S. 205, 210–11 (1975) (nudity on films shown at outdoor movie theaters); Lehman v. City of Shaker Heights, 418 U.S. 298, 308, 319 (1974) (Brennan, J., dissenting) (political advertising inside public buses); Cohen v. California, 403 U.S. 15, 21 (1971) (words "fuck the draft" on a jacket worn inside the hallway of a courthouse).

11. 491 U.S. 397 (1989).

12. *Id.* at 416.

13. *Id.* at 418 (citations omitted):

> It is not the State's ends, but its means, to which we object. It cannot be gainsaid that there is a special place reserved for the flag in this Nation, and thus we do not doubt that the Government has a legitimate interest in making efforts to "preserv[e] the national flag as an unalloyed symbol of our country. . . . National unity as an end which officials may foster by persuasion and example is not in question. . . .

14. Bork, *The Tempting of America: The Political Seduction of the Law* 353 (Free Press, 1990).

15. A fairly recent example is the Court's refusal to apply or expand the principle of federalism announced in National League of Cities v. Usery, 426 U.S. 833 (1976). This record itself became a reason for the explicit repudiation of *Usery* in Garcia v. San Antonio Metropolitan Transit Authority, 469 U.S. 528, 531, 539, 557 (1985).

16. Whitney v. California, 274 U.S. 357, 372, 375–76 (1927) (Brandeis, J., concurring) (footnote deleted).

17. Vincent Blasi calls Brandeis's opinion "arguably the most important essay ever written, on or off the bench, on the meaning of the first amendment." "The First Amendment and the Ideal of Civic Courage: The Brandeis Opinion in *Whitney v. California,*" 29 *Wm. & Mary L. Rev.* 653 (1988).

18. The only reference is to two quotations from Thomas Jefferson. 274 U.S. 375, n. 2. Professor Blasi terms Brandeis's historicism "a familiar move" and a "hoary tactic." *See* Blasi, *supra* note 17, at 671. It is true, as he argues, that the passage can be read as philosophy thinly clothed as history, but I doubt that the rhetorical consequences of repeatedly and emphatically mislabeling an argument are as simple or innocent as Blasi implies.

19. For a sobering account of the kinds of arguments advanced even by the opponents of the Alien and Sedition Act, see Walter Berns, "Freedom of the Press and the Alien and Sedition Laws: A Reappraisal," 1970 *Sup. Ct. Rev.* 109 (noting that most arguments were based on states' rights, not a vigorous con-

cept of freedom of speech). On Revolutionary censorship and intimidation by "the zealots of patriotism," who, for instance, destroyed a printing press that had published "wrong sentiments," see Leonard W. Levy, *Legacy of Suppression: Freedom of Speech and Press in Early American History*, at 176–82 (Harvard University Press, 1960). The views of Thomas Jefferson also were considerably more complicated than Brandeis suggests. Levy quotes Jefferson as referring to the press's "licentiousness and . . . lying" and as believing the solution to be "a few prosecutions of the most eminent offenders. . . ." *See id.* at 300. For some evidence implicating President Jefferson in acts of suppression, see *id.* at 297–307. Among contemporary scholars there is a trend toward a more optimistic view of the framers' thinking on free speech. *See, e.g.*, David M. Rabban, "The Ahistorical Historian: Leonard Levy on Freedom of Expression in Early American History," 37 *Stan. L. Rev.* 795 (1985); David Anderson, "The Origins of the Press Clause," 30 *UCLA L. Rev.* 455 (1983). Even Levy has revised his assessment in *Emergence of a Free Press* (Oxford University Press, 1985). The amount of detail and complication in these arguments, however, is itself a reproach to Brandeis's easy generalities. One of the strong defenders of the libertarian beliefs of the framers, for example, notes dryly that "the Framers sometimes seemed as eager to silence dissent as George III had been." Anderson, *supra* at 536. He copes with this by relying on the highly debatable claim that the framers' words are a more reliable indicator of constitutional meaning than their behavior.

Brandeis wrote, of course, long before any of this scholarship was published, but his concurring opinion in *Whitney* took no account of the problems suggested by historical scholarship that was available in 1927. *See, e.g.*, Edward S. Corwin, "Freedom of Speech and Press under the First Amendment: A Résumé," 30 *Yale L.J.* 48 (1920); Thomas F. Carroll, "Freedom of Speech and of the Press in the Federalist Period: The Sedition Act," 18 *Mich. L. Rev.* 615 (1920).

20. A well-known and effective condemnation of the justices' use of "mangled" constitutional history to establish political "myths" is Alfred H. Kelly, "Clio and the Court: An Illicit Love Affair," 1965 *Sup. Ct. Rev.* 119, 135, 136, and *passim*. A criticism of Justice Brennan's position on the historical meaning of the ninth amendment can be found in *id.* at 149–55. Kelly concluded, "[T]he present use of history by the Court is a Marxist-type perversion of the relation between truth and utility. It assumes that history can be written to serve the interests of libertarian idealism." *Id.* at 157.

21. This denial is partly rooted, I think, in the advocates' subjective sense that the preferred conclusion is inevitable, that it represents the one right answer. This mind-set has been vividly described and elaborately defended by one of the most respected legal philosophers of our time:

> Law as integrity replies that the grounds of law lie in integrity, in the best constructive interpretation of past legal decisions, and that law is therefore sensitive to justice. . . . So there is no way Hercules *can* report his conclusions [about the proper outcome of a case] except to say that the law, as he understands it, is [as he interpreted it].

Dworkin, *Law's Empire* 262 (Harvard University Press, 1986) (emphasis in original). Psychologically, if not logically, this viewpoint is linked to intolerance and hostility toward anyone who would qualify or challenge those dominating legal judgments that are truly believed by the many Hercules in our legal culture. For an example of this intolerance, see Ronald Dworkin, "Bork's Jurisprudence," 57 *U. Chi. L. Rev.* 657 (1990). There are, of course, many other illustrations. Justice Brennan, arguing against an interpretive method that would assign great weight to formalized marriage in determining child custody, described the method as "stagnant, archaic, hidebound . . . steeped in the prejudices and superstitions of a time long past." Michael H. v. Gerald D., 491 U.S. 110, 136, 141 (1988) (Brennan, J., dissenting). Occasionally, through the fervor emerges some partial recognition of the intellectual limitations inherent in a mind-set that conceives of preferred constitutional interpretations as ineluctable. Douglas Laycock firmly believes that the great bulk of modern decisions expanding individual's rights, including the right to abortion, can be justified as strict interpretations of constitutional text. *See* "Taking Constitutions Seriously: A Theory of Judicial Review," 59 *Tex. L. Rev.* 343 (1981). In response to my suggestion that if the issue of judicial review were historically fresh, it would seem plausible "that the Constitution either does not bear at all, or bears only in complex and indeterminate ways, on most specific public issues," Laycock wrote, "I find Nagel's assertions not merely implausible, but almost incomprehensible." "Notes on the Role of Judicial Review, the Expansion of Federal Power, and the Structure of Constitutional Rights," 99 *Yale L.J.* 1711, 1730 (1990). This is revealing; the passage is not meant, however, in the spirit of puzzlement or confession, but (as is common with those subject to Dworkinian true belief) in the fiercely self-righteous spirit of combat.

22. Although cynical explanations are, I think, too limited, they cannot be ignored. Justice Brennan, for instance, was relatively uncritical of some "unfocused" legislative objectives, such as enhancing the quality of life through aesthetic zoning and assuring a diversity of views through racial preference in broadcast licensing. *See* Penn Central Transportation Co. v. New York City, 438 U.S. 104 (1978); Metro Broadcasting, Inc. v. F.C.C., 497 U.S. 547 (1990).

Chapter 7

1. For example, Dinesh D'Souza's much-discussed book (*Illiberal Education: The Politics of Race and Sex on Campus* [Free Press, 1991]) depicts political correctness as essentially a modern phenomenon closely related to affirmative action.

2. 413 U.S. 376 (1973).

3. Virginia State Board of Pharmacy v. Virginia Citizens Consumer Council, Inc., 425 U.S. 748, 772 (1976).

4. Cohen v. California, 403 U.S. 15 (1971).

5. 395 U.S. 444, 447–48 (1969) (quoting Noto v. United States, 367 U.S. 290, 297–98 (1961)).

6. Ruth Bader Ginsburg, "Realizing the Equality Principle," in William T. Blackstone & Robert D. Heslep, *Social Justice & Preferential Treatment: Women and Racial Minorities in Education and Business* 135, at 137 (University of Georgia Press, 1977).

7. *See, e.g.,* the various opinions in Board of Education v. Pico, 457 U.S. 853 (1982).

8. Rust v. Sullivan, 500 U.S. 173 (1991).

9. A pathbreaking treatment of this general subject is *When Government Speaks: Politics, Law, and Governmental Expression in America* (University of California Press, 1983), by Mark G. Yudof. For a frank judicial acknowledgment not only that laws are expressive but also that one purpose of constitutional review is to prevent the expression of certain forms of collective judgment, see R.A.V. v. City of St. Paul, 112 S. Ct. 2538, 2550 (1992). For a scholarly acknowledgment, see Charles R. Lawrence III "If He Hollers Let Him Go: Regulating Racist Speech on Campus," 1990 *Duke L. J.* 431, 439–40. On the communicative aspects of suppressive laws, see Lee C. Bollinger, *The Tolerant Society: Freedom of Speech and Extremist Speech in America* (Oxford University Press, 1986).

10. Wallace v. Jaffree, 472 U.S. 38 (1985).

11. It is reported that in 1963, 70 percent of the American public disapproved of the Court's school prayer decisions. By 1984, 64 percent indicated that they would support a constitutional amendment to reintroduce prayer in the schools. *See* Joseph B. Tamney & Stephen D. Johnson, "Church/State Relations in the Eighties: Public Opinion in Middletown," 48 *Soc. Analysis* 1, 5 (1987).

12. This is a point later acknowledged by the Court in Planned Parenthood v. Casey, 00 U.S. 00, 112 S. Ct. 2791, 2824 (1992).

13. Maher v. Roe, 432 U.S. 464 (1977); Harris v. McRae, 448 U.S. 297 (1980).

14. 476 U.S. 747 (1986).

15. Planned Parenthood v. Casey, 112 S. Ct. 2791, 2822–24 (1992). Actually, this discussion of informed consent leaves open the possibility that the Court may soon return to something close to its position in *Thornburgh.* The *Casey* decision asserts that the proper inquiry is whether the specific information required presents a "substantial obstacle to obtaining an abortion." In this regard, the Court noted that the informed consent provision in question did not "prevent the physician from exercising his or her medical judgment."

16. Robert N. Bellah, Richard Madsen, William M. Sullivan, Ann Swidler & Steven M. Tipton, *Habits of the Heart: Individualism and Commitment in American Life* 121–41 (Harper & Row, 1986).

17. 476 U.S. at 762.

18. 391 U.S. 430 (1968).

19. *E.g.,* Dayton Board of Education v. Brinkman, 433 U.S. 406, 417 (1977); Keyes v. School District No. 1, Denver, Colorado, 413 U.S. 189, 211 (1973); Swann v. Charlotte-Mecklenburg Board of Education, 402 U.S. 1, 24 (1971).

20. Paul Gewirtz, "Choice in the Transition: School Desegregation and the Corrective Ideal," 86 *Colum. L. Rev.* 728, 738 (1986).

21. The Court has established an elaborate set of legal presumptions that allow trial judges to find illegal discrimination even where it cannot be directly proven. *See, e.g.*, Dayton Board of Education v. Brinkman, 443 U.S. 526 (1979); Columbus Board of Education v. Penick, 443 U.S. 449 (1979); Keyes v. School District No. 1, Denver, Colorado, 413 U.S. 189 (1973).

22. Brown v. Board of Education of Topeka, 347 U.S. 483, 494 (1954).

23. *See* Gewirtz, *supra* note 20.

24. *Id.* at 749.

25. *Id.* at 798.

26. This is true, for example, of the ferocious debate, described in Chapter 3, between Robert Bork and his academic opponents. It is also true of the acrimonious debate over affirmative action. *See, e.g.*, Stephen L. Carter, *Reflections of an Affirmative Action Baby* 99–123 (Basic Books, 1991). *See also* Donald P. Judges, "Light Beams and Particle Dreams: Rethinking the Individual vs. Group Rights Paradigm in Affirmative Action," 44 *Ark. L. Rev.* 1007, 1059–60 [and sources cited therein] (1991). Intolerance is not restricted to legal scholarship or to specific controversial issues. Academic inquiry is ultimately about what ideas we should not tolerate. *See* Phillip E. Johnson, "The Creationist and the Sociobiologist: Two Stories about Illiberal Education," 80 *Cal. L. Rev.* 1071, 1073 (1992); David P. Bryden, "It Ain't What They Teach, It's the Way That They Teach It," 103 *The Public Interest* 38 (1991). More generally, see Lee C. Bollinger, *The Tolerant Society: Freedom of Speech and Extremist Speech in America* (Oxford University Press, 1986).

27. These events were reported in the *Boulder Daily Camera*, Feb. 8, 11, 12, 13, 18, 19, and 28 (1992). President Judith Albino explained her position in a letter to the university community published in *Silver and Gold Record*, Feb. 20, 1992. Her articulation of the university's official position on gay rights is contained in *The President's Letter*, Nov. 1992: "There simply should be no doubt that the basic human rights of every member of this community—including gays, lesbians, and bisexuals—should be protected by our Constitution, laws, local ordinances, and under the policies of our most important public institutions."

28. Letter from Judith Albino, *Silver and Gold Record*, Feb. 20, 1992.

29. *See* D'Souza, *Illiberal Education*, *supra* note 1.

30. *See, e.g.*, Richard Delgado, "Words That Wound: A Tort Action for Racial Insults, Epithets, and Name-Calling," 17 *Harv. C.R.-C.L. L. Rev.* 133 (1982); Catharine A. MacKinnon, "Not a Moral Issue," 2 *Yale L. & Pol'y Rev.* 321 (1984); Mari J. Matsuda, "Public Response to Racist Speech: Considering the Victim's Story," 87 *Mich. L. Rev.* 2320 (1989).

Chapter 8

1. Evans v. Romer, Civil Action No. 92 CV 7223. Judge Jeffrey Bayless granted the motion.

2. In July 1993 the Colorado Supreme Court upheld the preliminary injunction. Evans v. Romer, 854 P. 2d. 1270 (1993). Subsequently, the district court

entered a permanent injunction, which is again on appeal to the state supreme court.

3. Brief in Support of Plaintiffs' Motion for Preliminary Injunction.

4. *See* Plaintiffs' Brief at 4, n. 8 ("A detailed description of the proponents of Amendment 2 is presented because of the plaintiffs' discussion of improper governmental purpose set out . . . below."). Judge Bayless granted the preliminary injunction in part on the ground that there is a reasonable probability that, by involving the state in "enforcing or encouraging private bias," Amendment 2 would be found to violate the fourteenth amendment. 92 CV 7223 at 28. Governments are, of course, constantly in the business of enforcing private decisions, preferences, and moral judgments; at this stage of the litigation, Judge Bayless has not yet fully explained why he thinks *bias* might be the appropriate word in this case.

5. A poll of Colorado voters (for what it is worth) indicated that the beliefs of the voters were complex and, on the whole, tolerant of homosexuals. *See Denver Post*, A1, A4 (Jan. 3, 1993) and A1, A7 (Feb. 23, 1993).

6. *E.g.*, Dayton Board of Education v. Brinkman, 443 U.S. 526 (1979); Columbus Board of Education v. Penick, 443 U.S. 449 (1979); Keyes v. School District No. 1, 413 U.S. 189 (1973).

7. Reitman v. Mulkey, 387 U.S. 369 (1967). *See also* Hunter v. Erickson, 393 U.S. 385 (1968); Washington v. Seattle School District No. 1, 458 U.S. 457 (1982).

8. Mississippi University for Women v. Hogan, 458 U.S. 718, 729 (1982). *See also* Craig v. Boren, 429 U.S. 190 (1976) (law permitting females to purchase beer at an earlier age than males termed "invidious").

9. Cleburne v. Cleburne Living Center, 473 U.S. 432 (1985).

10. United States Department of Agriculture v. Moreno, 413 U.S. 528 (1973).

11. Eisenstadt v. Baird, 405 U.S. 438 (1972). *See also* Zobel v. Williams, 457 U.S. 55 (1982) ("irrational"), and Reed v. Reed, 404 U.S. 71 (1971) ("arbitrary").

12. Church of the Lukumi Babalu Aye v. Hialeah, 113 S. Ct. 2217, 2222 (1993).

13. Wallace v. Jaffree, 472 U.S. 38 (1985).

14. Edwards v. Aguillard, 482 U.S. 578 (1987).

15. *Id.* at 592, n. 14.

16. Epperson v. Arkansas, 393 U.S. 97, 108 n. 16 (1968).

17. United States v. Eichman, 496 U.S. 310, 318–19 (1990). Analogously, the Court sometimes ignores evidence of, for example, valid public health objectives and depicts the public's purpose as protectionism or "economic discrimination." *E.g.*, Dean Milk Co. v. Madison, 340 U.S. 349 (1951).

18. Thornburgh v. American College of Obstetricians, 476 U.S. 747, 759, 764, 765–71 (1986).

19. *The Least Dangerous Branch: The Supreme Court at the Bar of Politics* 35-46 (Bobbs-Merrill 1962). *See also* note 40, *infra*.

20. *E.g.*, "Centennial Conference in Honor of Justice John Marshall Harlan," 36 *N.Y.L. Sch. L. Rev.* 1 (1992).

21. *E.g.*, Jeffrey Rosen, "The Leader of the Opposition," *The New Republic* 20, 27 (Jan. 18, 1993).

22. *Id.*; *cf.* Kathleen M. Sullivan, "Governmental Interests and Unconstitutional Conditions Law: A Case Study in Categorization and Balancing," 55 *Albany L. Rev.* 605, 617 (1992); "Post Liberal Judging: The Roles of Categorization and Balancing," 63 *U. Colo. L. Rev.* 293 (1992).

23. James B. Thayer, "The Origin and Scope of the American Doctrine of Constitutional Law," 7 *Harv. L. Rev.* 129 (1893).

24. *Id.* at 144.

25. For my acknowledgment that judicial discourse has influenced the vocabulary of political debate, see Robert F. Nagel, "Political Law, Legalistic Politics: A Recent History of the Political Questions Doctrine," 56 *U. Chi. L. Rev.* 643, 667–68.

26. See Robert F. Nagel, *Constitutional Cultures: The Mentality and Consequences of Judicial Review* (University of California Press, 1989).

27. Akhil Reed Amar, Comment, "The Case of the Missing Amendments: *R.A.V. v. City of St. Paul,*" 106 *Harv. L. Rev.* 124, 125 (1992). Similarly, Mark Tushnet describes *Texas v. Johnson* as "simple and straightforward." Review Essay, 24 *Law & Soc'y Rev.* 199, 209 (1990); *see also* note 29, *infra*. Professor Eisgruber describes the opinion as "admirably lucid and accurate . . . written in a way easily intelligible to citizens not trained in the law." Christopher L. Eisgruber, "Is the Supreme Court an Educative Institution? 67 *N.Y.U. L. Rev.* 961, 985 (1992).

28. Not to all lawyers, however. See Paul Campos, "Advocacy and Scholarship," 81 *Calif. L. Rev.* 817 (1993).

29. The Court itself had refrained from reaching the conclusion that burning the flag is "speech." Street v. New York, 394 U.S. 576 (1969); *cf.* United States v. O'Brien, 391 U.S. 367 (1968). Nevertheless, Mark Tushnet can say:

> [I]t seems to me clear that the general public understands that punishing people for burning flags is as pristine a violation of the core meaning of the first amendment as we are likely to see.

Tushnet, note 27, *supra*. Tushnet does not explain how he knows this, but the full passage strongly suggests that he is simply assuming that because his own opinions about the case are strong, they must be shared by "the general public." However, given that Tushnet is an unconventional thinker (a socialist, no less), his opinions are not likely to be an especially accurate index of the views of the average person.

30. The Texas statute, for example, applied only to public monuments, places of worship or burial, and the state and national flags.

31. To take one egregious example, the court-ordered desegregation plan for the Kansas City school system had a price tag of more than $460 million and involved the creation of a performing arts middle school, a twenty-five-acre wildlife area, and capital renovations "without parallel in any other school district in the country." Missouri v. Jenkins, 495 U.S. 33, 60–61 (1990) (Kennedy, J., concurring in part). When the citizenry declined to pay for this plan, the trial judge ordered a tax increase, explaining that he could see "no alternative." *Id.* at 51. For its part, the Supreme Court also adopted the language of moderation by invoking the need to respect the "integrity and function of local govern-

ment institutions." It concluded, therefore, that the lower court should have ordered the local authorities to raise taxes rather than raising them by itself. *Id.* This method, said the Court, would be entirely in keeping with the judicial function. *Id.* at 55.

32. *See* David A. Strauss, "The Ubiquity of Prophylactic Rules," 55 *U. Chi. L. Rev.* 190 (1988).

33. *See* Robert F. Nagel, "Controlling the Structural Injunction," 7 *Harv. J.L. & Pub. Pol'y* 395, 405–06 (1984).

34. 403 U.S. 15 (1971). For a fairly typical encomium, see Eisgruber, *supra* note 27 at 981 ("*Cohen* moderates the American spirit").

35. 403 U.S. at 28 (quoting Tinker v. Des Moines Indep. Community School Dist., 393 U.S. 503 (1969)).

36. *Id.* at 24.

37. For a discussion of the cultural aspects of opinions on the right to abortion, see Kristin Luker, *Abortion and the Politics of Motherhood* (University of California Press, 1984).

38. 367 U.S. 497, 522 (1961) (Harlan, J., dissenting).

39. *Id.* at 550 (quoting Boyd v. United States, 116 U.S. 616, 630 (1886)).

40. Planned Parenthood v. Casey, 112 S. Ct. 2791, 2815 (1992). This exalted self-image is based, I suspect, partly on the unfortunate influence of some hyperexcited academic commentary. This, too, is traceable to Thayer, who influenced (for example) Bickel, who once wrote that the independent federal judiciary is "a bulwark, or at any rate a symbol, that might just preserve and protect the very regime itself at some awful moment of supreme peril." Alexander M. Bickel, *The Supreme Court and the Idea of Progress* 180–81 (Harper Torchbooks, 1970).

41. 358 U.S. 1, 17 (1958).

42. *Id.* at 18.

43. Gerald Gunther, who was clerking for Harlan at the time, "vividly" remembers

> that the Justice pressing most insistently for added muscle in the decree was *not* one of the well-known liberals on the Court, but rather Harlan. More specifically, it was Harlan's voice and pen that was solely responsible for the toughest sentence in *Brown II.* . . .

"Another View of Justice Harlan—A Comment on Fried and Ackerman," 36 *N.Y.L. Sch. L. Rev.* 67, 68 (1991) (emphasis in original).

44. For differing positions of how restrained Harlan was, see the articles in the symposium cited in note 20, *supra.*

Chapter 9

1. A humorous treatment of the subject can be found in Henry Beard & Christopher Cerf, *The Official Politically Correct Dictionary and Handbook* (Villard

Books, 1992). For a different kind of effort at minimizing the phenomenon, see Mark Tushnet, "Political Correctness, the Law, and the Legal Academy," 4 *Yale J.L. & Human.* 127 (1992).

2. For a perceptive commentary on the place of white guilt in modern race relations, see Shelby Steele, *The Content of Our Character* 77–92 (Harper Perennial, 1991).

3. *See* James Davison Hunter, *Culture Wars: The Struggle to Define America* 135–61 (Basic Books, 1991).

4. One of the themes in the influential work of Richard Delgado, for instance, is the ineffectiveness of free debate in achieving immediate racial justice. *See, e.g.,* Richard Delgado & Jean Stefancic, "Images of the Outsider in American Law and Culture: Can Free Expression Remedy Systemic Social Ills?" 77 *Cornell L. Rev.* 1258 (1992). Much of the feminist literature evidences this same combination of despair, impatience, and ambition. *See, e.g.,* Catharine A. MacKinnon, *Feminism Unmodified* (Harvard University Press, 1987). For an argument that a legal norm of color-consciousness should be adopted for the purpose of altering "social relations and structures of thought and perception," see T. Alexander Aleinikoff, "A Case for Race-Consciousness," 91 *Colum. L. Rev.* 1060, 1122 (1991).

5. For illustrations, see the contributions of Professors Akhil Reed Amar, Peter B. Edelman, Owen N. Fiss, Thomas C. Grey, and Kathleen M. Sullivan to "Conference on Compelling Governmental Interest: The Mystery of Constitutional Analysis," 55 *Alb. L. Rev.* 535 (1992).

6. For an overview of the liberal record of the "conservative" Burger Court, see Robert F. Nagel, "Political Law/Legalistic Politics: A Recent History of the Political Question Doctrine," 56 *U. Chi. L. Rev.* 643, 659–61 (1989). On later developments, see David P. Bryden, "Is the Rehnquist Court Conservative?" 109 *The Public Interest* 73 (1992).

7. A good overview of the self-lacerations of constitutional theorists can be found in Mark Tushnet, *Red, White, and Blue: A Critical Analysis of Constitutional Law* (Harvard University Press, 1988). On practical problems with constitutional interpretations by the courts, see David L. Horowitz, *The Courts and Social Policy* (Brookings, 1977), and Gerald N. Rosenberg, *The Hollow Hope: Can Courts Bring About Social Change?* (University of Chicago Press, 1991).

8. Robert H. Bork, *The Tempting of America: The Political Seduction of the Law* 196, 201, 213–14, 219, 229 (Free Press, 1990).

9. *See, e.g.,* Ronald Dworkin, *A Matter of Principle* 40–53 (Harvard University Press, 1985).

10. Ronald Dworkin, "The Bork Nomination," *New York Review of Books,* August 13, 1987, at 10.

11. *Id.*

12. Dworkin, *supra* note 9, at 68.

13. *Id.*

14. *Id.* at 68, 366–67, 369, 371.

15. 491 U.S. 110 (1989).

16. *E.g.*, Stanley v. Illinois, 405 U.S. 645 (1972); Caban v. Mohammed, 441 U.S 380 (1979).

17. Eisenstadt v. Baird, 405 U.S. 438, 453 (1972).

18. 491 U.S. at 143 (Brennan, J., dissenting).

19. *Id.* at 130.

20. Jack H. Nagel, *The Descriptive Analysis of Power* (Yale University Press, 1975), at 12–22, 32–33.

21. See note 14, *supra*, and Ronald Dworkin, "Reagan's Justice," *New York Review of Books*, November 8, 1984.

22. Bruce Ackerman, "Constitutional Politics/Constitutional Law," 99 *Yale L.J.* 453, 536–45 (1989).

23. For a description and criticism of dialogue theories, see Earl Maltz, "The Supreme Court and the Quality of Political Dialogue," 5 *Const. Comm.* (1988).

INDEX